TROUBLED TRAILS

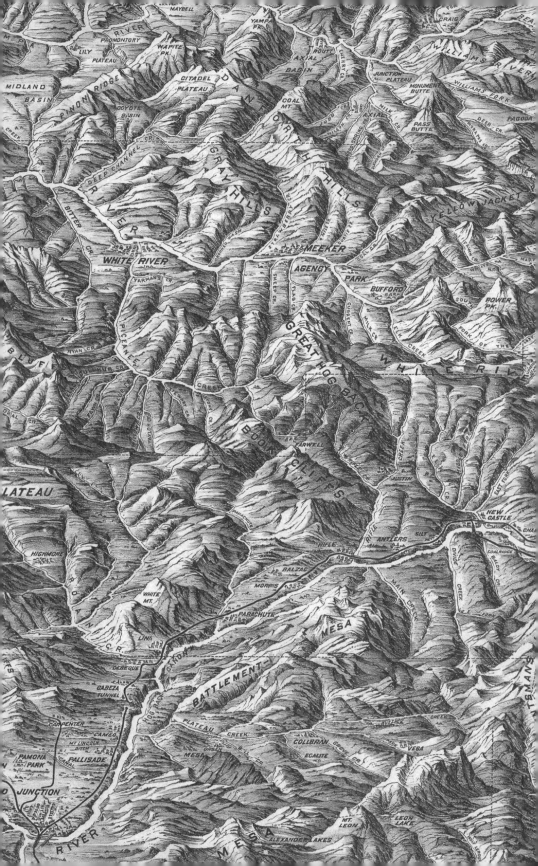

TROUBLED TRAILS

THE MEEKER AFFAIR AND THE EXPULSION
OF THE UTES FROM COLORADO

ROBERT SILBERNAGEL

With assistance from Jonas Grant Sr.
Maps by Robert Garcia

THE UNIVERSITY OF UTAH PRESS | *Salt Lake City*

The Defiance House Man colophon is a registered trademark
of the University of Utah Press. It is based upon a four-foot-tall,
Ancient Puebloan pictograph (late PIII) near Glen Canyon, Utah.

LIBRARY OF CONGRESS CATALOGING-IN-PUBLICATION DATA

Silbernagel, Robert 1952–
  Troubled trails: the Meeker affair and the expulsion of the Utes from Colorado /
Robert Silbernagel ; with assistance from Jonas Grant Sr., maps by Robert Garcia
    p. cm.
  Includes bibliographical references and index.
  ISBN 978-1-60781-129-9 (pbk. : alk. paper)
  1. Ute Indians—Wars, 1879. 2. Ute Indians—Relocation. 3. Meeker, Nathan Cook,
1814–1879. 4. Meeker, Josephine. 5. Indian captivities—Colorado. 6. Frontier and
pioneer life—Colorado. I. Grant, Jonas. II. Title.
  E83. 879.S55 2011
  973.8'3—dc22

Frontispiece: Map of Colorado, Library of Congress, Geography and Map Division.

TO MY WIFE, JUDY

*for putting up with me, encouraging me, and helping me through this project,
as she has with so many projects we've done together.*

CONTENTS

ILLUSTRATIONS

Maps

Plates
Follow page 118

FOREWORD

ONLY A FEW ENCOUNTERS WITH AMERICAN INDIANS BROUGHT FORTH
such a chain of events as the struggle of the Utes, the U.S. Army, and the
citizens of the state of Colorado known as "the Meeker affair." Popular
literature lists it as the "Meeker massacre," but a "massacre" is the killing
of the unarmed—and it was hardly that. Both sides were well armed.

A great number of books and articles deal with the Meeker affair and
the expulsion of the three Ute bands from Colorado. What is remarkable
is that there is so little new detail in these works. The volume presented
here breaks that tradition. It does not debunk the earlier works, but it does
expand the view of the times and the events.

One part of the book is geographical history. This was a need not
addressed until now. In the aftermath of the battle of Milk Creek, the
nation's attention was focused on the captives taken at the White River
Indian Agency. The fact that they were women and children especially
aroused the anger of a white American audience, and newspapers had a
field day. Despite the attention focused on the captives, few attempts have
been made to trace the trails used by the Utes as they retreated from the
White River with their hostages. Over many years Robert Silbernagel has
sought out the domains of that historic trek. His use of a wide variety of
sources indicates a devotion to truth and detail worthy of the best
historians.

Oral history is often more detailed and accurate in American Indian testimony than in the population at large, and an addition to this work, absent too often in others, is the perspective of the relatives of the participants through interviews with Jonas Grant Sr., one of the remaining descendants of the central characters in the drama—indeed, a descendant of She-towitch, the sister of the Uncompahgre (or Tabeguache) Ute leader Ouray. Grant's contributions significantly improve the validity of the work, and together, Silbernagel and Grant have produced a valuable addition to western history. Scholars of the Ute experience and members of the Ute tribes, as well as readers at large, will find it a rewarding read.

FLOYD A. O'NEIL
Director Emeritus
American West Center
University of Utah

PREFACE

IN WESTERN COLORADO, WHERE I LIVE, THERE ARE MANY REMNANTS OF old pathways that are still referred to as "the Ute Trail." That's hardly surprising, because for centuries the Ute Indians traversed every canyon, plateau, and mountaintop of this region, first on foot and later on horse-back. A few of the trails they once traveled, or portions of those trails, are still in use. But large sections of important trails—routes directly linked to the events of September 1879 and the Utes' subsequent exodus from Colorado—have been lost in time. This book is the result of my efforts to rediscover those trails, both the physical ones that cut across the rug-ged Colorado landscape, and the cultural and political ones that extended from Colorado to Washington, D.C.

There is a spot on the northeastern edge of the Roan Plateau, just out-side of Rifle, Colorado, from where you can see far to the north. With a good pair of binoculars, you can spot the meadow, nearly 40 miles away, where the White River Indian Agency stood in 1879. My wife, Judy, and I performed that reconnaissance in the autumn of 2005. It was an "Ah ha!" moment. Because of something that Josephine Meeker and Flora Ellen Price had said in 1879, we were searching for a place near Rifle from where we could see the old Indian agency site and the current town of Meeker a few miles upstream. The two women were among five whites held hostage by the Utes for twenty-three days in the autumn of 1879. A week of their captivity was spent camped along the Colorado River, west of the present-day town of Rifle. Both women reported that while camped there, Ute scouts would head up onto "the high peaks" near the camp and use their field telescopes to monitor activity near the White River. They were keeping track of U.S. Army troops near the site of the Indian agency, worried that the troops were preparing to move south in pursuit of the Utes.

This book project began as an attempt to determine the route that the Utes took with their hostages beginning on September 29, 1879, the day that the battle of Milk Creek began. It's also the day that Nathan Meeker and all the male employees at the White River Indian Agency were killed, and Josephine Meeker and her mother, Arvilla, as well as Flora Ellen Price and her two small children, were taken hostage by the Utes.

I had been struck in my research by the reference to the Utes' "high peaks" reconnaissance of the soldiers at the White River. Scanning the mountains from river level while driving along Interstate 70, it's hard to envision such a viewing spot nearby. That proved to be part of a problem that I had to learn to overcome: a tendency to evaluate the landscape and possible trail routes in terms of twenty-first-century travel—meaning wherever one could drive a car or a four-wheel-drive vehicle. Instead I had to consider where the Utes might have been able to go on their sturdy mountain ponies—and that was almost anywhere.

I am a horseman and have ridden many hours in the backcountry of Colorado. In fact, this project began after a horseback trip I took with my friend Alan Moore on the South Fork of the White River. After completing that trip, I began to wonder about the trail taken by the Utes and their hostages in 1879, and whether we could follow it on horseback. When I realized that little solid information had been published about the trail, I resolved to do what I could to find it.

The Utes of 1879 had a well-developed network of trails, but to those of us accustomed to pavement and pickup trucks, the routes aren't always obvious; however, the Hayden Survey maps of Colorado, completed in 1877, provide invaluable insight. They show a multitude of horse trails crisscrossing the terrain of northwestern Colorado, along with the handful of wagon roads that then existed. Like the view from atop the Roan Plateau, they challenged my previous ideas. But geography wasn't the only arena that required me to adjust my thinking.

Most of what I initially knew about the events of 1879 came from books written by white authors many decades after the fact. Some of them were sympathetic to the Utes; others were less so. But it wasn't until I

began to delve into the historical documents and listen to the Utes themselves—reading their statements recorded in official documents and books
of the time, and hearing modern-day Utes tell the story as it had been
handed down for generations—that new understanding started to emerge.

I didn't set out to write a treatise on U.S. relations with American
Indians, nor a detailed history of U.S. involvement with the Utes. But
some historical context was required, and it is offered here. Much more
than that, however, I wanted to understand the individuals involved in
these events—both Ute and white.

I came to see Nicaagat, Josephine, She-towitch, Flora Ellen, Colorow,
Charles Adams, Quinkent, and others as complicated individuals with
complex motives. They weren't simply stereotypes caught in one more conflict of cultures. I hope I have managed to convey to readers something of
these complex personalities. As one measure of respect, I have tried to use
the Ute names for the Indians whenever they were available. If they were
known by other names to the whites, those names are in parentheses.

Learning more about She-towitch was especially fascinating. She was
known to the whites as "Susan," the sister of the esteemed Ute leader
Ouray. She was also Jonas Grant's great-great-grandmother, and it was
intriguing to listen to his family's lengthy oral history about her and other
Utes. I felt privileged to learn what his family history told of the events of
1879. That connection also led me to examine articles published by the
Chicago Tribune. Its journalists thoroughly covered the events at the White
River Agency, providing a perspective much different from those in
Colorado.

I was also surprised to learn that travel during the late nineteenth century could be much speedier than I realized. Cruising along on an interstate highway at 75 miles per hour, it is easy to picture the people of 1879
plodding slowly along on horseback. But much of this book is a narrative
of people in frenetic motion. It wasn't just the Utes and their hostages, but
army units moving with well-organized haste, riders racing to send messages, and rescue teams and others galloping across much of western Colorado. Travel may have been primitive, but it was hardly slow. Time after
time I read of people on horseback covering 50, 75, even 100 miles in a day
on isolated mountain trails. Since a day-long ride of 25 miles leaves me
bone-achingly weary, I was impressed.

I have tried to maintain a sense of that movement and urgency
throughout the book. In some cases, my research turned up information

that I found relevant but which seemed to slow down the story. This information is included in appendices that serve as supplements to several
chapters in the main narrative.

My hope is that readers will experience some of the adventure and
growing awareness that occurred for me as I searched for the trails related
to the Utes' exodus from Colorado.

ROBERT SILBERNAGEL
Palisade, Colorado
March 2010

ACKNOWLEDGMENTS

A PROJECT SUCH AS THIS BOOK INVOLVES THE AID OF MANY PEOPLE, AND
it's impossible to name them all, but I wish to recognize some who were
particularly important.

Andrew Gulliford, professor of history at Fort Lewis College in
Durango, Colorado, served as my historical adviser and provided invaluable suggestions for my research and writing, as well as much-needed
encouragement at critical times.

My wife, Judy, and friend Alan Moore joined me on many expeditions
related to this project, assisted in research, and added curiosity and enthusiasm to my own.

Jonas Grant Sr. graciously related parts of the oral history of his family to me and provided invaluable insight about Ute history and language
and corrected mistakes in my manuscript. He and his wife, Joy, welcomed
me to their home and helped greatly when I visited Fort Duchesne on several occasions.

Other Utes who generously offered information about their own families, or on tribal history, include Loya Arrum, Adelbert Tavashuts, and
Clifford Duncan. Mr. Duncan read much of my manuscript and offered
valuable suggestions. So did James Jefferson, of the Southern Utes.

Floyd O'Neil, director emeritus of the American West Center, University of Utah, also offered important historical perspective and sugges-

tions, as did James A. Goss, professor emeritus of anthropology at Texas Tech University and Peter Decker, author of *The Utes Must Go!*

Joe Sullivan and Edith Starbucks, along with members of the Rio Blanco Historical Society, escorted us on horseback on the Sullivan ranch, where some of the events in this book took place. They also welcomed us to a number of events in Meeker related to what occurred in 1879.

People at various libraries, museums, and other facilities were invariably helpful and pleasant when I visited and sought assistance. They included Mike Perry, Dave Bailey and staff at the Museum of Western Colorado in Grand Junction; Peggy Ford with the City of Greeley Museums in Greeley, Colorado; Lori Cox-Paul with the National Archives, Lakewood, Colorado, branch; and staffs at the Mesa State College Library, Mesa County Public Library, the Denver Public Library, Colorado Historical Society, and Pioneer History Museum in Colorado Springs.

INDIVIDUALS INVOLVED
IN THE MEEKER AFFAIR AND ITS AFTERMATH

Utes

Canalla: Known to the whites as "Johnson" or "Johnson 2." He and his wife, She-towitch, helped care for the hostages during their time in captivity.

Canavish: The father of Canalla. Also called "Johnson" or "Johnson 1."

Chipeta: Ouray's wife and a powerful woman within the Ute community. She was popular with whites, and remained so until her death in the 1920s.

Colorow: White River Ute leader well known to whites prior to the events of September 29, 1879. He was a leader with Nicaagat during the battle at Milk Creek.

Henry Jim: An interpreter at the White River Indian Agency who was present at the Milk Creek battle site but was not implicated in the killings at the agency.

Jane Redjacket: Worked as a house servant and sometimes as an interpreter at the White River Agency.

Tim Johnson: Son of Canalla and She-towitch who was taken to federal prison in Virginia for his part in the events of September 29, 1879. He was released after more than a year.

Nicaagat: A leader of the White River Utes, including in the battle with the soldiers at Milk Creek. He was known to whites as "Captain Jack," "Ute Jack," or simply "Jack."

Ouray: Leader of the Uncompahgre, or Tabeguache, Utes. Designated by white officials in Washington, D.C., as the leader of all the Utes, although many Utes never accepted that designation. He worked with whites to end the fighting at Milk Creek and to free the hostages.

Pahsone: A young Ute who took charge of Josephine Meeker during her captivity. He wanted the young white woman to be his wife.

Piah: White River Ute leader who was strongly opposed to white interlopers. Frequent companion of Colorow. Sometimes listed as an ally of Nicaagat, but occasionally as an enemy.

Quinkent: A leader of the White River Utes known to whites as "Douglas" and believed to have been present when the killings at the White River Indian Agency occurred. Arvilla Meeker spent most of her captivity with him.

Sapivanero: Ouray's brother-in-law who once tried to kill Ouray but later became his second in command. He was sent by Ouray to assist Charles Adams in freeing the white hostages.

She-towitch: Wife of Canalla and sister of Ouray, known to the whites as "Susan." She was the most outspoken protector of the hostages. Some historical accounts say her Ute name was "Tsashin" (pronounced "Shawsheen"), but her descendants say "She-towitch" is the proper Ute name.

Sowawick: Close friend and traveling companion of Nicaagat. He accompanied Nicaagat to Denver to meet with Governor Frederick Pitkin and later traveled with him to Washington, D.C.

Yanco: Uncompahgre Ute who raced from Milk Creek to the Los Pinos Agency to deliver news of the battle to Chief Ouray.

Whites

Charles Adams: Arranged release of hostages. A former Indian agent at both the White River and Los Pinos agencies, he was a member of the first official investigation into the 1879 events at White River and accompanied the Utes to Washington, D.C., for congressional hearings.

Joe Brady: A miller at the Los Pinos Indian Agency in the Uncompahgre Valley. Sent by Ouray with a small group of Utes to Milk Creek to tell the White River Utes to stop fighting.

William Byers: Founded the *Rocky Mountain News* in Denver. Owned land at Hot Sulphur Springs in an area the Utes still considered their hunting grounds. He was friendly with the Utes and a friend of Governor Frederick Pitkin.

Lieutenant Samuel Cherry: An officer of Thornburgh's command who was out in front of the rest of the troops and involved in the first confrontation at Milk Creek.

Captain Francis S. Dodge: Leader of a troop of black soldiers (also called Buffalo Soldiers) who arrived to aid Thornburgh's troops at Milk Creek.

E. A. Hayt: Commissioner of Indian affairs for the Department of the Interior at the time of the White River events.

Samuel S. Kirkwood: Succeeded Carl Schurz as secretary of the Department of the Interior in 1881.

Colonel Ranald Mackenzie: Army commander who oversaw the removal of the Uncompahgre Utes from Colorado in 1881.

Otto Mears: Western Colorado entrepreneur who was friendly with the Utes but helped ensure that most were removed from Colorado to Utah.

Arvilla Meeker: Wife of Nathan Meeker. Taken hostage on September 29, 1879.

Josephine ("Josie") Meeker: Youngest daughter of Nathan and Arvilla Meeker. Taken hostage on September 29, 1879.

Mary Meeker: Middle daughter of Nathan and Arvilla Meeker. Lived in Greeley in September 1879.

Nathan Meeker: Agent at the White River Indian Agency, 1878–1879. Killed September 29, 1879.

Ralph Meeker: Son of Nathan and Arvilla Meeker. A journalist working in New York in September 1879, he rushed to western Colorado to meet his mother and sister after their release.

Rozene Meeker: Eldest daughter of Nathan and Arvilla Meeker. Lived in Greeley in September 1879.

Colonel Wesley Merritt: Army officer sent from Cheyenne, Wyoming, to rescue troops besieged at Milk Creek.

Captain J. Scott Payne: Second in command under Major Thomas T. Thornburgh. Assumed command at Milk Creek after Thornburgh's death.

Governor Frederick Pitkin: Governor of Colorado in September 1879. Made money in the San Juan mining district, on what had once been the Ute reservation. An outspoken advocate of removing Utes from Colorado.

Flora Ellen Price: Her given name was "Sophronia." Wife of a carpenter killed at the White River Agency on September 29, 1879. She and her two small children were taken hostage that day along with the two Meeker women.

Joe Rankin: Scout with Major Thornburgh's command. Rode more than 140 miles in 28 hours to get the news out that Thornburgh had been killed and his troops were under siege.

M. Wilson Rankin: Nephew of Joe Rankin. Delivered the message to Colonel Wesley Merritt ordering him to stop pursuing the Utes. Later wrote a memoir that included details about the 1879 uprising.

Carl Schurz: Secretary of the Department of the Interior and thus overseer of Indian affairs in 1879.

Henry Teller: U.S. senator from Colorado in September 1879 and a vocal advocate for removing the Utes from Colorado. He was later secretary of the Department of the Interior and Josephine Meeker's employer.

Major Thomas T. Thornburgh: Leader of the troops sent from Fort Steele, Wyoming, to aid Nathan Meeker at the White River Indian Agency. Killed at Milk Creek on September 29, 1879.

UTE BANDS

Muache, Capote, and Weminuche: Three smaller bands who lived along the Colorado–New Mexico border. They were not involved in the events of September 29, 1879, and were not forced to move from Colorado. The Muache and Capote bands later became the Southern Ute tribe, and the Weminuche became the Ute Mountain Utes. Both still have reservations in Colorado.

Uintah Utes: Utes who historically lived in Utah, including the Salt Lake Valley prior to the arrival of the Mormons. By 1879 they resided on the Uintah Reservation in northeastern Utah.

Uncompahgre Utes: Also called the Tabeguache Utes, they lived in west-central Colorado and were served by the Los Pinos Agency. Ouray was their tribal leader in 1879. Few Uncompahgre Utes were involved in the events of September 29, 1879, but they were forced to move from Colorado in 1881 nonetheless.

White River Utes: Sometimes called the Yamparika. This was the band living in northwestern Colorado and the primary one involved in the events of September 29, 1879. They had no single, unequivocal leader, but Canalla, Canavish, Colorow, Nicaagat, Quinkent, and Piah were all leaders with their own groups of followers.

MAPS

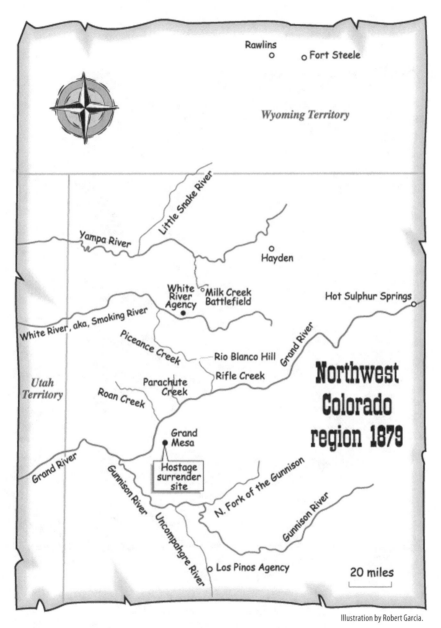

Rawlins

Fort Steele

Wyoming Territory

Little Snake River

Yampa River

Hayden

White River Agency

Milk Creek Battlefield

Hot Sulphur Springs

White River, aka, Smoking River

Piceance Creek

Grand River

Rio Blanco Hill

Rifle Creek

Parachute Creek

Utah Territory

Roan Creek

Grand Mesa

Northwest Colorado region 1879

Hostage surrender site

Grand River

Gunnison River

N. Fork of the Gunnison

Gunnison River

Uncompahgre River

Los Pinos Agency

20 miles

Illustration by Robert Garcia.

Map 1. Northwest Colorado region, 1879

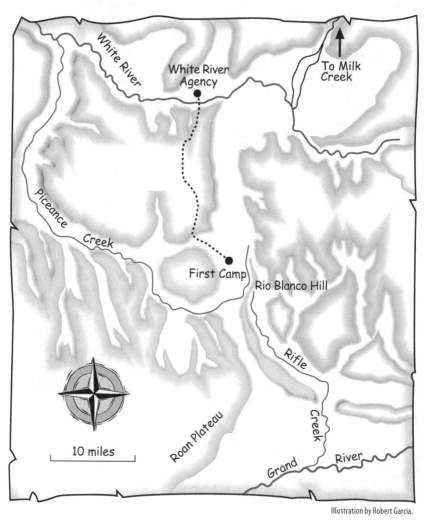

White River

White River
Agency

To Milk
Creek

Piceance   Creek

First Camp

Rio Blanco Hill

Rifle

Creek

10 miles

Roan Plateau

Grand   River

Map 2. Trail Section No. 1, September 29 to October 7, 1879

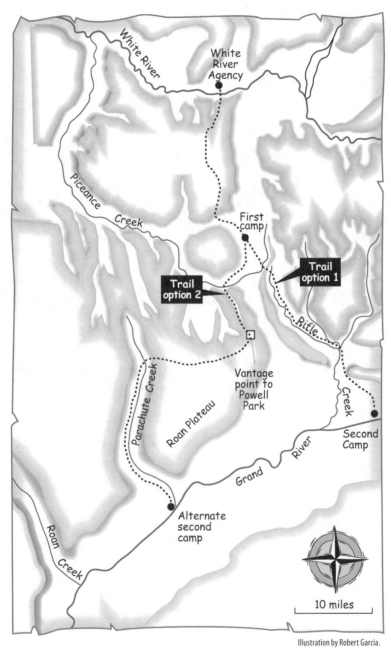

White River

White River Agency

Piceance Creek

First camp

Trail option 1

Trail option 2

Rifle

Vantage point to Powell Park

Creek

Second Camp

Parachute Creek

Roan Plateau

Grand River

Alternate second camp

Roan Creek

10 miles

Illustration by Robert Garcia.

Map 3. Trail Section No. 2, October 7, 1879

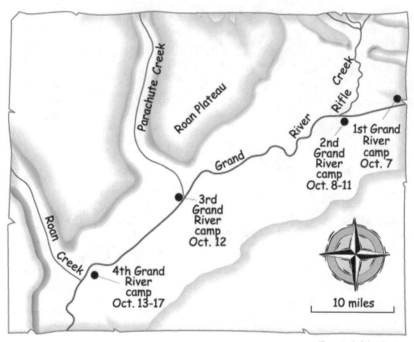

Map 4. Trail Section No. 3, October 7-17, 1879

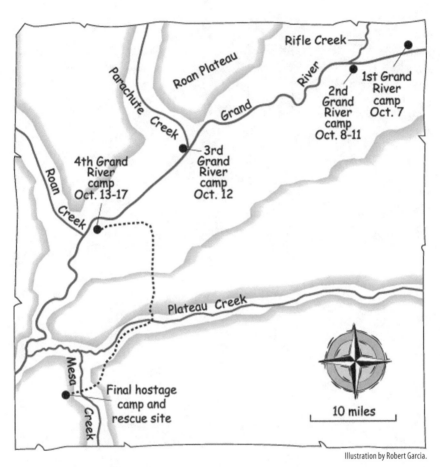

Rifle Creek

Roan Plateau

Parachute Creek

Grand River

2nd Grand River camp Oct. 8-11

1st Grand River camp Oct. 7

Roan Creek

4th Grand River camp Oct. 13-17

3rd Grand River camp Oct. 12

Plateau Creek

Mesa Creek

Final hostage camp and rescue site

10 miles

Illustration by Robert Garcia.

Map 5. Trail Section No. 4, October 17-21, 1879

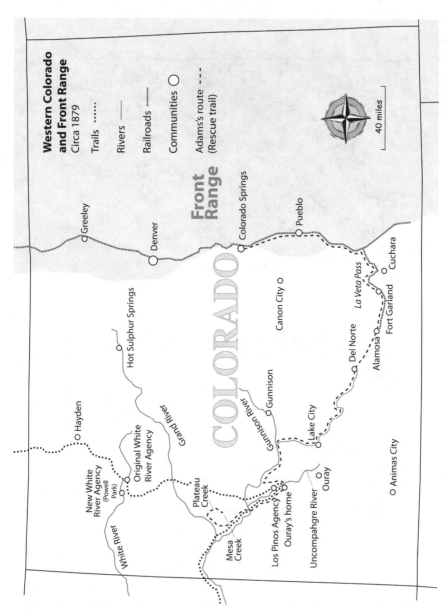

Western Colorado and Front Range

Circa 1879

Trails · · · · · ·

Rivers ——

Railroads ········

Communities ○

Adams's route – – –
(Rescue trail)

Front Range

Greeley

Denver

Colorado Springs

Pueblo

Hot Sulphur Springs

COLORADO

Canon City ○

Cuchara

La Veta Pass

Fort Garland

Alamosa

Del Norte

Gunnison

Gunnison River

Hayden

New White
River Agency
(Powell
Park)

Original White
River Agency

Grand River

White River

Plateau
Creek

Mesa
Creek

Los Pinos Agency

Ouray's home

Uncompahgre River

Ouray

Lake City

Animas City

40 miles

Map 6. Western Colorado and Front Range, Circa 1879

Illustration by Robert Garcia.

TROUBLED TRAILS

NICAAGAT CONFRONTS JOSEPHINE

THE UTE MAN WAS FRUSTRATED AS HE LAID OUT HIS COMPLAINTS TO the white woman being held in a teepee deep in the Colorado mountains in the autumn of 1879. Josephine Meeker was a hostage in Ute territory where few non-Utes had ventured. She and four others had been herded far south from the White River Indian Agency, force-marched over rugged terrain on tough Ute ponies. Now she was alone in a teepee with this angry Indian. The man confronting her was an intelligent and popular Ute leader named Nicaagat. He had come into the teepee not to threaten or terrorize Josephine, but to explain—to try to make her understand how things had gotten so far beyond the control of either of them.

Six days earlier Josephine's father, Nathan C. Meeker, had been killed along with all of his male employees at the White River Indian Agency in northwestern Colorado. Of the whites who were there, only Josie and her mother, Arvilla, along with Flora Ellen Price, the young wife of one of the agency workers, and her two young children had survived the attack.

But the Utes had also been attacked—on the same day that Meeker was killed. Roughly 140 soldiers had marched onto their reservation that morning, an action that the Utes viewed as an invasion. When that occurred, Nicaagat had every reason to believe his own people were about to be murdered, or bound in chains and manacles and hauled away. Major Thomas T. Thornburgh had told him as much a few days before the invasion, as the soldiers from Wyoming were headed south toward the White River Agency and the Ute reservation.[1]

Despite Nicaagat's continued efforts to convince the soldiers to halt outside the reservation and allow the officers, Ute leaders, and Nathan Meeker time to discuss their differences, the soldiers had marched onto the reservation, sparking fears among the Utes for the safety of their wives, their children, and their homeland. Given what had happened in other parts of Colorado and in other territories, the Utes had ample reason to be afraid.[2]

The result of the army's action was a battle at Milk Creek, at the northern boundary of the Ute reservation, beginning in the late morning of September 29, 1879. The commanding officer, Major Thornburgh, was killed along with twelve other soldiers and civilians. At least nineteen Utes were also killed.[3]

Despite their casualties, the Utes were able to keep the soldiers pinned down in a broad valley for six days. The siege ended the morning of October 5, the same day that Nicaagat confronted Josephine in the teepee. Army reinforcements from Wyoming had arrived almost simultaneously with a messenger from Chief Ouray, the powerful Ute leader to the south. Ouray demanded that the White River Utes cease fighting. Colonel Wesley Merritt's 400-plus reinforcements added incentive for the White River Utes to honor Ouray's request.

Nicaagat—also known as "Captain Jack," "Ute Jack," or just "Jack"— had been at the Milk Creek battle. He had tried, right up until the first shots were fired, to prevent a violent confrontation.[4] But Nicaagat had not been at the White River Indian Agency, 20 miles to the southwest, when Indian agent Nathan Meeker and his employees were killed, also on September 29. Nor had he been there when Josephine and the other women were taken hostage later that same day. Still, there was little question in his mind that one man was primarily to blame for all of the resulting violence.

"Jack came to see me and laid before me all his grievances against the agent, against the soldiers and all of them," Josie told a congressional hearing early the next year.[5] "He said that if the agent had done as he ought to have done, there never would have been any massacre....he said, too, that the agent was continually writing to get Washington to get the soldiers here; that those wild and exaggerated stories which they had seen in the Denver papers about the agency being burned, and about the 'Utes must go' had been written by father."[6]

It was not the first time Nicaagat had angrily denounced Nathan Meeker. He had said almost the same thing to Major Thornburgh, the army commander, several days before the battle at Milk Creek began, when he urged the major not to bring his troops onto the Ute reservation.[7] Thornburgh ignored Nicaagat's advice and was one of the first people to die at the battle of Milk Creek. Nicaagat had also voiced his concerns about Nathan Meeker's misdeeds during a meeting he had arranged with Colorado governor Frederick Pitkin barely a month before the battle— and to other people on different occasions.[8]

Records of the events leading up to the battle of Milk Creek and the killings at the White River Indian Agency detail a series of missteps, miscalculations, misleading statements, and outright lies on the part of numerous people. But Nicaagat's actions show a concerted effort to avoid conflict while he attempted to make others aware of the problems Meeker was creating. His is also a story of increasing frustration and growing anxiety, despite the fact that he had been a friend of white men for more than a decade.

Nicaagat had made trips to Washington, D.C., to help negotiate treaties and had also scouted for General George Crook in the campaign against the Sioux and Cheyenne. He believed most of the whites were people with whom he could reason, even if Nathan Meeker was not. He believed that if he presented his case to Major Thornburgh, Governor Pitkin, and officials in Washington, they would take appropriate action. When everyone ignored his pleadings—when soldiers came and refused to honor the Ute reservation boundaries—he quite reasonably feared his people were under attack and facing possible slaughter.

Although Nicaagat was portrayed in some contemporary accounts as a warmonger spoiling for a fight, one who had planned an ambush of Thornburgh, there is virtually no evidence to suggest that he sought a battle. He simply wanted his people's lands to be protected from white interlopers. And he desperately wanted a new Indian agent to be installed at White River, someone more truthful and less condescending and dictatorial than Nathan Meeker.

But that didn't happen. Instead, Nicaagat found himself an enemy of the whites, and he and his people pursued by American soldiers. Although Major Thornburgh's 140 troops had been pinned down for six days, Merritt had arrived with 400 new troops. And Nicaagat was under no illusion that those were all the soldiers who would come. He had seen the army deploy thousands of troops in pursuit of Plains Indians.

Now Nicaagat found himself facing a young white woman, one of the hostages that some of the Utes believed would enable them to negotiate with the whites so that the soldiers would not annihilate their people. Nicaagat had known twenty-one-year-old Josephine Meeker for a little more than a year, since she first arrived at the White River Agency. They apparently had a cordial relationship, even if they weren't close friends.

Records from that time suggest that the two of them—Nicaagat and Josephine—were both extremely popular among the 800 or so Utes who lived in and around the White River Agency.[9] Perhaps Nicaagat thought Josephine would understand his grievances because she had shown herself to be a friend of the Utes at the White River Agency, sometimes to the consternation of her father.

Nicaagat was in his late thirties or early forties, tall and striking in appearance. More than that, he was an undisputed warrior. When he returned from serving with Crook in the campaign against the hated Sioux, he was "idolized" by the young Ute men. He had fought side-by-side with the white soldiers, helped corral the Sioux, and had come back to the Ute reservation a hero.[10]

His standing no doubt rose even more in the horrible winter of 1877–78, when food and other supplies that were supposed to go to the Utes were held up in Rawlins, Wyoming, because of a crooked private contractor and bureaucratic bumbling on the part of the federal government. Nicaagat and his rival Quinkent—known to the whites as "Chief Douglas"—had worked together to break through the bureaucracy and get the supplies from the warehouse to the hungry Utes.

Most of the time Nicaagat and the much older Quinkent were in competition for the hearts of the White River Utes. While a small group of older Utes followed Quinkent, a much larger band—made up of perhaps 200 families—had gravitated to the younger, more energetic, and less compromising Nicaagat.[11]

Josephine had arrived at the White River Agency in July of 1878, a few months after her father took over as the agent. She was to serve as a teacher to the Ute children and run a boardinghouse for agency employees. When few Utes opted to send their children to her school, she went out to their nearby camps to socialize. This led her parents to worry that she was spending too much time with the Utes in their encampments and becoming too Indian.[12]

Many of the male Utes found Josie intriguing and sought to court her, including, according to one account, some of the older, prominent leaders (although Nicaagat is not mentioned among the suitors).[13] She clearly enjoyed the Utes' company, laughing at their jokes and learning a few Ute words. She went riding with some of the Ute women in the hills near the agency.[14] Josie also smoked tobacco with the Utes and enjoyed watching their traditional horse races. And they reciprocated by inviting her to healing ceremonies that were rarely open to outsiders.[15]

Now here she was, listening to a Ute leader berate her dead father. Nicaagat was trying to convince her that Nathan Meeker was to blame for the horrific events that had transpired. Josephine did not record how she responded, only what Nicaagat told her.[16]

These two strong-willed, charismatic people were caught up in one of the last major confrontations between American Indians and a ceaselessly expanding white population. Both would survive the events of 1879, and both were key participants in two official investigations conducted following the uprising—one in western Colorado and one in Washington, D.C. They even met and visited amicably one last time, in February 1880, during the Washington hearings before a congressional committee on Indian affairs.

Josie never returned to the Ute reservation after being released from captivity. Nicaagat went back, but he left within two years for Wyoming rather than follow his people to a smaller, more restricted reservation in Utah. Just over three years after their confrontation in the teepee, Josephine and Nicaagat were dead. Both of their deaths may have been related to the events that brought them together in the fall of 1879.

THE BATTLE AT MILK CREEK
AND THE KILLINGS AT THE WHITE RIVER
INDIAN AGENCY

RELATIONS BETWEEN NATHAN C. MEEKER AND HIS UTE CONSTITUENTS at the White River Indian Agency in northwestern Colorado had deteriorated steadily through the spring and summer of 1879. Things had been relatively amicable when Meeker arrived in May 1878, but his patronizing attitude—he had the Utes refer to him as "Father Meeker"—and his unceasing efforts to turn the seminomadic horseback hunters into ground-tilling farmers grated on most of the Utes.[1]

Meeker had come to the agency at the age of sixty-one for several reasons. First, he firmly believed he could, with kindness and his own hardworking example, turn the people he viewed as "savages" into civilized, productive members of society. He had a blueprint for this effort in his own writings. Some twenty years earlier he had written a novel called *The Adventures of Captain Armstrong,* in which the hero is marooned on an island in the South Pacific. After facing initial challenges and threats to his safety, he ultimately convinces the natives of the benefits of hard work and Christian values.[2]

Furthermore, Meeker was a utopian who had twice been involved in idealistic efforts to create planned agricultural communities—not quite communes or experiments in socialism, but far more communal than the independent, solitary farmer ideal that was the free-market model of the time. The first had been in Trumbull Phalanx, Ohio, shortly after he and Arvilla Smith married in 1844, but it failed rapidly. The second was in what would become Greeley, Colorado, about 40 miles north of Denver, beginning in 1870. Meeker was the leader of the Union Colony there until he left to take over at the White River Agency.[3]

This second endeavor had the advantage of financial backing from New York *Tribune* publisher Horace Greeley—he of the famous "Go west, young man!" exhortation. Meeker worked for Greeley as a correspondent during the Civil War and later as an agricultural writer. Greeley shared Meeker's enthusiasm for establishing a new sort of agricultural community in the West. He helped him advertise for participants, hosted the first meeting in New York, served on the board of directors of the Union Colony, and bankrolled Meeker's trips to Colorado to look for suitable land. He also purchased the land, which was to be resold to Union Colony members, and paid for improvements such as fences and irrigation ditches through loans that were to be repaid by the colony as a whole.[4]

While Meeker's wife, Arvilla, was deeply religious, Meeker was less so. He'd had a falling out with church people early in his life and didn't trust them. Even so, he had a puritanical nature.[5]

The Union Colony was to be a dry community, and members grew angry when an outsider tried to establish a saloon nearby. In soliciting for colony members, Meeker advertised for temperate men who didn't use foul language and were willing to work hard. And while he initially was seen as the unquestioned leader of the community—its elected president, resident of the largest house, agricultural planner, and publisher of the community newspaper—the same condescending attitude that would later anger the Utes upset members of the Union Colony as the enterprise continued. Although it fared better than the earlier agricultural community that he had joined in Ohio, the Greeley project didn't flourish initially. Irrigation ditches didn't reach as much of the colony as quickly as Meeker had promised. Drought, heat, dust storms, and rugged winters discouraged

some of the eastern-born colony members who had believed they were
moving to the Eden of the West. Many packed up and left. But worst of
all, Greeley's money began to dry up.[6]

In 1872 Greeley made an unsuccessful bid for the Republican nomina-
tion to become president of the United States. Not long afterward, he fell
ill and died. His heirs, two daughters, began demanding that Meeker pay
off the debts he owed their father.[7] And that was the second reason Meeker
became the agent for the White River Indian Agency: he needed money.

With the exception of his years in the newspaper business and his
other writings, Meeker had not been financially successful in any undertaking—not farming, being a storekeeper, or leading a communal agricultural colony. He sincerely wanted to repay the debts he owed to the family
of his friend and mentor, so he began actively lobbying Colorado's congressional delegation for a post at an Indian agency, where the guaranteed
salary would allow him to gradually honor his financial obligations.[8]

At the time there was a national debate over who should be in charge
of the Indian agencies and how they should be run. The U.S. Department
of the Interior was in charge of Indian reservations, as it is today, but officials with the Department of War believed that they could do a better job
and solve what was called "the Indian problem" once and for all. Many of
the Indian agents had religious backgrounds, were affiliated with churches
back east, and were firm believers that Christian charity and education
were the best ways to civilize the Indians. But after a decade of Indian
wars from Arizona to Idaho to the Dakotas, trust in that theory was rapidly ebbing away. Secretary of Interior Carl Schurz, who feared what
would happen if control of the agencies was turned over to the War
Department, was sympathetic to the Indians but also eager for a plan that
would move them more quickly from being what he and others viewed as
little more than government-supported children on reservations to peaceful, productive members of society. Meeker's agricultural ideas seemed to
fit that bill, and he won the agency appointment, replacing Reverend
Edward Danforth, a Unitarian who'd had a relatively cordial relationship
with the White River Utes.[9]

Meeker's patronizing attitude and his farming plans were not the only
problems creating friction with the Utes. As occurred elsewhere throughout the West, white pioneers, driven by the allure of precious metals and
prime agricultural ground, were encroaching ever more on lands that had
once belonged to the Utes. Ever since the United States had gained con-

trol of western Colorado through the 1848 Treaty of Guadalupe Hidalgo with Mexico, the government had been pressuring the seven Ute bands to give up more and more of their territory to white interlopers. The most recent effort had resulted in the 1874 Brunot Agreement, which opened large chunks of the southwestern mining district around the new towns of Silverton and Ouray to those seeking gold and silver.[10]

In the northwestern corner of the state there was less pressure by whites to move onto Ute land. But ranchers and miners were moving into areas such as North Park and Middle Park, which were not part of the Ute reservation according to the 1874 agreement but were regarded as primary hunting grounds. Furthermore, the White River Utes, like most of their relatives throughout western Colorado, viewed the reservation more as a boundary to keep the whites out than an enclosure in which they were bound to remain. So they traveled repeatedly to North Park, Middle Park, and the area north from the White River toward Wyoming. They encountered miners, ranchers, white hunters, and others and, according to some accounts, threatened a number of them if they didn't leave the area.[11]

The summer of 1879 was also exceptionally dry. Meeker wrote to Governor Pitkin saying there had been no rain at the agency for more than two months. Snows the preceding winter had been lighter than normal, and as a result, forest and brush fires burned throughout much of western Colorado that summer.[12]

Most whites blamed the Utes for starting the fires, and it's true that the Utes were known to set blazes to drive game and improve forage for their horses. But the West during a dry year is also prone to wildfires caused by lightning and careless campfires. The Utes probably got blamed for many fires that were either ignited by lightning or caused by reckless miners and hunters.[13]

It didn't matter. By midsummer whites in Colorado were in an uproar over the fires and pleading for the army to do something about the wandering Utes. Meeker received letters from the residents of North Park and Governor Pitkin demanding that he keep the White River Utes on the reservation. Pitkin also wrote to federal officials, noting the problems and seeking army assistance to corral the Utes.[14]

Meeker continued to push for the creation of an agrarian society at the White River Indian Agency. He moved the agency 15 miles downriver in the spring of 1879 to a location more amenable to cultivation. Nicaagat and his band of followers refused to move to the new location because they wanted nothing to do with farming, a viewpoint that was the source of considerable dispute between him and Meeker. Even so, when Meeker's efforts to plow up grasslands at the new site created antagonism among many of the Utes who had moved downstream, Meeker turned to Nicaagat for assistance. On at least two occasions he sent a rider 15 miles upstream for Nicaagat, who came down to talk with the angry Utes, even though they were members of the bands led by Quinkent (Douglas) and Canalla (Johnson 2), not Nicaagat. Nicaagat managed to soothe hard feelings and strike a compromise that allowed the plowing to continue within specific parameters.[15]

Nevertheless, two incidents occurred with the plowing that helped hasten the hostile encounters of September 29. First, in late August some Utes fired rifle shots as agency employee Shadrick Price was plowing near the Utes' horseracing track. One of the shooters was the son of Canalla, and he maintained that he and his friend were engaged in target practice only, shooting away from Price. But Price insisted that he had heard bullets zinging over his head and immediately quit plowing.[16]

Then, in mid-September, after Nicaagat had helped reach an agreement on the plowing, Canalla approached Meeker angrily. He hadn't been present when the agreement was reached, and he was furious about the new plowing that was taking place. Accounts differ about what happened during their confrontation. Canalla said that while he spoke angrily to Meeker, he did no more than grab him by the shoulder to emphasize his point. Meeker, however, maintained that he had been assaulted, thrown out of his office, and shoved against a hitching rail in front of the Indian agency headquarters. If other employees of the agency had not been nearby, Meeker wrote in letters to authorities, he probably would have been killed.[17]

After Meeker sent several urgent messages stating that he believed his life, his family members, and the agency employees were all in danger, government officials reacted. Secretary Schurz contacted his counterpart at the Department of War, which sent word to generals in the field who authorized Major Thomas T. Thornburgh, commander of Fort Steele near Rawlins, Wyoming, to proceed to the White River Agency with a suitable number of troops. Although technically under different administration than Colorado, the Wyoming post was closest to the White River. Thornburgh was ordered to protect Meeker and his employees, and arrest any Utes who were believed to be causing problems, including two who had been accused of setting fires that reportedly had destroyed a ranch home earlier that summer.[18]

Thornburgh was no Indian-hating soldier. In fact, he had met Meeker on a train from Cheyenne earlier that summer, as Meeker was returning from a visit to Greeley, and found the White River Indian agent overly excitable and prone to exaggeration about the Utes. Thornburgh even conducted an investigation of claims made by Meeker earlier that year—questioning ranchers, freighters, and others who worked in the Snake River country between the White River and Rawlins. He found little to indicate that the Utes were actively threatening white settlers in the region or that they were responsible for most of the fires they were accused of setting.[19]

Even so, Thornburgh was a loyal army officer, bound to his duty. Moreover, the year before he had led an unsuccessful expedition into the Sand Hills of northwestern Nebraska to round up a few Sioux who had left their recently established reservation in the Dakotas. He had failed miserably, getting wagons bogged down in quicksand, following decoy trails, and allowing his prey to escape. With this new assignment, he was determined to demonstrate that he could efficiently and quickly deal with Indian disputes.[20]

Thornburgh mustered three units of cavalry, two infantry units, wagons and teamsters with supplies—at least 180 men altogether—and headed south over the wagon road from Rawlins toward the White River Agency in late September. As he moved forward, he sent messages to Meeker by swift civilian riders, and he and the Indian agent traded several brief messages as the army approached the agency.[21]

But Thornburgh also had a critical conversation with Nicaagat a few days prior to the battle. Nicaagat had heard that soldiers were approaching and met a young officer, Lieutenant Samuel Cherry, at Peck's store, about 15 miles north of the reservation, on September 27. Nicaagat asked repeatedly why the soldiers were coming, and Cherry said he should go speak with his commanding officer. Nicaagat agreed to do just that. Late in the evening, Nicaagat and four other Utes rode into Thornburgh's camp. After being introduced to Thornburgh, Nicaagat repeated the question he had put to the young officer. Thornburgh explained that he had been ordered to the reservation by his superiors in Washington. When Nicaagat said the Utes didn't want to fight the soldiers, and that it would be wrong for brothers to fight, Thornburgh replied that it didn't matter if they were brothers—

if the Utes tried to prevent him from doing his duty, he and his troops would have no choice but to fight.[22]

Nicaagat urged Thornburgh not to enter the reservation with the full body of his troops, but to stop just short of the boundary. Then Thornburgh and four or five of his key officers could proceed onto the reservation, meet with Meeker and the Ute leaders, and try to resolve the dispute peacefully. He had good reason for making such a request. Nearly all of the Utes were aware of the Sand Creek Massacre, east of Denver, in 1864. That attack was led by Colorado Territorial Militia Colonel John Chivington, a Methodist minister. Cheyenne and Arapaho Indians under Chief Black Kettle were camped peacefully along Sand Creek and had pledged not to fight with the whites. But in retaliation for attacks against a stagecoach committed by other Indians, they were brutally murdered in a surprise dawn attack. Women and children were among those killed. Only a few Indians escaped.[23]

Additionally, Nicaagat had served as a scout for General George Crook in his campaign against the Sioux and Cheyenne Indians in Montana, Wyoming, and the Dakotas in 1876, the year Custer was killed, and in 1877. Nicaagat was present later that year when the army attacked a Sioux village led by Chief American Horse, destroying it and killing many of the inhabitants, women and children among them. American Horse died in U.S. custody a few days after the attack. Nicaagat probably also witnessed an attack that obliterated a Cheyenne village on the brutally cold morning of November 25, 1876. Most of the Cheyenne escaped to the surrounding hills, many to die there. Lacking shelter, Indian babies froze in their mothers' arms.[24] Furthermore, Meeker had stated loudly to Nicaagat only days before that the soldiers were coming to put many of the Utes in chains and haul them away.[25]

In short, Nicaagat could envision nothing good happening to his people if all of Thornburgh's troops entered the reservation—only death or captivity. Thornburgh even told him he wanted to arrest several Utes suspected of setting fires that summer, namely two Indians called Chinaman and Bennett, as well as other unnamed troublemakers. Because of his combative relationship with Meeker, Nicaagat had reason to fear he might be on the arrest list as well.[26]

Initially, Thornburgh seemed receptive to Nicaagat's proposal that he enter the reservation with only a few men, but it is not clear if he ever told Nicaagat that. He did, however, send a message to Meeker saying he would keep the bulk of his troops outside the reservation and come in with five officers on September 29 to confer with Meeker and the Ute chiefs. Meeker responded that it seemed a suitable plan. But when Thornburgh discussed the plan with his own officers, some of them believed it was a trap by which the Utes hoped to murder Thornburgh and whatever officers accompanied him to the agency. Thornburgh then wrote to Meeker again, recalling that his orders specifically called for him to proceed to the White River Agency, and leaving the largest body of his troops behind would not be fulfilling those orders.

If that hadn't been enough to anger the already agitated Utes, Thornburgh added a further wrinkle. He decided he could trick the Indians. He wrote Meeker saying he would proceed as if he and a few officers were coming to the agency, but instead of leaving the bulk of the troops behind, they would wait until nightfall to hurry through a canyon where they feared ambush and would be only a short distance from Thornburgh if he needed them. Meeker again agreed, although Thornburgh never received the Indian agent's final response: it was found in possession of a White River Agency employee who was killed on his way to deliver it.[27]

On the morning of September 29, Thornburgh and his troops crossed Milk Creek, the accepted northern boundary of the reservation even if it wasn't the actual surveyed boundary. Eight or ten Utes under Nicaagat went out to meet them with nothing but peaceful intentions, Nicaagat would later tell members of Congress. But fifty or more other Utes, not under his control, followed not far behind. All of the Utes became suspicious when they saw the troops divert from the regular wagon road, thereby avoiding a canyon where the soldiers believed they could be easily ambushed, and start through a broad valley toward a rise that would lead eventually to the agency. According to Nicaagat, he wanted to go forward to meet with the troops and discuss their plans, and he ordered the others to stay back out of sight. But some of those, not members of his party, rejected his orders. They displayed themselves where the troops could see them among the pinyon, juniper, and sagebrush on the hillside overlooking the approaching forces. Fearful of attack, Thornburgh and other officers ordered the troops to deploy in traditional skirmish lines, an action that Nicaagat recognized as typical preparation for an attack.[28]

Even so, Nicaagat said he told the Indians not to shoot. Lieutenant Cherry, at the front of the leading troop, proceeded farther toward the hillside where the Indians were, stopped, and waved his hat. He said it was meant as a form of greeting. Nicaagat told Congress he didn't see the hat being waved, but other Utes later reported it to him. Whatever its intended meaning, it triggered the start of hostilities.[29]

Cherry said the Utes fired first, whizzing one or two bullets past him and injuring one of his soldiers and a horse. The Utes unanimously reported that unidentified soldiers touched off the first shots, and they only responded after being fired upon.[30]

Cherry and his troops dismounted and retreated under heavy fire. The rest of the troops circled wagons and made a barricade that was quickly added to with the bodies of dead horses and mules. They were in a small basin—"the cellar," the Utes called it—with the Indians surrounding them on the high ground and raining deadly shots directly down on them.[31]

In the immediate aftermath of the battle, and for more than a century afterward, the primary white version of the story would be that the Utes had planned an ambush of Thornburgh and his troops. The Utes, however, have always maintained that wasn't the case. First they note that the Indians had no reason to believe the soldiers were going to take the route they did onto the reservation. They expected the troops to follow the conventional wagon road. Additionally, when the shooting began, the Utes held the high ground, had better long-range weapons, and many experienced marksmen. If their intent had been to annihilate the soldiers, they could have easily done so. Finally, after the initial burst of gunfire, no other soldiers were killed during the week-long siege. The Utes kept them pinned down but were careful not to kill them, their descendants say.[32]

In the midst of the first, frenetic fighting, Thornburgh galloped alone across an open meadow between one group of his besieged troops and another. He died alone when a Ute bullet struck him in the head. Soldiers witnessed his death and reported it to Captain J. Scott Payne, who assumed command of the troops.[33]

Nicaagat said he witnessed the start of the fight and then fell back in despair. He left Milk Creek the following morning to round up some of his horses that had strayed.[34]

Other Utes testified that it was unclear who the primary leader of the Utes was during the battle. In the highly independent social structure of the Utes, it is very likely that no single person was in charge. But Nicaagat and Colorow were the two most frequently mentioned as leaders at the Milk Creek battle.[35]

Within a few hours after the fighting begin, at least one of the Utes left the battle site and galloped back to the White River Agency, some 20 miles to the southwest. There he informed Quinkent and other Utes of the battle—information that triggered the killing spree at the agency. Although Quinkent and a few other Utes had enjoyed a cordial luncheon with Meeker and his family that day, an hour or so later some Utes began firing at the male employees who had been working on the roof of one of the agency buildings.[36]

The shooting went on sporadically for hours, during which time Josephine and Arvilla Meeker, Flora Ellen Price, her two children, and an agency employee named Frank Dresser dashed from the main house to a brick milk house a few yards away. They cowered there until around 5 p.m., when it became clear the Utes were setting the buildings on fire. Hoping they wouldn't be spotted, they made a break for the sagebrush hills, running first across an open field.[37]

The Utes saw them, ordered them to stop, and fired shots in their direction. One grazed Arvilla's leg, causing a painful but not life-threatening wound. The women halted, and the Utes surrounded them. Dresser escaped, and although he had also been wounded, the women believed he had survived. After their release they learned that he had crawled to a small cave or mine entrance, where he died.[38]

Arvilla was ordered to go back into the burning agency headquarters for money and her medicine kit. She also grabbed her treasured copy of *A Pilgrim's Progress*. The Utes found the medicine kit too large and ordered her to leave it behind. On the way out of the agency building, she found the body of her dead husband, clothed only in a shirt, with a bullet through his head. She knelt, considered kissing him, but thought better of it because her Ute captor was standing over her. So she told Nathan good-bye and hurried down toward the river where the other captives were being held.[39]

After some initial bickering among the Utes over who should be in charge of which captives, the women were ordered onto horses with little more than blankets for saddles. That was particularly painful for Arvilla, then sixty-four years old, with a wounded leg and limited horseback experience. Flora Ellen's young daughter was tied onto a horse with Josephine, while Flora Ellen kept her year-old son with her. Surrounded by agitated and drunken Utes, the small party made its way southward onto what, for the past 130 years, has been a largely forgotten trail.[40]

HOSTAGES IN THE BORDERLANDS

AMONG THE MANY CULTURAL CHASMS THAT EXISTED WHEN THE UTES and their hostages headed down the trail, one of the broadest involved the different concepts of hostage taking and the use of captives for bartering purposes. When the Utes at the White River Agency took the women and children hostage, they were continuing an ancient tradition that extended well beyond their own territory and culture. They were doing what their ancestors and people in many other cultures around the world had done for centuries—capturing women and children who might serve as slaves, be adopted as family members, or be traded to others. In this case, the captives were viewed as insurance—or at least protection—against reprisals from the army.

When Spaniards came to the New World, they expanded the American Indians' hostage practice based on their own lengthy tradition of hostage taking and trading with Muslims during the long history of conquest, reconquest, and peaceful coexistence on the Iberian Peninsula.[1] Unlike the slave trade involving captured Africans that occurred in other parts of the Western Hemisphere, captives under this arrangement weren't treated as subhuman creatures, barely more than livestock. Although the practice of taking captives in the American Southwest was often violent, especially during raids in which hostages were captured, those seized were frequently adopted by their American Indian or Spanish captors. They might become household servants, be baptized into the Catholic faith, and even be allowed to marry other members of the culture to which they were being assimilated.[2]

Some captives undoubtedly received brutal treatment, but others were met with compassion, even kindness. A significant number of the American Indians captured by or traded to the Spanish became *genizaro*—servant soldiers who worked with the Spanish military to protect settlements from marauding Indians and even joined the Spaniards on slave raids to tribal villages. Often the genizaro had their own communities or their own neighborhoods within diverse Spanish settlements.[3]

Nearly all of the American Indians living under Spanish rule had access to the Spanish legal system. Some even traveled to Mexico City to press their legal claims, although that system was clearly weighted in favor of the Spanish colonists and against the Indians.[4] Furthermore, intermarriage between captives and conquerors was frequent and accepted. Eighteenth-century Spanish records from New Mexico list different types of residents, including Spaniards, *genizaros*, Indians, and "coyotes" (mixed breeds). Some list Spaniards with Indian or coyote wives, or coyotes with Indian wives, even *genizaros* with coyote spouses.[5] That cultural tradition no doubt played a part in the Ute warrior Pahsone's belief that Josephine Meeker was not only a hostage but was going to be his wife.[6]

In Spanish society the captured outsiders might have little chance of reaching the top tiers of social status, but they were not treated as cattle, to be sold on an auction block. In contrast, Spanish women and children taken by Indians, or Indians captured by competing tribes, were able to attain powerful positions among their new families. Ouray, Colorow, and Nicaagat all became leaders of the Utes, even though Ouray had an Apache mother, Colorow was probably a Comanche, and Nicaagat's lineage was uncertain.

Because of that long history of hostage taking and trading, it's no surprise that several individuals deeply involved with events related to the White River hostages had experiences with captives, slaves, or hostages at some point during their lives. And those experiences affected how they reacted during the crisis.

Ouray grew up near Taos, New Mexico, and he and his brothers were hired out by their father as sheepherders for the Spaniards. They were also baptized and taught the Catholic faith by local friars. As a result, as a young man Ouray was able to closely observe the Spaniards and the few Americans living near Taos, as well as representatives of various Indian tribes. He spoke Spanish fluently, English tolerably, and several American Indian languages. He also understood other cultures, particularly that of the expanding Anglo-Americans, far better than most Utes.[7]

Additionally, Ouray lost a young son to Arapaho raiders while on a hunting trip to Colorado's eastern plains. Years later, when American leaders from Washington, D.C., were trying to persuade the Utes to give up additional territory through what became the Brunot Agreement of 1874, one of the enticements they offered to win Ouray's support was the promise that the U.S. Indian Commission would find his son for him. Authorities did find among the Arapahos a youngster of approximately the right age who had purportedly been taken captive as a youngster, but the boy maintained that whatever his ancestry, he was now an Arapaho and the Utes were his enemies.[8]

Ouray's sister She-towitch [Susan] was also taken captive by the Arapahos as a teenager. But perhaps because she was already a teenager and was held captive only two years, she never assimilated into that tribe. Although treated roughly during captivity she was freed—although whether it was through her own efforts or that of the Colorado Militia is unclear.[9]

There's little doubt that that experience played a pivotal role when She-towitch, then the wife of White River Ute leader Canalla [Johnson 2], took Josephine and the other captives under her wing. Josie, Flora Ellen, and Arvilla repeatedly referred to She-towitch in their later testimony as the friendliest of their Ute captors—someone who protected them from violence, made sure they had adequate food, held and comforted Flora Ellen's children, and wept over their fate.

Another Ute woman, Jane Redjacket, who worked as the Meekers' house servant and sometimes served as Nathan's confidant, had been sold to a white judge in Wyoming Territory in the 1860s according to one account. There she also worked as a house servant and developed her English skills. The judge, William A. Carter, eventually agreed to free her so she could return to the Utes and marry a man named Pauvitz.[10]

And then there is Nicaagat. Details of his early life are sketchy. Conflicting accounts of his early years say he was born to the Apaches of New

Mexico or the Goshutes of western Utah.[11] It is believed he was sold by his own tribe or taken captive by Spanish or Ute traders who dealt him to a Mormon family in Utah as a small boy. He learned English, was baptized and raised in the Mormon religion—and suffered unbearable treatment from a woman in the household who wielded a buggy whip. When he could no longer take it, he threatened her with a knife, jumped on one of the family's horses, and rode east until he reached first the Uintah Utes of northeastern Utah, and later the White River Utes in Colorado.[12] Or so he told his Ute friends later in his life.[13] Accounts from various historical records differ.

When he fled the Mormon household as a teen, Nicaagat found acceptance in the welcoming embrace of the Utes. But he would never forget his experience living with the Mormons. Sometimes he would recall it as a time of captivity.[14] Other times, he seemed to view it as a source of honor.[15]

The practice of hostage taking was viewed in a much different manner by the culture that was rapidly expanding across the United States. From Colorado to the East Coast, whites considered taking women and children hostage an abomination. They understood slavery and human captivity primarily in terms of blacks living in the South. Most had also heard of Cynthia Ann Parker, abducted by Comanches in Texas as a child. She was rescued nearly twenty-five years later, only to find she no longer felt comfortable in white culture. She became depressed and silent, and never fully reverted to white ways.[16]

The whites also knew hundreds of stories—many of them more myth than reality—about how Indians treated captives. They had long heard stories of scalpings and burnings, rapes and eviscerations. Few had any knowledge of the cultural history of hostage taking in the border country of the Southwest. Even if they did, it mattered little, because such a culture was completely foreign to them and an affront to their Christian beliefs, even if those beliefs had allowed many of them to accept the enslavement of Africans.

When word of the events at the White River—and the Utes' taking of hostages—reached the rest of the nation, most Americans assumed the captives were being subjected to the worst atrocities imaginable. If they survived at all, most believed it would only be after horrendous suffering.

4

TRAIL SECTION 1

FROM COLORADO HIGHWAY 64 NEAR MEEKER, ONE LOOKS SOUTH TO view the site of the old White River Indian Agency. And south is the direction the Utes headed with their hostages on the evening of September 29, 1879, following the killings at the agency and the battle with the soldiers at Milk Creek. "Just after dark, after we had been mounted [we] started across the river directly south," Josephine Meeker recalled several months after the events.[1]

Immediately south of where the White River Indian Agency stood in 1879 are the broad, open meadows of Powell Park, now primarily in alfalfa or grass for pasture. Meandering through the park is the White River itself. It is a cold, clear stream about 50 feet wide at this point, and shallow enough to cross on horseback in late September, when Josephine and Arvilla Meeker and Flora Ellen Price and her two children crossed it with their Ute captors.

Riding south, they would have traversed a gradually rising landscape that is now primarily pasture for cattle. In those days it provided the rich grasses so important to the Utes' horses. Perhaps the caravan stopped at a little spring of clear, cold water on land that, at the time of this writing, was owned by Joe Sullivan, his daughter Kathleen, and her husband, Reed Kelly. The deed for their ranch, which Joe purchased in the early 1950s, records the name of that water source as "Josephine Spring."

Beyond the spring they would have entered the rugged sagebrush country in what is now known as Josephine Basin, so named by cowboys in the late nineteenth century.[2] It was already dark when they began their ride, but a nearly full moon would have offered abundant light.[3] If they turned and looked back down the mountain toward the White River, they might have seen smoke and even flames from the buildings set ablaze at the agency they had just left.

That night they rode about 12 miles, Josephine stated. "It took us until one or two o'clock to get in, but we stopped on the way."[4] This was part of Josephine's statement to the White River Ute Commission, which gathered near present-day Montrose, Colorado, beginning in November 1879, less than a month after the women were released by the Utes. The commission consisted of Chief Ouray, Charles Adams (the man who arranged the release of the hostages), and Major General Edward Hatch, head of the U.S. Army in New Mexico. The testimony of the three women was actually taken by Adams in Greeley shortly after their release from captivity. He read their statements to the other members of the commission.

"Was there any water there by the trail?" Adams asked Josephine.

"No; right off from the water. We turned and went up into a little canyon," she said.

All the evidence suggests they rode to what whites referred to as "the squaw camp," which was either on Piceance Creek or a tributary of that stream. They were probably closer to 15 miles south of the White River.

On September 28, the day before the battle, according to M. Wilson Rankin—a cowboy, courier, and mail carrier who knew the territory and would personally visit the site of the White River Indian Agency less than a week after the killings—the Ute women and children "were moved with their tepees from their camp at the agency to the head of the east branch of Piceance Creek, twelve miles south of the agency, where they made camp, which was known as 'Squaw Camp.' Four tepees were left standing at the agency where ninety-four had been. One of these was Douglas' tepee."[5]

This is no easy jaunt, even in modern times. The landscape of grass and sagebrush rises gently at first, until a mile or so south of Josephine Springs (which is about 4 miles south of the White River). Then it climbs rapidly to the mesa top, where pinyon and juniper trees thrive. Even riding horseback on an old jeep road, as we did in the autumn of 2005 with Joe and Kathleen Sullivan and their friends, our horses were breathing heavily during the climb. We had to stop a couple of times to let them catch their breath. For the hostages of 1879—riding at night, traumatized by the killings at the agency, with no idea of what was going to happen to them—the trek must have been a terrifying ordeal.

"The road over the large mountains was so steep it was all I could do to sit on the horse. By this time it was quite dark," Flora Ellen Price said.[6]

"It was now dark and Douglas lost no time in getting started. Being lame from having had a thigh dislocated three years ago, and not being used to riding, I asked to ride behind Douglas," recalled Arvilla Meeker. "The moon came out so clearly that the night seemed like day. We forded the river and trotted off toward the mountains to the south."[7]

Mrs. Meeker continued:

> My limb ached so terribly that I could scarcely sit on the horse. Douglas held it awhile, then he strapped it in a kind of a sling to his saddle. I asked if I should see my daughter, Josephine. Douglas replied, "Yes." As we rode a villainous looking Indian trotted alongside and slapped me on the shoulder and asked me how I would like to be his squaw, and he made indecent proposals. Chief Douglas listened and laughed. He said the Indian was an Arapahoe and I would kill Utes if I married an Arapahoe.[8]

Arvilla Meeker also said Douglas's breath smelled of whiskey. "The other Indians all took out bottles of whiskey, which they held up between their eyes and the moon as they drank so as to see how much was left," she recalled.[9]

"There were about twenty-five or thirty there when we came out of the agency," said Josephine. "They all had their guns and were well armed. They had plenty of ammunition and plenty of whiskey. Most of them were drunk."[10]

Flora Ellen also thought some of the Indians had been drinking. "Jim Johnson, a White River Ute, rode out in the party with us. He did not say anything to me only that he was going to take me to the Utes' squaw camp, and he said the Utes 'no hurt me.' I think he had a little whiskey in him."[11]

Josie told Charles Adams she believed the Utes obtained the whiskey from the army wagons they had taken from Thornburgh's troops, saying that's where the Indians claimed they had gotten the alcohol. She said none had been kept at the agency, which was probably true given Nathan Meeker's strong antipathy toward alcoholic beverages.[12]

Army officers who testified before Congress a few months later denied they had carried any large amounts of alcohol with them, though the medical officer had some. They suggested that the liquor came from nearby trading posts, such as Peck's store, just off the reservation.[13] The presence of liquor no doubt increased the women's fear that the Indians had only spared them temporarily so that they could terrorize and torture them later on.

Flora Ellen recalled that as she walked away from the burning agency, "I had read so much about their treatment of captives that I was afraid they would want to torture me. They said, 'No kill white squaw; heap like them.' I said, 'You are going to burn me,' and they said, 'No burn white squaw.' Then they took me out through the brush."[14]

In addition to the killings that had already been committed, the Utes gave them some reason to fear the worst. Arvilla recalled getting ready to ride out immediately after seeing the body of her dead husband. "We left the trail and came to a little canyon in the mountains, with high rocks on all sides. All dismounted and the prisoners were searched by the Indians, even to our shoes and stockings," she said. They rested, but it was a disturbing rest. Douglas held a gun to Arvilla and threatened to kill her. She cried out and, to her relief, heard Josephine call out, "I am all right, mamma; don't be afraid!"[15] In other accounts, she and Josie both described a gun being pointed at Josie as she was threatened with death.

"After resting for half an hour, we remounted and rode until midnight, when we reached the Ute women's camp," Arvilla said. "Douglas ordered me roughly to get off the horse. I was so lame and in such pain that I told him I could not move. He took my hand and pulled me off and I fell on the ground because I could not stand."[16]

One Ute seemed delighted to present Flora Ellen with a souvenir from the killings. Riding beside her, the unnamed man pulled out a watch on a strap and put it around her neck, asking her if she recognized it. She did. It had belonged to William Post, one of the employees at the agency who had been killed that day.[17] Even so, there were acts of kindness from the Indians. "When we arrived at camp that night a squaw came and took my little boy from the horse and cried over him like a child," Flora Ellen said. "I dismounted and sat down in Pahsone's camp. I wasn't at all hungry and when they offered me coffee, cold meat and bread I could not eat."[18]

After being pulled roughly from her horse by Douglas, the aging Mrs. Meeker received some needed assistance. "An Indian and a squaw soon came and helped me up and led me to a tent. When I went to bed, Douglas and his wife covered me with blankets and I was more comfortable that night than at any other time during my captivity."[19]

Still, there were quite understandable questions about who might rescue them, and when.

"We camped that night with the rest of them in this canyon....In the morning, early, all the men cleaned up their guns, supplied themselves well with ammunition and started, as they told us, to fight the soldiers. Of course we were wondering why the troops did not come in. Meanwhile, for two days, all the squaws were busy in going back to the agency and carrying off more flour and more goods."[20] When asked by one of the members of Congress how far this first camp was from the White River Indian Agency, Josie replied, "I should think we were about ten miles."

Differing mileage estimates and time frames are typical of the various accounts about the hostage trail. There are even different reports from the same person. But given their shock, their travel through unfamiliar country, and their fear, it's amazing the three women were able to give such cogent accounts as they did.

M. Wilson Rankin also talked of the initial night for the hostages based on stories he had heard, accounts he read later, and his own personal interview with Flora Ellen about three years after the events. Although his story meshes with theirs on the broad details, he offered a few details that the victims themselves did not report.

Mrs. Meeker, at the age of sixty-eight [she was actually 64] was not a strong woman, and the night ride to the squaw camp taxed her endurance to the limit. She was taken in charge by Douglas and mounted on a pony, with blankets for a saddle. When too weak to ride alone, she was tied on with a rope, and at times rode behind Douglas. Mrs. Price was taken in charge by Cojo, and mounted on a pony with blankets for a saddle, with her baby boy in her arms. Josephine was the only one furnished with a saddle. It was a government saddle, taken from the horse that Thornburgh rode. [How

Rankin obtained that bit of information is not known. Nothing else refers to it as Thornburgh's saddle.] Price's three-year-old girl rode behind Josephine, tied on with a blanket.

With their caravan of pack ponies and government pack mules, they crossed White River to the south, going by the rough mountain trail to the squaw camp.

During the night ride, the Utes were hilarious, and drinking from bottles of liquor. One greasy and uncouth-looking Indian rode alongside Josephine and said, "Good squaw. You my squaw."

From the loot, the captives were furnished with sufficient blankets for bedding. Some of the squaws assisted them to be comfortable. Susan [She-towitch] wept, and felt sorry for them. The next day, Jane and Douglas' squaw, "Quana," went back to the agency garden to get vegetables.[21]

Josephine told the congressional committee, "The massacre was on Monday, the 29th, and we staid there in this canyon until Thursday (October 2)....On Thursday we moved on about ten miles farther and camped again. [The stories are inconsistent about whether they camped in one place or two prior to October 7.] On Sunday night, they told us that a white man from Uncompahgre had come in and that we would see him."[22]

The white man was Joe Brady, who was sent by Chief Ouray from the Los Pinos Indian Agency, also called the Uncompahgre Agency, more than 100 miles to the south (near present-day Montrose). He had a message from Ouray demanding that the White River Utes cease fighting. Brady never saw the women and didn't learn until later that he had been in the same camp with them, apparently on Saturday, October 4.[23]

Also while at this camp, the hostages witnessed an unusual event, staged by the Utes, which both frightened and intrigued the white women. The Utes had collected pieces of clothing from some of the troopers killed at the Milk Creek battle, and "On Sunday they made a pile of sage brush as large as a washstand and put soldiers' clothes and a hat on the pile," Josephine recalled. "Then they danced a war dance and sang as they waltzed around it."

They were in their best clothes, with plumes and fur dancing caps, made of skunk skins and grizzly bear skins, with ornaments of eagle feathers. Two or three began the dance, others joined, until a ring as large as a house was formed. There were some squaws, and all had knives. They charged on the pile of coats with their knives and pretended they would burn the brush. They became almost insane with frenzy and excitement. The dance lasted from two o'clock until sundown. Then they took the coats and all went home.[24]

Flora Ellen also offered an account of this event, adding that "They wanted Miss Josie and me to dance with them. We told them we could not, 'We no sabe dance.'"[25]

There is more confusion about when they left the Ute women's camp on Piceance Creek. For instance, Rankin wrote that on the same day that Brady arrived, the women's camp was moved, "the first day to Parachute Creek, and the next day to Grand River, near the mouth of Roan Creek."[26]

And Josephine gave this account in a book she wrote about the ordeal. On Wednesday, October 1,

the squaws and the few Indians who were there packed up and moved the camp ten or twelve miles, into an exceedingly beautiful valley, with high mountains all around it. The grass was two feet high and a stream of pure soft water ran through the valley. The water was so cold I could hardly drink it.... Mr. Brady had just come up from the Uncompahgre Agency with a message from Chief Ouray for the Indians to stop fighting the soldiers. This was why so many came back.[27]

If Brady had just arrived, this would have been Saturday, October 4, not Wednesday, October 1. But one can forgive Josephine Meeker some confusion in recalling precise details of what was undoubtedly a very stressful situation.

However long they stayed in the Ute women's camp, their next movements along the hostage trail are even more difficult to discern from the historical distance of more than 130 years.

NICAAGAT

Nicaagat was guarded when he spoke to whites, even deceptive. He regularly downplayed his abilities as an English speaker and sometimes hid them altogether. But occasionally, events or emotions made him reveal his skill. That was the case when he purchased potatoes from rancher Tom Emerson, west of the present-day town of Craig. Nicaagat—often referred to as "Captain Jack"—had been hunting antelope in an area known as Jackrabbit Springs. He stopped at Emerson's ranch and bought some potatoes. "Be sure to bring back the sack," Emerson said to him. "I've only got a few and can't let any of them go."

Several days later Nicaagat's wife returned the potato sack to Emerson, but the rancher decided to have some fun with the Ute leader the next time he came by the ranch. He asked Nicaagat, in all seriousness, why he had failed to return the sack. "Wife bring sack," Nicaagat replied.

But Emerson continued to pretend it hadn't happened. He lectured Nicaagat, telling him that Indians should be honest and trustworthy. He demanded to know why the Ute hadn't returned the potato sack as he had promised. An angry Nicaagat replied in impeccable English, "Mr. Emerson, I am telling you for the last time, my wife did return your sack."[1]

In most accounts written around the time of the Milk Creek battle, Nicaagat's comments were recorded as broken English, the kinds of words whites came to believe all American Indians used. He reportedly told Nathan Meeker as the soldiers were on their way from Fort Steele to the White River that the Utes desired to "have heap more talk." And he supposedly told another white man days before the battle that "Fort Steele soldiers no fight, Utes heap fight."[2]

However, the potato sack incident wasn't the only account in which much better linguistic skills appeared. For instance, there was the time he reportedly encountered a freight contractor named T. S. Garrett along the Little Sandy River in Wyoming. The Ute was riding a good horse and leading a large, young mule. Garrett asked him, "How? Where you catchie mule?" Nicaagat responded, "Stole him, by-God, can't you speak English?"[3]

He was even coy about his language abilities when testifying before an official congressional committee, according to one newspaper account. "At first he positively asserted he did not understand and could not speak English. Several questions were put to him in English, but he preserved the most stoical appearance of indifference," the *Chicago Tribune* reported. "The questions were then put to him in Spanish, through an interpreter, with no better result. The Committee were about to abandon the examination when Jack suddenly surprised them in very good English."[4]

The Utes also regarded Nicaagat as proficient in English. "This Nicaagat was a man who knew a great deal of the Maricat'z [white man's] ways and had more of their words than any of the People, except perhaps, Ouray," one account reported.[5]

Despite the newspaper account mentioned above, however, according to official records, when Nicaagat testified before the House Indian Affairs Committee in the spring of 1880 about the events of September 1879, he spoke Ute, and his words were translated by two interpreters, one of whom was Chief Ouray. (When Ouray himself testified to the same committee, he spoke Spanish, and his comments were translated by an unidentified interpreter.) Even so, the transcript of Nicaagat's testimony is longer, his transcribed language is more grammatically correct, and his words more precise than any of the Utes except Ouray.[6]

Also, there was this exchange between the chairman of the committee and Nicaagat. The congressman was probing for information about how much alcohol Major Thornburgh and his troops had with them on their expedition to the White River, and whether they had dispensed it freely when Nicaagat visited their camp.

"Did you see any firewater in the soldier's camp?" the congressman asked. "Did you see anybody who had taken too much of it, and did you get any of it?"

Nicaagat replied, very properly for the official record, "No, I did not see anybody that appeared under the influence of liquor and they did not give me any."[7]

Was this Nicaagat's way of showing, even when speaking through an interpreter, his disdain for words like "firewater" and his understanding of proper English? Was it Ouray or another interpreter who chose to use "under the influence of liquor" instead of "firewater," the word so many whites used when talking to Indians about alcohol? It is impossible to know.

But if Nicaagat could speak English very properly when the occasion required, he could also keep his language abilities hidden if it suited him. When he traveled to places such as Denver, where there were significant numbers of white people, "Ute Jack had a sly way of getting information. If he saw two or more whites in conversation on the street or other convenient place, he would stick around, pretending not to be interested. If he were spoken to, he would shake his head and grunt, pretending, 'no savvy.'"[8]

It's unclear why Nicaagat felt it necessary to be highly selective in displaying the full extent of his English skills. Perhaps he felt whites would be threatened if he came across as too intelligent, too proficient in speaking their language. Maybe, as the last anecdote suggests, it was an intelligence-gathering device—a belief that whites around him would discuss in greater detail events affecting the Utes if they thought he had only a rudimentary ability to understand. But there is no question how Nicaagat developed his English skills. That occurred when he lived as a young boy with a Mormon family named Norton near Salt Lake City. Exactly how he came to live with them, how long he lived there, and where he came from originally are questions with far less certain answers.

Nicaagat's ancestry has been variously described as "mixed-blood, Apache-Ute,"[9] as having "some Mexican blood and possibly some Apache."[10] Or he was originally a "Goshute," a tribe in west-central Utah with close ties to the Utes,[11] or "born of the Southern Utes, and had a taint of Mexican blood in his veins."[12] Several accounts say he was orphaned as a young child[13] and became the property of the Norton family through trade or sale.

One man who grew up in northwestern Colorado a few years after the Utes were moved out—and referred to Nicaagat as "a great American patriot"—said of Nicaagat's beginnings: "He and other children were sold to white people as slaves. A family named Norton bought this lad. Early in life he herded goats, then became a teamster."[14]

Another pioneer who lived and worked in southern Wyoming and northwestern Colorado in the 1870s and 1880s said that when Nicaagat was a small boy, he was adopted or traded for, along with other Indian children. "There were unscrupulous Mexicans trading with the Mormons, who would deal in Indian children during the first years of Mormon settlement in the Salt Lake Valley." The Norton family, with whom Nicaagat lived, called him "John" and taught him both English and Spanish.[15]

In 1948, author Robert Emmitt interviewed Saponise Cuch, then an old man living on the Ute reservation in Utah. But he had been a teenager in 1879 and had participated in the Milk Creek battle. In his book *The Last War Trail,* Emmitt reported the Ute perspective of the battle based on his interviews with Saponise Cuch. According to Emmitt, Nicaagat had been stolen from his own people by the Spanish-speaking people who sold him to a Mormon family.

> He had lived in the house of those people all the years he was growing up; he had gone to their school and to their church; he had read their Book and been dipped into their water. Then there were the other children—the white children who belonged to those people. Although he had been too small to remember when he was taken from his own people, he had always known that he did not belong in that house, or in the school or the church where he was made to go. Those people explained to him that their God had made his people dark long ago because they did bad things. They said that if he tried to be a good Saint he might someday become white; but Nicaagat always knew that he did not want to become white.[16]

A few years later, another writer said Nicaagat was among a batch of Indian children put up for sale in Salt Lake "by the famed Ute chief and Mormon elder, Walkara, when Brigham Young legalized slavery in Deseret":

Walkara usually castrated boy slaves because he sold them to Navajo chiefs who didn't trust complete males in their female hogans. But Jack was bought by a Salt Lake City family named Norton. Mr. Norton didn't see any point in castrating him.... The Nortons raised Jack, taught him English and got him a job driving a Salt Lake City ice wagon. Six months on the ice wagon convinced Jack that white men lived a crazy life. He joined the Uintah Utes, married a Yampa Ute named Tatseegah, and went to White River.[17]

According to one Ute family's oral history, Nicaagat was actually a half brother of Ouray and She-towitch. That would fit with accounts that said he was half Apache. He ended up in California in the 1850s before being rescued by a Mormon family and moving to Utah with them.[18] Many sources point to the Norton family in Salt Lake City as the Mormons who raised Nicaagat, but the modern Church of Jesus Christ of Latter-day Saints—the Mormon Church—was not able to find any record of him with such a family.

Nicaagat was born sometime around 1840, based on his later claims of age. According to the various accounts, he was orphaned or captured, adopted or enslaved well before his tenth birthday. The 1850 Utah census, which was actually enumerated in the spring of 1851, lists three Norton families living in and around Salt Lake City at that time. But none reported having a son named John, adopted or otherwise, of approximately the age Nicaagat would have been. Church records through the 1850s show several more Norton families, but none with a son named John.[19]

As with his origins, Nicaagat's reasons for leaving Salt Lake City are also a matter of dispute. There is the story mentioned above that he simply got tired of being a teamster, living amid the crazy world of the whites, so he left. Emmitt wrote that his departure occurred after one of Mr. Norton's wives, for whom Nicaagat served as a virtual slave, took a whip to him one too many times. He objected, threatened the woman with a knife, then tossed it to the floor, ran out of the house, stole a family horse, and headed for Ute country. Once there, Emmitt said, Nicaagat quickly lost his white ways, and the English words he had learned began to slip away from him.[20]

But years later Nicaagat seemed proud of his time with the Mormons, at least according to an aide to General George Crook. Captain John Bourke reported meeting Nicaagat—whom he and other army officers referred to as Ute John—with a group of Indian scouts who called themselves the Mountain Volunteers. They were mostly Shoshone, but Bourke said, "One of the most important of these volunteers was 'Ute John,' a member of the tribe of the same name, who claimed to have been thoroughly civilized and Christianized" because he had spent six months driving a team for the Mormons in Salt Lake City. "John's proudest boast was that he was a 'Klischun' [Christian], and he assured me that he had been three times baptized in one year by the 'Mo'mons,'" Bourke said.[21]

As with his language skills, Nicaagat acknowledged his Mormon background when he found it advantageous to do so. Frequently described as the most intelligent of the White River Utes, Nicaagat was a careful observer of people, and he presented different personas to different people. Whether he did so with Utes as well as whites is unknown. But it is clear that he quickly rose to prominence among the White River Utes.

Not much is known about his early years with the Utes, after he left the Norton family and fled east. Emmitt said he arrived in the White River country in the spring, just in time for the annual bear dance, where he found a wife—or *pe-you*. And since Ute men traditionally joined the clan of his wife's family, Nicaagat was from then on a Ute in all respects.[22]

There are no pictures of him or written descriptions until a few years later, but it is clear Nicaagat stood out among the compact-bodied Utes. Some reports said he was nearly 6 feet tall, although he doesn't appear that tall in contemporary photographs. He was among the most knowledgeable of all the Utes save Ouray himself. His narrow face and prominent nose were different than the round faces of many Utes. Furthermore, according to a pair of contemporary observers, Nicaagat was "something of a dandy and had a good deal of ornamental work on his clothing as well as on his pipe, and gun cases embroidered with colored porcupine quills and beads." Nicaagat, they said, "usually dresses in a complete suit of buckskin, but wears a black slouch hat."[23]

He may even have been something of an Indian Lothario, based on the story of one white man who knew him. Captain William Merrill, who had been an Indian agent for the Utes ten years before the White River outbreak, described Nicaagat for a newspaper interview as "the Beau Brummel and Gay Deceiver of the Northern tribe." "At one time he had great influence. But he had been driven away on account of his love affairs," Merrill added. He told of one occasion in which Nicaagat's dalliance with the wife of a subchief cost him two ponies, five blankets, a rifle, a foot of lead and a handful of powder." The woman, Merrill said, was executed.[24]

Despite that story, Merrill revealed his respect for Nicaagat, who he said had once saved his life. He described how the Ute leader came upon him one cold winter evening as he was riding to Denver. "I found myself freezing—and perfectly willing to give up and go to sleep, and sat down for that purpose," Merrill recalled. "Jack pulled me up, took out his knife and pricked me in the sides and cheeks and kicked and pounded me, and in that way kept me on the move for three hours, and when we reached Denver I was nearly exhausted."[25]

Another leading Colorado citizen, former territorial governor Alexander Hunt, also held Nicaagat in high regard. He had lived briefly at Hunt's house, Hunt recalled. The former governor considered Nicaagat "a brave and honorable Indian."[26]

Nicaagat loved to ride and hunt through mountain territory of the White River Utes. "He is generally armed, even in time of peace, with a first-rate Winchester rifle and his belt is full of cartridges. His pose and manner are dignified and graceful, and he is exceedingly jovial in disposition; though a serious, thoughtful look comes into his eyes when he is at business. He knows more of the world than his fellows and consequently respects and fears the whites more."[27]

In 1868, when he was approximately twenty-eight years old, Nicaagat was chosen with a handful of other White River Utes to join Chief Ouray of the Uncompahgre Utes, along with representatives of the other bands, on a trip to Washington, D.C., to negotiate a treaty.[28] Perhaps it was his English-speaking skills that won him what surely was a high honor for a young man who was a relative newcomer to the White River Ute band. Maybe he had already demonstrated his leadership qualities in other ways. In any event, he went to Washington with the other Ute leaders, met President Andrew Johnson, received a large medallion that he still proudly wore almost a decade later, and participated in the negotiation of a treaty with the U.S. government.

Ouray was the lead negotiator for the Utes, and the agreement reached was said to be the most favorable treaty ever entered into by an Indian tribe dealing with the U.S. government. It established millions of acres of mountain and high desert lands that would belong to the Utes "forever," set provisions to keep whites off the Ute lands, and created annual annuities

in food and clothing that were to go to the Utes. It also established three
Indian agencies on the Ute reservation lands. Nicaagat may have closely
observed the manner in which Ouray dealt with the whites, how he maintained his dignity but refused to yield on critical points as he pushed for
the favorable treaty.

That treaty lasted not even five years before whites in Colorado were
demanding a renegotiation—specifically, access to the rich silver ore
regions of the San Juan Mountains in southwestern Colorado. Nicaagat
did not go to Washington for the final signing of the Brunot Agreement
of 1874, but he was present at the original Los Pinos Agency—south of
present-day Gunnison—when the preliminary negotiations were taking
place in 1872.

There he caught the eye of an army officer sent to escort negotiator
Felix Brunot and his entourage. "Major A. J. Alexander, the Fort Garland
officer, talked with Chief Jack of the White River Utes, and confided to
Brunot later that Jack's military knowledge was 'broader than his own.'"[29]
How Nicaagat obtained that knowledge of military affairs is unknown,
since the meeting in question took place four years before Nicaagat joined
General Crook as a scout. But it is a testament to Nicaagat's intelligence
and ability to impress others when he chose to do so. And the time he
spent with the U.S. Army would be a defining period for the young Ute
leader.

Nicaagat became an army scout after Crook put out the word to
Indian agents working with what were considered friendly Indian tribes
that he was seeking scouts.

> In a request for daring scouts from the White River Ute Indians, a num-
> ber proclaimed their willingness to serve, but because of lack of serviceable
> mounts at that time (it being in early spring), they were prevented from ral-
> lying to the call.
>
>   U.M. Curtis, interpreter, realizing the eagerness of Ute Jack...arranged
> for his transportation. Jack, an active, adventurous Indian, was about thirty-
> five years of age.
>
>   Jack, dressed in native garb and mounted on a Ute pony, accompanied
> the mail carrier from the Agency to Snake River, thence by buckboard to
> Rawlins, where he was met by Lieutenant Eckner, Crook's representative,
> who furnished him with a complete new outfit, including a buckskin jumper,
> sombrero hat, pants and cowboy boots, purchased at the Jim France store.

An eagle feather was furnished him to decorate his new hat, by a feed stable attendant, before he left for Fort Laramie. He was the only Ute Indian employed by Crook, and was known to Crook's men by the name of Ute John.[30]

With Crook's forces, Nicaagat met Bourke and other officers and spoke readily with them. But when it came to military affairs, Bourke reported, "'Ute John' had one peculiarity: he would never speak to any one but Crook himself in regard to the issues of the campaign. 'Hello Cluke,' he would say, 'how you gittin' on? Where you tink dem Clazy Hoss en Settin' Bull is now, Cluke?'"[31]

Initially, Bourke offered a very uncomplimentary picture of Nicaagat. "'Ute John' was credited by most people with having murdered his own grandmother and drunk her blood, but, in my opinion, the reports to his detriment were somewhat exaggerated, and he was harmless except when sober, which wasn't often, provided whiskey was handy."[32] Few other sources refer to Nicaagat ever being intoxicated, even though other Utes were reportedly drinking heavily during and after the events of September 29, 1879.[33]

In any event, Bourke later developed a measure of respect for the Ute scout, as when they entered a Sioux burial ground along Rosebud Creek. "There were dozens of graves affixed to the branches of the trees, some of them of great age, and all raided by our ruthless Shoshones and Utes," he wrote. "There was one which the Shoshones were afraid to touch, and which they said was full of bad 'medicine,' but 'Ute John,' fortified, no doubt by the grace of his numerous Mormon baptisms, was not restrained by vain fears, and tumbled it to the ground."[34]

Later that summer there was worry that Crook's expedition might have to be abandoned because the Shoshone scouts decided they'd had enough of army life. A Colonel Burt was dispatched to the Crow reservation to seek replacement scouts, but he was unsuccessful in his mission, "and all our scouts left with the exception of the much disparaged 'Ute John,' who expressed his determination to stick it out to the last."[35]

Utes back at the White River waited eagerly for word of Nicaagat's exploits with Crook—word that occasionally arrived in the mail with Mr. Curtis. Some even set out with Curtis to join Nicaagat and Crook, but turned back before reaching the battlefield. And when Nicaagat returned home after the campaign, which lasted into 1877, he was "idolized" by young Ute warriors.[36]

Nicaagat joined Crook's army in early summer of 1876—approximately a month before Colonel George Armstrong Custer and his troops were annihilated at Little Bighorn, and probably just before Crook and his army were forced to retreat at the battle of Rosebud Creek. In witnessing the second event, and no doubt hearing a great deal of talk about the first, Nicaagat learned that well-armed Indians could defeat the U.S. Army under certain circumstances, at least temporarily.

But Nicaagat also saw first-hand what happened when the army was adequately prepared to retaliate in large numbers. He was present when Crook's forces destroyed the Sioux village where Chief American Horse was residing, and probably when a Cheyenne village was attacked in late 1876. In both cases he witnessed the deaths of many women and children.

His experience with Crook, as much as anything, made him eager to prevent hostilities in 1879, when Major Thornburgh and his troops were marching toward the White River. Several accounts claim that Nicaagat's visit to Thornburgh's camp prior to the battle was a reconnoitering effort as much as a peace mission, and it is probably true that he used the visits to assess the strength of Thornburgh's forces. But nothing in Nicaagat's background suggests he was eager to fight the soldiers. He knew some of Thornburgh's troops from his service with Crook, and they called to him when he entered their camp.[37] And while he might have thought there were enough White River Utes to hold off Thornburgh and his 140 soldiers, he knew with absolute certainty from his own experience that killing this small band of soldiers wouldn't be the end of it.

He also had reason to fear that when substantial numbers of armed soldiers headed to Indian villages, they weren't planning only to talk. When he repeatedly tried to persuade Thornburgh to leave the bulk of his troops outside the reservation and come in to the White River Agency to meet with Meeker and Ute leaders, it was not—as some would later claim—a ruse to ambush Thornburgh away from his troops. Nicaagat knew too well the consequences of such action. It was a sincere attempt to use diplomacy to avoid armed conflict.

The portrait often painted of Nicaagat was of a fiery Ute leader unwilling to bend to white men's ways. "Jack had no desire to settle down and coexist with white people as a fellow farmer, which was what the white people wanted," wrote Charles Wilkinson. "He had the opposite desire. Ute country was for the Ute and for the Ute alone."[38]

That picture is accurate, to a point. Nicaagat was more reluctant than many Utes to give up the nomadic hunting life and become a farmer. He told Nathan Meeker, Josie Meeker, Governor Frederick Pitkin, and others that such work—manual labor—wasn't appropriate for Ute warriors. He argued against sending Ute children to Josie Meeker's school because that would only educate them in white men's ways and push them toward becoming farmers.[39]

However, that portrait doesn't give the full measure of this pragmatic man, who had been to the cities of the East Coast and had witnessed the power of the U.S. Army in its campaigns against Indians in the West. He had no illusions that the nomadic Ute way of life would last forever. In the spring of 1879 he had White River Agency clerk W. H. Post write a letter to Denver postmaster and former newspaperman William Byers that illustrates that view.

> Dear Sir:
>
> I happened to mention your name in Ute Jack's hearing last evening, and he at once wanted me to write you. He has just returned from Snake River, where he has been since October last....Jack belongs to the opposition party, and objects to the removal of the agency and of Indians working, &c. *He claims, however, that when the game is used up, then it will be time enough to work* [emphasis added].[40]

Nicaagat was a complicated man—both warrior and peacemaker; erudite or linguistically crude as the situation demanded; romantic yet a realist; a man to whom even harsh critics of the Utes ascribed a great deal of honesty and integrity, but who nonetheless found it necessary at times to deceive whites—at least about his English-speaking abilities.

But not always. Some who observed him during the waning days of the official investigation at the Los Pinos Agency made this observation: "He talks English quite well and likes to talk."[41]

6

HELLBENT FOR HELP

IN THE DAYS AFTER THE FIGHT BEGAN AT MILK CREEK AND THE KILL-ings occurred at the White River Indian Agency, galloping horses and their riders raced across the mountains of western Colorado. Some were running for help. Others—whites and Utes—rushed to deliver messages. And in less than a week, the cavalry was literally charging to the rescue.

Colonel Wesley Merritt led the U.S. Army mission to rescue Major Thomas Thornburgh's besieged troops, but he would not have been able to do that until word got out that the troops were under attack. Joe Rankin sounded the alarm, and there is no question he made a historic ride beginning shortly before midnight on September 29. Under cover of darkness, he sneaked out of the valley where the beleaguered troops were trapped, grabbed one of the cavalry horses not yet killed by the Utes, and then raced toward Rawlins, Wyoming. Twenty-five hours and 140 miles later, on the morning of October 1, he reached the telegraph office. He had switched horses at least three times.[1]

But Rankin was not alone. Some military officials gave credit to one of their own for arriving first at Fort Steele, near Rawlins, with news of the

Milk Creek battle. Private Edward Murphy made a 170-mile ride in 24 hours, ex-soldier E. V. Sumner claimed years later—with no word on how often or where he might have changed horses.[2]

While Rankin and Murphy were heading north, at least one Ute was racing south to deliver the news of the White River hostilities to Chief Ouray at the Los Pinos Agency—about 140 miles away in the Uncompahgre River valley. Rankin and Murphy had a well-established wagon road to follow for much of their run to Rawlins, and no major mountain passes to ascend. Ute messenger Yanco, however, had to cross the divide between the White and Grand rivers, climb Grand Mesa to an elevation of at least 10,000 feet, then drop down to the Gunnison River valley and ride on to the Uncompahgre Valley.[3]

We don't know exactly the route Yanco took. His testimony before the White River Ute Investigation Commission is not that detailed. But maps of western Colorado prepared by the Hayden Survey point to a likely route. Ferdinand Hayden's crews were in the field surveying in 1874, '75, and '76, and the exquisitely detailed maps were first published in 1877. Although trails were recorded throughout the region, one trail is specifically marked as the "route from White River to Los Pinos."[4]

That map suggests that the most probable route for Yanco—heading south toward Los Pinos after witnessing the outbreak of fighting at Milk Creek—would have been southwest along the White River to near the site of the present-day town of Meeker, then south along Flag Creek to the top of what is now known as Rio Blanco Hill. From there he would have dropped into Rifle Creek and followed it to the Grand (now Colorado) River, then crossed it and headed south. Climbing steeply along Mamm Creek toward the two Mamm Peaks, he would have been near the Battlements at the east edge of Grand Mesa. He would have circled south of Leon Peak and crossed the mesa to Surface Creek, which drops off the south side of Grand Mesa into the Gunnison River drainage. From there it would have been a relatively easy gallop up the Uncompahgre Valley some 30 or 35 miles to the Los Pinos Agency and Ouray's home.

Roughly as long as the route covered by Rankin, the ride south to the Uncompahgre involved much more rugged terrain and a considerably greater climb than anything the white riders encountered. The fact that Yanco arrived at Los Pinos on October 2—a day later than Rankin made it to Rawlins—is testament to his equestrian skills and the endurance of the hardy Indian ponies.

The message delivered by Rankin propelled Colonel Merritt into action from Cheyenne, beginning what would be a historic military march. And Yanco's message to Ouray prompted the Ute chief, along with Los Pinos Indian agent Major W. M. Stanley, to send a relief force of their own—although far smaller and much different than Merritt's. Both Ouray and Stanley wrote messages. Ouray's was to be delivered to the leaders of the White River Utes who were fighting Thornburgh's troops. It said:

> To the chiefs, captains, headmen, and Utes at the White River Agency:
>
> You are hereby requested and commanded to cease hostilities against the whites, injuring no innocent persons, or any others further than to protect your own lives and property from unlawful and unauthorized combinations of horse-thieves and desperadoes, as anything farther will ultimately end in disaster to all parties.
>
> OURAY
> Head Chief, Ute Nation[5]

Stanley's message was more of a plea to the army officials—since he had no authority over the military—that they stop fighting as well.

> To the officers in command and the soldiers at the White River Agency:
>
> Gentlemen: At the request of the chiefs of the Utes at this agency I send by Jos. W. Brady, an employee, the enclosed order from Chief Ouray to the Utes at the White River Agency.
>
> The head chiefs deplore the trouble existing at White River and are anxious that no further fighting or bloodshed should take place, and have commanded the Utes there to stop.
>
> I hope that you will second their efforts, so far as you can consistently with your duties under existing commands.
>
> Thus much for humanity.
>
> Very respectfully, your obedient servant.
> W. M. Stanley
> United States Indian Agent[6]

Stanley and Ouray selected Los Pinos Agency employee Joe Brady, accompanied by Ouray's brother-in-law Sapivanero and several other

Utes, to ride to the White River immediately with the messages. Although his mission did not receive the notoriety of Joe Rankin's run to Rawlins, Brady's feat was an amazing one nonetheless.

First, Brady was not a particularly skilled horseman. He was a miller at the Los Pinos Agency and was probably far more familiar with driving a team of horses pulling a wagon than galloping on horseback over rough mountain terrain. His job did not require him to spend much time in the saddle. Additionally, Brady indicated that he knew little of the White River country prior to his ride. He entrusted his life to his Ute guides, riding into what was unknown territory for him and into the middle of a battle between Utes and whites. He had no way of knowing how he would be received by the angry White River Utes when he delivered his message from Ouray.[7]

Brady left the Los Pinos Agency at 2:30 p.m. on October 2. He arrived at the main Indian camp on a small creek that he couldn't identify (almost certainly Piceance Creek) at 7:15 p.m. on October 4. He didn't know it then, but the three women and two children held hostage by the Utes were in the same camp. He slept in a Ute teepee until early the following morning, when he headed to where the Utes were fighting Thornburgh's troops. He and his Ute entourage arrived at Milk Creek from the south within hours of Merritt's arrival with his relief forces from the north—on October 5.[8]

But days before either of them made it to Milk Creek, another group had arrived at the battle site: the Buffalo Soldiers.

Captain J. Scott Payne had taken command of the troops at Milk Creek following Major Thornburgh's death, and on the night of September 29 he understood how dire the soldiers' situation was. Surrounded by the Utes, a dozen of their troops dead and many more wounded, most of their horses killed or dying, with limited food and ammunition, they needed reinforcements quickly or they were likely to be annihilated. Late that first night, Payne asked for volunteers to creep through the Ute lines to attempt to get word of their plight back to Rawlins and Fort Steele. Four men heeded the call: Rankin, Murphy, Corporal George Moqwin, and teamster John Gordon. They were expected to sneak out as best they could and take separate routes away from the battlefield in the hope that one or more of them would make it through. But the Utes' lines around the besieged troops were far from impregnable, and all four of them were successful.

Rankin and the other couriers left the entrenchment, picking their way through the brush, moving beyond the sleeping Utes, and avoiding the guarded passes. Their route probably followed the cover of Milk Creek upstream for about two miles to where the creek bends south. To avoid noise, the couriers may have led their horses to this bend, mounted and ridden north toward the divide between Milk Creek and Stinking Gulch, where they would be in rugged country well beyond the main Indian lines. The four men rode quietly to the north for about four or five miles under cover of aspen groves, evergreens and tall brush. The four split shortly afterward.[9]

Murphy and Gordon reached the ranch of Tom Iles on the Yampa River. There they met a man named Jimmy Dunn, whom they instructed to find Captain Francis Dodge and his Company D, Ninth Cavalry—all of whom were African Americans except the officers. Dodge's unit had been sent north from southern Colorado in July as a result of settlers' complaints about Utes reportedly burning the forests. The unit was known to be in the vicinity of Steamboat Springs at the time the Milk Creek battle began.

On his way to Steamboat Springs, Dunn met surveyor Ed Clark, who was headed to the White River Agency to perform some work for Nathan Meeker. Dunn convinced Clark to help him locate Dodge and his troops. Clark began the effort but then decided his life might be in danger and headed for the safety of the Iles's ranch. Before he did so, however, he wrote a brief note for Dodge: "Thornburgh killed. His men in peril. Rush to their assistance. E.E.C." Then he tied it to a piece of sagebrush alongside the road between Steamboat Springs and Hayden. Amazingly, Dodge found the note.[10] Or, to be more precise, Sandy Mellen, a guide hired by Dodge, found the small scrap of paper in the brush on October 1. Dodge and his men rushed on to Hayden, which they found deserted. But as they were looking around, John Gordon and some other men rode up—another bit of luck since Dodge didn't know where Thornburgh's troops were.

Dodge and thirty-five black cavalry troopers, one other officer, and four civilians rode through a snowy night and reached Milk Creek early on October 2, having covered roughly 80 miles in 23 hours.[11] Dodge held his military unit back and sent Mellen and Gordon ahead to signal the surrounded troops. In the early morning darkness, the soldiers within the barricade at first thought that the two were English-speaking Utes trying to trick them into showing themselves. But soon they recognized Gordon's voice and began cheering. Captain Dodge and his troops then came galloping into the fortifications—without a shot being fired at them by the Utes.[12]

Exactly why the Utes let them go in unchallenged is unclear. It wasn't because they were so surprised at the sight of African American soldiers. Nicaagat and others had already encountered Dodge and his troops, and most of the other Utes had undoubtedly heard of black soldiers. They wouldn't have been stunned to inaction by the vision of dark-skinned troopers. A more likely explanation, offered by Dodge himself, was that the Utes feared that Dodge and his troopers were just the advance guard of a much larger force, and they did not want to reveal their positions.[13] It's also possible that the Utes simply understood, as Dodge didn't seem to, that having the Buffalo Soldiers join the white soldiers within the barricades did little to improve their situation.

As it turned out, Dodge's decision to race into the pit to join Thornburgh's beleaguered soldiers was a strategic mistake. Company D of the Ninth Cavalry accomplished nothing but adding to the number of bodies within the small confines of the barricade of dead livestock. Although they were allowed into the enclosure without shots being fired, the Utes began shooting a few minutes later. Dodge's troops and all the others were soon under a heavy fusillade from Ute marksmen. Within hours, all but seven of the Buffalo Soldiers' horses had joined the ranks of dead and dying animals. And, like the white soldiers, the black troopers would remain trapped behind the breastworks of rotting carcasses until Merritt and his 400 soldiers arrived a few days later.[14]

There is no doubt, however, that the arrival of Dodge and his soldiers offered moral support to the remnants of Thornburgh's troops. First, it provided concrete evidence that some of their messengers had gotten through. If Dodge and his troops had received word of their predicament from the four couriers—and Gordon's presence with him proved that he had—then perhaps the news had also made it as far as Rawlins and Fort Steele. More troops might very well be on the way.

Additionally, the black soldiers proved to be as fearless and as hard-working as the white soldiers. For many of the whites, who had never encountered blacks in any capacity except as servants—or perhaps as slaves prior to the Civil War—that was unexpected. Statements made later detailed the amazement and joy with which they greeted the "colored soldiers": "We forgot all about the danger of exposing ourselves and leaped up out of the pits to shake hands all around. Why we took those darkies in right along with us in the pits. We let 'em sleep with us, and they took their knives and cut off slips of bacon from the same sides as we did."[15]

What's more, the black soldiers demonstrated that their courage was equal to the whites'. Sergeant Henry Johnson, one of the Buffalo Soldiers, was later awarded the Congressional Medal of Honor for leaving the security of his rifle pit under heavy fire to check on soldiers in the other trenches, as well as for undertaking a water-gathering excursion to Milk Creek, also under heavy fire.[16] Another, unidentified black soldier risked his life to scurry to a supply wagon and back—drawing the attention of Ute marksmen—to grab some wood so he could start a fire and cook coffee for a wounded white soldier who was pleading for it.[17]

Still, there was little change in the soldiers' day-to-day life: Keep your head down during the day. Have a few volunteers sneak cautiously out for water at night. Hope that a Ute bullet or arrow wouldn't find you. Listen to the taunting of the Utes who knew a few English words, hollering from behind trees and rocks on the nearby rises. Listen to the ping of bullets as the Utes sporadically fired down into the barricaded enclosure, infrequently hitting a human, much more regularly hitting horses and mules. That routine might have lasted days longer if Colonel Merritt had not been so well organized and determined to reach the trapped troopers quickly.

After Rankin's arrival in Rawlins, word of the soldiers' plight was telegraphed to the adjutant general, Omaha Barracks, Nebraska. It was received at 2:25 a.m. on October 1, Omaha time (an hour ahead of Wyoming and Colorado time). By daylight, orders had been telegraphed to Fort D. A. Russell, just outside of Cheyenne, where Merritt was commander (but lying sick in bed when he received the message).[18]

Cheyenne is roughly 120 miles east of Rawlins, but both towns were on the main line of the Union Pacific Railroad. Within hours, Merritt had risen from his bed and had designated four companies of the Fifth Cavalry—about 234 enlisted men and 20 officers—for the relief effort. He ordered them to prepare horses, tack, and provisions, and to be ready to board the train heading west, which they did shortly after noon the same day. He telegraphed to Rawlins for wagons and teamsters to haul his infantry to the battle site, and arranged to have three companies of the Fourth Infantry from Fort Laramie—approximately 150 additional soldiers—meet him there. They were waiting at Fort Steele, just east of Rawlins, when Merritt and his forces arrived early on the morning of

October 2. As mules and horses were harnessed and wagons packed, Merritt contacted Joe Rankin, sending him ahead to the Snake River to enlist the aid of frontiersman and trapper Jim Baker in guiding them to Milk Creek.[19]

Merritt executed a textbook rapid march using techniques he described in several essays he later wrote. They left Fort Steele at 11 a.m. on October 2 and covered 45 miles, halting at 9 p.m. The horse soldiers were assigned a meticulous, rigorous schedule with frequent brief halts and occasional longer stops to unsaddle the horses and let them roll, eat, and drink. It was a routine that saved their animals' strength and allowed the soldiers to better endure the long trek. Merritt firmly believed that careful consideration for both men and animals—and the arrest of any officer or enlisted man who failed to follow his orders to the letter—was the best way to ensure the success of a long cavalry march.[20]

The result was that Merritt and his reinforcements covered the 170 miles from Fort Steele to Milk Creek in a little more than two and a half days—not quite the speed with which Rankin made the trip to nearby Rawlins racing in the opposite direction, but a remarkable time for that many people, horses, wagons, and supplies, nonetheless. Add in another thirty hours or so from the time Merritt first received his orders and rose from his sickbed, then organized his troops and got them on the train to Fort Steele, and the whole event must be viewed as an exceptional military maneuver.[21]

They arrived at Milk Creek before dawn on October 5, with Joe Rankin accompanying them, but were unsure exactly where their fellow troopers were, or even if they had survived. A bugle blast from Merritt's trumpeter solved the dilemma. The bugler within the barricades responded, amid cries of joy from the men trapped inside. Merritt led his men into the valley where the Thornburgh troops were entrapped and had some of his troops deploy in skirmish lines to confront the Utes. A few shots were fired, with minimal harm to either side, and Merritt pulled his troops back to protect the other soldiers and supplies.[22] The Utes pulled back as well and waited.

Then Joe Brady arrived. Accompanied by Sapivanero and other Uncompahgre Utes, he had made the difficult journey over Grand Mesa and up to the Indian women's camp in a little over two days, leaving Los Pinos at 2:30 p.m. on October 2 and arriving at the main Indian camp at 7:15 p.m. on October 4. He left that camp at 2 a.m. Sunday morning,

October 5, and rode to the battle site, arriving at 10 a.m., after stopping for about an hour to build a fire. An Indian woman they met on the way told them that reinforcements—Merritt and his soldiers—had just arrived. Brady reported hearing sporadic gunfire as they rode up to the Indian "headquarters," hidden behind a bluff from Merritt and his forces.[23]

Once at the Ute front lines, Brady was greeted warmly by all of the White River Utes present, shaking hands with each of them while he still sat on his horse. Then he dismounted and was introduced to Nicaagat, or "Captain Jack," as Brady called him. Brady said Nicaagat appeared to be the leader, so he read him the message from Ouray in English. He then discovered that Sapivanero had brought another message from Ouray, which he delivered personally to Nicaagat. There was little argument from Nicaagat or the other Utes. Whether as a result of Ouray's demand or Merritt's reinforcements, they recognized it was time to stop fighting. "Captain Jack said, 'That's all right; we will not fight anymore,'" Brady recalled.[24]

As they hunkered down behind a large rock, Brady said they would need a white flag of truce to show the soldiers their intentions. He pulled a handkerchief from his pocket and searched for a stick on which to fasten it. But Nicaagat said, "Wait a minute, there will be a larger one here.... [A]nd in a short time they brought a sheet and teepee pole, and we tore it and tied a fourth of the sheet to the pole." They posted it behind a rock where the soldiers could see it and waited. After a brief time, Brady, looking through a crevice in the rocks, noticed that the soldiers had pulled back, and a single officer had ridden out toward the Indian line. "After I waited a sufficient length of time, I got my horse and went down and met an officer, whose name I disremember now."[25]

Once again Joe Brady displayed incredible courage—for which he never received adequate credit. Alone and unarmed, carrying nothing but the makeshift white flag and knowing that countless rifles would be trained on him, he rode some 300 yards from the Utes' position, on the ridge to the south, to the valley floor, where Thornburgh's troops had been entrenched, and where Merritt and his reinforcements were now encamped.

Brady arrived without incident. He asked to see the commanding officer and said he had a message for him. What followed sounds surreal now. Brady was clearly still miffed about it when he described it a month later. He was taken to a wagon, under which a road-weary Colonel Merritt was sprawled. The officer who accompanied him handed the note to Merritt under the wagon. Merritt read it and handed it back.

"As he sent no answer I got down off my horse and went to where he was and asked him if he had any written answer to send back," Brady stated. "He said he believed not. I remarked that I would like to take some answer back to the Indians, and he remarked that he believed he had not anything to send back. That was about all that passed between the officer in command and myself."[26]

Spending no more than twenty minutes in camp—enough time to have a cup of coffee—Brady then remounted and rode back toward the Ute lines, accompanied by the same unidentified officer. They separated about midway between Merritt's lines and the Utes', but another officer then approached Brady. "He told me to tell Captain Jack the best thing he could do would be to come in the next morning with four or five men under a flag of truce, and they would meet them where they met me and hear what they had to say," Brady reported.

The officer left, and Brady continued to the Ute lines, where he told Nicaagat and others of the suggestion. Nicaagat was at first eager to go down immediately to meet with Merritt and the other soldiers. He walked around in a frenzy of indecision, peering several times over the rocks toward Merritt's troops, before he finally concluded there were just too many soldiers to risk riding into their camp. Several other Utes prepared to ride with Brady back to Merritt's camp, but they also changed their minds after seeing the assembled soldiers.[27]

At this point, the patient Brady seems to have lost his temper. "By this time I began to feel a little provoked at the way they [the Utes] were acting, and I turned and rode back to where the Indians were and told them that I was going to start home."[28]

It didn't matter. The Utes were clearly done fighting. Some even talked of going down to shake hands with the soldiers, believing the white soldiers would generously accept the Utes' declarations that it had been a "pretty good fight," would laugh and slap them on the back. Fortunately for those naive Utes, Nicaagat and others who knew better talked them out of making such a gesture. Instead, they quietly pulled back from the Milk Creek battlefield.[29]

Before retracing his route from the Uncompahgre Valley, Brady stopped at another camp—almost certainly the one where the hostages were being held, since he met Quinkent (Douglas) there. Brady estimated it was 38 to 40 miles from the site where he had met Merritt and his soldiers. Since he was heading south toward the Uncompahgre, that mileage estimate would place the camp of at least sixty teepees along Piceance Creek near the top of what is now known as Rio Blanco Hill. That's where the hostages and most of the Indian women and children stayed while the battle at Milk Creek was in progress.

But the Indians kept the hostages hidden, and Brady had no idea they were there. In fact, he didn't even know whether they were still alive. Queries to his Indian guides about what had happened at the agency brought the response only that Agent Meeker had been killed. There was no word on what had happened to any of the other whites there.[30]

The hostages knew Brady had arrived from the commotion in camp, after which the Utes told them that a white man had come up from Ouray's agency. They must have hoped that the unknown white man had come to rescue them, but those hopes were dashed when it became clear that the Utes were not going to allow Brady to see them.[31]

By midday on October 6, Brady was on his way back to Los Pinos to tell Ouray that the White River Utes would heed his command to stop fighting, but he didn't know what the soldiers were going to do. He arrived on October 9—having been transported the last few miles in Ouray's personal carriage—after traveling more than 300 miles in a week over rugged terrain occupied by Utes whom many Coloradoans believed were initiating a widespread war against all whites in western Colorado.[32]

Merritt would spend several more days at the Milk Creek site, attending to the wounded and seeing that Thornburgh's and Dodge's troops were rested and readied for their trip back to Fort Steele. On October 11 he moved his troops from Milk Creek to the White River, and then downstream to the site of the White River Agency, where buildings were still smoldering, and the bodies of Meeker and his dead employees were discovered.[33]

For the Utes who had besieged Thornburgh's troops for a week at Milk Creek—one of the longest continuous engagements ever between the U.S. Army and Native Americans—it was also time to leave the area. They headed to the camp on Piceance Creek where the hostages were being kept, and the next morning they all began the next significant move along the hostage trail.

HORSE POWER

IN 1868, WHEN NEWSPAPERMAN SAMUEL BOWLES VISITED HOT SULPHUR
Springs, just outside the northeastern boundary of the newly defined Ute
reservation in Colorado, he found a group of Utes at one of their favorite therapeutic natural spas. But the Indians didn't limit the therapy just
to humans. Bowles described the Utes "taking ailing horses into the hot
springs for their cure."[1]

Bowles's observation is just one example of how much the nineteenth-
century Utes treasured their horses. They were the Utes' primary form of
transportation and their freight system. They were hunting companions,
war machines, and escape mechanisms. And they provided the Utes with
one of their favorite forms of recreation.

Nathan Meeker came to recognize how deeply the Utes cared for their
horses—or "ponies," as they were routinely called—but he had no empathy
for that human–animal bond. Rather, he viewed it as one of the Utes'
greatest vices. They could hop on their ponies and go loping off the reservation just when he wanted them to stay and work. They also devoted
thousands of acres of prime grassland to feeding their ponies—land that

Meeker believed should be used for grazing sheep and cattle, or plowed up to raise crops. The ponies allowed the White River Utes to remain semino-madic when, as far as Meeker was concerned, they should be learning to be farmers. Furthermore—and contrary to Meeker's Puritan ethic—the ponies allowed the Utes to frequently engage in one of their favorite pas-times: horse racing. Worse, racing gave them the opportunity for constant gambling.

Meeker naively thought he could persuade the equestrian Utes to give up most of their beloved ponies and become foot-bound farmers. When that didn't work—when it only created additional tension between the Indian agent and the Utes—Meeker made things worse by angrily declar-ing that the Utes would have to shoot most of the horses.

The events at the White River Agency in September 1879 did not transpire only because Meeker ordered the plowing of the Utes' racetrack. But it is clear much of the friction that eventually led to the agency attacks stemmed from the Utes' love of their ponies, and Meeker's belief that their horses were the greatest obstacle to the Utes becoming civilized—at least as he understood that term. He appeared oblivious to the fact that he had centuries of Ute tradition to overcome.

By the time of the White River incident, the Utes had been horsemen and -women for at least 240 years, possibly longer. They had also become experienced breeders and horse traders. The Utes' original acquisition of the horse was made possible by their proximity—or at least the proximity of the southern Muache and Capote bands—to the Spanish settlements near Santa Fe.

At first frightened by the large animals, the Utes used horses like the large dogs that had been their pack animals before horses arrived. "When they first got these ponies, the stories told that the People [the Utes] did not know what to do with them. They first used them as they did the great dogs and they did not ride them for a long time."[2]

Some say the Utes at first considered the marvelous new animals to be "magic dogs" because they had no other frame of reference for these huge beasts that could pack their goods and, later, the Utes themselves.[3] But others, including modern Ute researchers, say the Indians quickly adopted a corruption of the Spanish word for horse, *caballo*, as the name for their ponies: *kava'u*, which is plural, and the singular *kava*. A short Ute–English vocabulary written by an early Mormon pioneer in Utah lists two Ute words for horse: *ka-vah'-u*, but also *teah*. Neither is close to the word listed for dog: *sar-rich*.[4]

In any event, the Utes likely were responsible for spreading horse culture to northern tribes, including the Shoshones, Nez Perces, and perhaps even the Comanches. The availability of horses among North American Indian tribes spread first north and west from the Santa Fe area—directly through Ute territory, some experts on horses and Indians contend. The Utes, possibly the earliest American Indian equestrians in what is now known as the American West, may have acquired their first horses even before 1600.[5]

Others date the first Ute acquisition of horses a few decades later, to 1640, three years after the first recorded battle between Spanish settlers in New Mexico and the "Yuta" Indians to the north. A number of Utes were taken captive in that 1637 battle, but in 1640 "some Utes escaped from Santa Fe and took their first horses, the beginning of a new era for the nomads."[6]

Twentieth-century writer Marshall Sprague claims that

> The Colorado Utes were among the first, if not the very first North American horse Indians to acquire horses.... In contrast to most, the imaginations of the Utes were fired by horses to such a pitch as to completely change their tribal personality. From the start, they revered the horses out of gratitude for being freed from the horseless millenniums of misery and inferiority. They put them in the same beloved class of personal property as wives, children and dogs.[7]

While some tribes looked on dogs, and later horses, as a source of food, the Utes did not. They might work their dogs and horses hard as beasts of burden, hunting partners, and weapons of war, but they didn't eat them.[8]

Some Utes also subscribed to a legend, similar to that of several other equestrian tribes, of a giant white mustang, a superhorse that could outrun all others and was invincible in battle. If it could be captured and bred, its descendants and their riders would also be invincible.[9]

It didn't take long after acquiring their first ponies for Utes to become adept horsemen and -women. They traded and raided, and, before long, were breeding horses more suited to the mountains than the early Spanish stock. Trapper William Ashley was impressed with the Ute ponies he saw in the 1820s. He noted that they were generally better animals than those belonging to the Plains Indians to the east, and that the Utes had more horses per person than most other tribes.[10]

The Utes' culture changed significantly as a result of the horse.

> In addition to being able to move heavy hide tepees from place to place, Utes added horse trappings to their most highly valued possessions—acquired as trade items, as loot from raids or as the handiwork of the Ute men. Often they rode bareback, or leather pads sufficed for saddles with short stirrups, allowing riders to guide their horses with their knees and leaving hands free for shooting arrows rapidly. Quickly the proud, vigorous Utes became renowned for their skill as horsemen, as well as their large herds. Ownership of ponies became the Ute Indians' principal symbol of wealth and source of pride.[11]

They developed their own saddles, sometimes using animal horns to make the pommel in the front of the saddle and the cantle in the back, and they made or purchased individualized bridles.[12] Although the Great Plains tribes became renowned for their equestrian skills, the Utes were unquestionably skilled riders, "expert mountain horsemen, reportedly loping down steep slopes in pursuit of deer or elk at full speed, over places where a white man would dismount and lead his horse." They also developed a special stirrup that hung from the horse's mane, allowing the rider to drop to one side and shoot under the horse's neck during a battle.[13]

In the early nineteenth century, any Ute hunter with wanderlust had a vast territory across which to travel on horseback. From Taos in northern New Mexico to as far north as the Yampa River, and from the mountains just outside of present-day Denver to the Great Salt Lake in Utah, it was all Ute territory—virtually unsettled by white men. Different bands controlled different regions of the millions of acres of mountains, high deserts, canyons, forests, and mesas, but all were generally friendly with the others, and very few members of other tribes ventured far into Ute lands.

The Utes also traveled well beyond the lands they claimed as their own. In the eastern plains of what is now Colorado, they hunted buffalo and occasionally raided Arapaho and Cheyenne villages. Artifacts found by modern-day historians show that they roamed as far east as the Republican River, near the present border between Colorado, Kansas, and Nebraska.[14]

Utes along the southern border of their territory regularly traveled far into New Mexico and what is now Arizona, as well as parts of Oklahoma and Texas. Sometimes they partnered with Comanches, Apaches, and Navajos, as well as the Hispanics of these territories, but just as frequently they engaged in raids against them.[15]

In their mountain strongholds, with horses attuned to the high country, they were feared and respected by neighboring tribes. In 1821, Apaches in northern New Mexico warned explorer Jacob Fowler to beware of the "Utaws" to the north.[16] In the mid-nineteenth century, U.S. Army Colonel R. I. Dodge reported that despite the Utes' relatively small numbers, "all the powerful plains tribes, though holding them in contempt on the plains, have an absolute terror of them in the mountains."[17]

In the 1840s, Ute leader Walkara famously led small bands of raiders from central Utah to southern California along the Old Spanish Trail. He and his companions stole horses from the Spanish settlements and drove them over a thousand miles of desert and rugged rock passes to sell or trade them with other Indians and Hispanics in New Mexico.[18]

Horses, especially breeding stock, were so important to the Utes that one of the key provisions of the 1863 agreement (not a formal treaty) between the U.S. government and Ouray's Uncompahgre band of Utes was that the government would provide five good American stallions that the Utes could use to replenish and improve their herds. As with so many promises made to the Utes, and other Indians, the United States never fulfilled that pledge.[19]

Some Utes believed Chief Ouray became too much like a white man as he grew older, with his adobe house, a farm, a vegetable garden, and a stylish horse and carriage. But Ouray never abandoned his love of the Ute ponies. After moving to his farm south of the present-day city of Montrose in the mid-1870s, Ouray's wealth was in his 40,000 head of sheep and his 100-acre farm. "But his pride was his herd of several hundred beautiful horses, some of them acclaimed racers."[20]

Even Nicaagat, who reportedly had no taste for status or tribal importance, valued his horses greatly. The ponies Nicaagat owned, along with teepees, were his only important possessions. And when the initial barrage of gunfire had died down during the battle at Milk Creek, and Nicaagat was despondent about the future, he did the only thing that made sense to him. He went searching for his ponies, which had been abandoned when he went to battle and his family had been forced to move its campsite.[21]

Even those Ute horses that weren't racers were highly valued for their endurance and stamina in the mountains, not just by the Utes but by the Europeans who encountered them. "For all practical purposes, there is no limit to the number of his ponies, strong of limb and sure-footed, fleet as the wind, tough and hardy as their masters," one report said in 1879. The Ute ponies could carry a rider 100 miles in a day, climb those steep mountains, swim river torrents, and subsist on mountain grass, summer and winter, "pawing when necessary, through the snow to find it."[22]

But racing was a favorite pastime for virtually every Ute. "The Utes loved horse racing and indulged in it at every opportunity. Besides transportation, the main use of the horse to the Utes was racing, and every Indian who could afford horses kept some primarily for racing. To them, any individual who did not have a horse to run in a race was 'a nobody.'"[23] And it was horse racing—loved by the Utes and despised by Meeker—that created one of the greatest cultural chasms at the White River Indian Agency in 1878 and 1879. Just how great is illustrated by the story of a Ute leader whom Meeker thought he had converted to the ways of the farmer.

Canavish, who was known to the whites as Johnson, was a powerful medicine man and one of the leaders of the White River Utes. Thus in late 1878, when Canavish showed an interest in becoming a farmer, Meeker was thrilled. He picked out land for him, started building a house, and gave him some cows. Canavish told Meeker that if he was going to be a farmer, some of his ponies would have to learn to work in harness, pull wagons, and start doing harder work than they had done before. To do that, he said, his harness ponies would need oats and other grains that were given to the white men's horses. Meeker agreed, and soon Canavish's horses were eating the extra rations. After receiving some instruction from the white employees at the Indian agency, Canavish and his sons were seen driving teams of ponies pulling heavy wagons rapidly around the agency.

Through the winter they practiced and trained, and on into early spring. Then came the annual bear dance, when Utes from many different bands, and even a few members of other tribes, gathered to celebrate the new year—the awakening of the bear. Dancing continued for days as mates were chosen and old friends greeted. There was feasting and games. And horse racing.

It soon became clear that Canavish and his sons had an edge over the rest of the racers. Their ponies had been in heavy training all winter, and they had been getting grain to supplement the dried grass of Powell Park. They won again and again and again, and Canavish and his sons gathered many treasures from other Utes in the gambling that inevitably accompanied the racing.

"Toward the end of the Bear Dance feasts, everyone saw the joke, and they laughed about it for a long while."[24] But Nathan Meeker didn't laugh. Much to Canavish's surprise and dismay, Meeker didn't think the Ute leader's big joke was funny at all. He accused Canavish of being a liar, a cheat, and a bad Ute. Now, Meeker declared, Canavish would get nothing more from the agent, not even the food that was due him and his family. It was the end of Meeker's amicable relationship with the one Ute he had earlier thought was most attuned to his wishes, the one most likely to become a farmer.

Canavish spent days brooding, talking with his sons and other Utes, trying to figure out what had gone wrong with his horse-racing joke. He had been certain Meeker would be amused by it. And more important, he was sure it would demonstrate to Meeker how important the ponies were to the Utes—including the racing and the land to pasture them—and make him abandon the idea of using these critical lands for agriculture.[25]

But Meeker drew no such lesson from the joke. He only became more convinced than before that most of the Utes were lazy and not to be trusted, more interested in horse racing and gambling than in doing what he considered an honest day's work. And he became more and more certain that the best way to get the Utes to change their ways was to eliminate their ponies—or at least most of them. "Within three months of his arrival, Meeker understood that in order for him to succeed in moving the Utes toward 'civilization' he needed to break, if not destroy…the Utes' horse culture."[26] In this, as with so many of the conclusions Meeker reached regarding the Utes, his thinking was a significant part of the problem, not the solution.

Because of the Utes' great love for, and dependence on, their horses, it is easy to understand that when Nathan Meeker strode arrogantly onto the grounds at the White River Indian Agency and quickly concluded that eliminating the Ute horse herds was the best way to "civilize" the tribe, he was igniting a firestorm. Furthermore, Meeker greatly underestimated, or simply chose to ignore, the hostility that would be generated by his suggestion that the Utes kill off many of their ponies. One hostile encounter occurred with Canavish, the same Ute who tricked Meeker into believing he was turning his racing ponies into draft horses. It came during a meal in Meeker's house, to which Canavish had been invited. "Meeker told Johnson he must shoot some of his ponies to make room and grass for working horses. Johnson grew so infuriated he got up and left the meal."[27]

Although Meeker was not successful in forcing the Utes to kill or abandon most of their ponies, the events he set in motion with his arrogance and pompous pronouncements would eventually cost them many of their beloved horses.

8

TRAIL SECTION 2

THE UTES AND THEIR HOSTAGES DIDN'T MOVE IMMEDIATELY AFTER THE army reinforcements arrived. In fact, according to Josephine Meeker, the Indians were confused and near panic following the arrival of Merritt and his troops at Milk Creek. "On Sunday night Jack [Nicaagat] came and made a big speech, also Johnson [Canalla]. They said more troops were coming and they recited what orders they say had been brought from Chief Ouray. They were in great commotion and did not know what to do. They talked all night, and the next morning they struck half their tents and put them up again. Part were for going away and part for staying."[1]

It was also on that Sunday night that Nicaagat confronted Josie in her teepee and they had the conversation related in chapter 1. But it was two days later—Tuesday, October 7—that the anxious Utes finally decided to strike camp and head south toward the Grand River, known today as the Colorado River. All three of the women hostages agreed it was a rugged, exhausting trip. Josie reported that the group "left on Tuesday for Grand River, and we had a long ride. The cavalcade was fully two miles long. The wind blew a hurricane and the dust was so thick we could not see ten feet

back on the line....We traveled all day without dinner or water. Mother
had neither saddle or stirrups, but merely a few thicknesses of canvas
strapped on the horse's back. She did not reach Grand River until after
dark."[2] Flora Ellen Price said they began breaking camp that day around
3 a.m. The hostages had no breakfast, "And we rode all day in the thick
dust without water." The group she was with reached the Grand River
about sundown and camped in the sagebrush.[3]

But where exactly did they go?

From the large camp near the top of Rio Blanco Hill on Piceance
Creek, the shortest and easiest route to the Grand River would have been
due south—either along Government Creek, or east across a low hogback
and down Rifle Creek. Several pieces of evidence support the proposition
that Rifle Creek was their route. Author Marshall Sprague claimed that
this was essentially the route taken, although he did not offer any additional evidence.[4] Additionally, the Hayden Survey maps clearly show the
main route between the Los Pinos Indian Agency and the White River
Indian Agency running south along Rifle Creek to the Grand River—the
same route Joseph Brady is believed to have taken after delivering his message from Ouray to the White River Ute leaders.[5]

On a warm autumn day in an extremely dry year, it's easy to imagine
the dust rising thickly on the trail, as the hostages described. But what's
harder to fathom is the time of the ride if this were the route taken. It
doesn't seem far enough to account for the extremely long and arduous
trip the three women described. Measuring the distances on the Hayden
map from the campsite near the top of Rio Blanco Hill to the top of the
divide between Flag and Rifle creeks, and then down Rifle Creek (now
called West Rifle Creek) through Rifle Gap, then traveling east a few miles
to follow the main trail shown on the Hayden map, the route would have
covered about 30 miles.

On May 5, 2007, my wife, Judy, our friend Alan Moore, and I traveled
the route along existing roads and recorded our mileage. It came out to
just a little less than 30 miles to the spot where the Hayden map shows the
trail crossing the Grand River. Thirty miles is a good day's ride, even for
experienced horsemen. Furthermore, the three women from the White
River Indian Agency were not accustomed to spending long days in the
saddle. This was probably the longest single-day ride of their entire trip,
and it was no doubt grueling. As someone who rides horses during the

summer two or three times a week, I can attest to the fact that a ride of even 20 miles is plenty long. It leaves me exhausted and sore.

However, even if the 2-mile-long cavalcade that Josie described moved slowly—averaging only 3 miles an hour—it still would have covered the distance in 10 hours, not the 12 hours or more described by the hostages. Sunrise to sunset at that time of year at that latitude was about 11.5 hours.[6] Furthermore, the terrain doesn't seem to mesh with Arvilla Meeker's description of the ground over which they rode: "We traveled rapidly over mountains so steep that one would find it difficult in walking over them on foot....One of the mountains was so steep that after making part of the ascent, Douglas' party had to turn back and go around it."[7]

Wilson Rankin, the nephew of scout Joe Rankin, who made the famous ride from Milk Creek to Rawlins, arrived at the White River Agency within days after Merritt had moved his troops from Milk Creek to the agency. Rankin had his own ideas of the trail the Utes and their hostages took once the fighting at Milk Creek halted: "On the same day Brady left the Ute camp, the camp was moved, the first day to Parachute Creek and the next day to Grand River, near the mouth of Roan Creek."[8] Others have suggested that the Utes took their hostages as far west as the Roan Creek headwaters before heading down to the Grand River. But that doesn't fit for several reasons. First, it would require a much longer day than even the hostages reported. Also, the hostages clearly stated that in subsequent days, after arriving on Grand River, they moved downriver from their initial camp; however, from Roan Creek, that would put them in De Beque Canyon, and neither the hostages nor other sources indicate that they ever entered it.

There are problems with Rankin's narrative as well. First, the report that they stopped one night and took two days to reach the Grand River from what he called the "squaw camp," which he agrees was near the head of Piceance Creek, clearly contradicts the women's stories that they covered the entire distance in one grueling day. Also, while the bulk of the Utes eventually camped at the mouth of Roan Creek, where it spills into the Grand River—the site of the present-day town of De Beque—the hostages never mentioned joining the main camp of the Utes at Roan Creek after reaching the Grand River. Even if they did, they certainly didn't make it there on the first night after leaving the camp near Rio Blanco Hill.[9]

Additionally, there is little indication, either from the Hayden maps or from settlers who moved in shortly after the Utes moved out, that the Utes used Parachute Creek as a frequent north-south route. The upper ends of the various forks of Parachute Creek are all so steep that it would have been difficult to get a horse up or down them, although one fork was used by ranchers later to get cattle to the top of the Roan.[10] That terrain sounds to be a much better fit with Arvilla's description of mountains so steep one could barely hike them than the moderate climbs and descents along the Rifle Creek route. But that doesn't mean that the party Douglas was leading, including Arvilla, couldn't have done some steep climbing along Rifle Creek. If they got behind others in the long cavalcade and tried to catch up by taking a short cut, they could easily have made some very steep climbs over portions of the hogback that separates Rifle Creek from the drainage now known as Government Creek, just a few miles to the west.

There is, however, another factor that argues for the Government Creek or Rifle Creek route, although it doesn't entirely preclude the Parachute Creek route: field glasses. After the Utes and their hostages reached the Grand River, scouts regularly rode to the nearby mountain peaks to look back toward the White River using field glasses—hand-held military-style telescopes—to reconnoiter Merritt and his troops. Josie recalled that "A number of them had glasses. They would go up on these high mountains and watch the progress of the soldiers for distances of 20, 30, or 40 miles."[11] She described a scene of pandemonium on Saturday, October 11, when the Ute sentries detected Merritt and his troops moving southward. The Utes were in such a panic, she said, that they spooked their horses and had trouble catching them. Once again, according to Josie, the Ute leaders couldn't decide whether to move farther away from the army troops or stay where they were.[12]

But where, in the vicinity of the Grand River, could the Utes have ridden to a mountaintop and looked back to the White River where the soldiers were camped? The options are limited.

In February of 2006, I flew with Alan Moore and flight instructor Jeff Johnson over the area between the Colorado River and the White River, aerially examining potential routes. One thing quickly became evident. In nearly all of the area from west of Roan Creek to a dozen miles or so east of Parachute Creek, even from a height of several hundred feet above the highest points on the Book Cliffs, it is impossible to see the site of the old

White River Indian Agency. The lower hills immediately south of the White River blocked the view. On horseback at ground level, even on the highest points on the Book Cliffs, it would have been impossible for the Utes with their army telescopes to spot the soldiers—except for a couple of places.

In September 2005, Judy and I drove from Piceance Creek south up Cow Creek to the top of the Book Cliffs, also known as the Roan Plateau. At the northeasternmost point of the plateau, overlooking Government Creek, we could look due north with binoculars and easily see Powell Park, where the White River Indian Agency was located nearly 130 years ago, and upstream near where the town of Meeker now sits. Given that hundreds of army troops were there with great numbers of horses, mules, and wagons, and it was an extremely dry year, the dust from their movements would have been abundantly evident from that vantage point.

The Utes might have climbed to the top of the Book Cliffs by the same route we took—west along Piceance Creek from the top of Rio Blanco Hill, then up Cow Creek to the top of the Book Cliffs. There are also several locations south of Piceance Creek along the Government Creek drainage where it appears one could get a horse to the top of the Roan Plateau and to the site where we viewed Powell Park. There is another location—not on the Book Cliffs, but on the peak of the hogback between Government and Rifle creeks—where the Utes might also have ridden and looked back on the White River with their field glasses. It now serves as the location for several communication towers because of its height over the valley.

If the Utes traveled down Rifle Creek to the Grand River, they could easily have sent a few riders back to either of those sites to watch Merritt and his troops. Even on the hardy Ute ponies, it would have taken three or four hours to reach the top. It is a linear distance of about 20 miles from the river to the spot on the northeast corner of the Book Cliffs or the peak on the hogback from where they could see the White River.

However, if the Utes and their hostages had taken the Parachute Creek route south to the Grand River and camped near the mouth of that stream, the high-mountain surveillance would have required traveling a greater, but not impossible, distance. Still, it would have been a considerably more difficult ride for the Ute scouts. The linear distance would have been close to the same, but they would have had a much steeper climb back up Parachute Creek, then northeast, avoiding a number of deep canyons, to the spot where Powell Park is visible. It would have been a longer ride than the one to Government Creek, but it would have been possible in a single day. From Roan Creek, though, the distance becomes prohibitive—at least 30 linear miles from the mouth of Roan Creek to the viewing point over very rugged terrain.

Based on the hostages' narratives, it's clear that the Utes sent scouts to more than one location. They also sent out runners to learn what the scouts had seen and then report that information quickly to the Utes along the Grand River. They may also have sent scouts out in relays or pairs so that if movement by the soldiers was detected, one scout could race down to the main camp along the river to report to tribal leaders while the other remained in place to continue the surveillance.

The hostages and most of the Ute women, children, and elderly spent nearly a week at the Piceance Creek camp while the Milk Creek battle was raging. It appears that from there to the Grand River the Indians and their hostages traveled east about 5 miles to the head of the Rifle Creek drainage, then south and slightly east toward the Grand River. Although there are some discrepancies between this route and the women's descriptions of their journey, it still seems to fit better than any of the other potential routes. Furthermore, it had the advantage for the Utes, who were frightened that Merritt and his soldiers wouldn't be far behind them, of being a familiar trail on which they could quickly reach the Grand River with relatively little difficulty.

Once on the Grand, there was abundant food for their animals, and large parks where their camp of almost a hundred teepees could be set up. There were plenty of side drainages and nearby high mountains where they could hide their women, children, and hostages, and sites where they could make a stand against the soldiers. They were also far removed from any area where other white men were likely to venture. It seems likely that once they realized Merritt had arrived with additional troops, the Utes would have taken the swiftest and most familiar route to the Grand River.

JOSEPHINE MEEKER

GALLOPING THROUGH GREELEY ONE SUMMER DAY IN 1875, EIGHTEEN-year-old Josephine Meeker tumbled from her horse and "was rendered insensible," according to her father's newspaper, the *Greeley Tribune*. It's not clear whether the austere Nathan Meeker wrote the article about his daughter's fall and apparent concussion, but the story did admonish the young woman and her companions: "Girls should be more careful about racing their horses."[1] Josie Meeker, however, often did things others thought she shouldn't do, and she did things differently than convention dictated. She was independent, eager to participate in the world, and un-daunted by what society thought a woman's place should be. That no doubt pleased her mother, Arvilla, who in January 1876 was named vice president of the Colorado Territorial Women's Suffrage Society.[2]

Furthermore, Josie was eagerly preparing herself for a career. Not con-tent to be just a housewife, she wanted to become a secretary, a novel endeavor for a young woman in the 1870s. In 1876, her older brother Ralph, who was working at a newspaper in New York, sent her a Yost Writing Machine—a typewriter. She evidently became skillful in using it, typing much of her personal correspondence from then on.[3] In early 1878, just months before she and her mother joined Nathan Meeker at the White River Indian Agency, Josie was attending a business school in Denver to further her training in secretarial skills.[4]

Josie was also adventurous. Her propensity for racing horses through the town of Greeley was only one indication of that. In September of 1874, at the age of seventeen, she climbed Long's Peak, a landmark peak in northern Colorado and also one of the state's highest at more than 14,200 feet in elevation, with her Aunt Elida Meeker and others.[5] The trek was no easy excursion. Just a year earlier, in September and October of 1873, Englishwoman Isabella L. Bird took three days to reach the top of the mountain with an experienced mountain man as her guide and two young men as assistants. They started at Estes Park, more than 30 miles closer to the peak than Greeley.

Bird wrote about her experience in letters to her sister in England, which later became a book called *A Lady's Life in the Rocky Mountains*. Although she was awestruck by the grandeur of the mountain and its scenery, Bird wrote that she reached a point "of extreme terror":

> I was roped to "Jim" [her guide] but it was of no use; my feet were paralyzed and slipped on the bare rock...progress on the correct line of ascent was blocked by ice; and then for two hours we descended, lowering ourselves by our hands from rock to rock along a boulder-strewn sweep of 4,000 feet, patched with ice and snow, and perilous from rolling stones. My fatigue, giddiness and pain...were so great that I should never have gone half-way had not "Jim"...dragged me along with a patience and skill.[6]

Interestingly, Bird also visited the Union Colony at Greeley on that 1873 trip, when Nathan, Arvilla, and Josie Meeker were all residents there. Bird found it to be one of the most pleasant communities in Colorado. In her book she did not record meeting any of the Meekers, but it seems unlikely she would have visited that town—and been written up in the *Greeley Tribune* as she was—without meeting the town's leading citizen, the newspaper editor, and his family. And it's easy to imagine that Josie, then sixteen, would have been awestruck and inspired by Isabella Bird, a woman of independent means traveling alone through the West, a lady who was an excellent horsewoman, a fearless adventurer, and someone competent enough to both make her own travel arrangements and mend her own clothes. Bird was likely one of many people—members of the Meeker family included—who inspired and encouraged the independent and adventurous spirit that defined Josie Meeker.

Born in 1857 in Hiram Center, Ohio, Josie was the youngest of five children. Eldest brother Ralph doted on her, whether sending her a typing machine while she was a teenager or inviting her to stay with him and his wife in New York after the White River tragedy. And Josie clearly returned his affection. But she was fondest of her sister Mary, who was just three years older than her. After Josie was released along with the other hostages, Mary was the first family member she sought to contact. She wrote poignant letters to Mary from Washington, D.C., where she moved in the aftermath of her captivity with the Utes.[7]

Josie seems to have corresponded little with her eldest sister, Rozene, but the two feuded mightily after the events at the White River over government reimbursement for the family and what should be done with the Utes. Rozene even made numerous public presentations in which she told of the horrors she and her family had faced at the hands of the Indians. In letters to newspapers and public officials, Rozene demanded that the Utes be removed from Colorado or exterminated.[8]

Little is known about Josie's relationship with her brother George, ten years her senior and a year younger than Ralph. He died in Colorado while accompanying his father on a trip to establish the Union Colony in Greeley.[9]

When Josie was born, Nathan Meeker was operating a store in Ohio. Later he ran a store and a small farm in southern Illinois, neither of which was very profitable. By the time Josie was four, he was spending long periods of time away from his family to cover the Civil War for Horace Greeley's *New York Tribune*. Unlike his other occupations, Nathan proved successful as a war correspondent and was able to send his family money from his writing. He also began a lengthy relationship with Greeley that led to him becoming an agricultural correspondent for the *Tribune* after the war, and ultimately resulted in the creation of the Union Colony and the town of Greeley in 1870, when Josie was thirteen. A few years later Ralph went to work as a reporter for a rival paper to Greeley's, the *New York Herald*.[10]

Whatever the source of Josie's independent streak, it was cultivated throughout her early life, especially during her years in Greeley. And that character trait was in full blossom by midsummer of 1878, when she and her mother joined Nathan Meeker at the White River Indian Agency in the wilds of northwestern Colorado.

Just a few weeks before Josie and her mother were scheduled to leave for the White River, Ralph wrote a letter thanking her for heading to the Indian agency to take up her responsibilities as teacher and boardinghouse mistress. She responded to Ralph on August 11, 1878, a few weeks after she had arrived, with an emphatic personal disclaimer: "I cannot imagine why you wish to thank me for coming out here. I get paid for it, or I would not have come; as for duty, I never do anything because I think it my duty. I either do a thing from necessity or because I like to."[11]

Evidently, she liked her assignment as a teacher to the Ute children, even if she sometimes left her father miffed by her activities and views. She spent her first few weeks at the agency meeting and getting to know the Ute families. She rode out to visit them with Henry Jim, a young Ute who served as an agency interpreter. She not only tasted Indian foods such as boiled jerked meat, but also

> became absorbed in learning about Ute customs, and she talked at home about the things she had learned and seen among the Indians. When she brought home a pair of moccasins that one of the women had made for her, [Nathan] Meeker was forced to remind her gently but firmly that she was here to teach, not to learn, and should set a careful example of the American way. She dutifully put the moccasins away to be shown later in Greeley.[12]

Josie eventually succeeded in recruiting three students for her school. One was Freddie, the son of Quinkent (Douglas). Another was the son of one of Nicaagat's close followers. The third was "a little girl whose mother had died recently and whose father was happy to have Josephine care for her."[13] But even that limited success in recruiting children to her school was a source of frustration for her father. "Meeker and his wife Arvilla became concerned with the way Josie adapted herself to agency life. She was a friend to all the Utes and although she had been hired to teach the Ute children, she sympathized with the [Ute] parents in their stand about school....She also participated in many Ute activities, with evident joy."[14]

Josie further worried her parents by discussing the Utes' "savage customs with almost too much sympathy and admiration. She taught the girls how to freshen themselves with eau de cologne and how to keep fastened with hooks and eyes." And in recreational travel that foreshadowed her experience as a hostage, Josie "went fishing with Ouray's sister Susan [She-towitch] up Piceance Creek to the top of the Roan Plateau."[15] Beyond that, and in a direct affront to her father's puritanical views, Nathan Meeker "suspected that Josie played Spanish monte with the [Ute] men. Once he saw a squaw offer her a cigarette while they sat watching the races at Johnson's track."[16]

As for her responsibilities at the boardinghouse as hostess to the agency's white employees, even her mother despaired of her abilities. Arvilla Meeker wrote at one point that she had joined in a meal at the boardinghouse and became sick for the second time on Josie's cooking.[17]

To the Utes, Josie Meeker was intriguing, and they welcomed her with far more acceptance than they showed her father. Vivacious, friendly, and attractive, she soon drew suitors among the Ute men, "many of whom occupied first rank as chiefs," including Quinkent—age sixty-plus.

> They made all kinds of offers to her, those that were married agreeing to put away their other wives, and those that were not swearing that their love and admiration for the white maiden would never be dimmed or diminished by affection for any other woman.... One moccasined lover had hardly been sent away until another succeeded in his plea at the shrine of love.[18]

But if some of the Utes were romantically attracted to her, others, particularly Ute women, wondered if something was wrong with her.

> She was long past the age when a woman should have a man with her, but this woman, who was the Agent's daughter, had no man.... There was something about this woman that made a person like her. She was sad, the women said, because she had no man to be with. They felt sorry for her, and they listened to her talk because they did not want to hurt her feelings.[19]

Quinkent told the other Utes that Josie had come to be with the Ute children to act like a big sister to them. So the Utes called her Pa-chits, "big sister," and she went out often to talk with the women about their children and about the school where she hoped to teach them. The women asked their children if they wanted to go to school and live with Josie at the agency, but most of the children did not. Josie kept asking, and the Ute women continued to give her the same answer. She "did not understand that the women would not make the children do what they did not want to do." The Utes thought the whites "were very cruel to their children, always making them do things they did not want to do."[20]

That Ute acceptance of—or deference to—Josie continued even after she and the others were taken captive. Flora Ellen Price would complain after their release from captivity that "they made me do more drudgery than they did Josephine. They made her cook and they made me carry water."[21] Furthermore, because the young warrior Pahsone made it evident to everyone, including Josie, that he considered her his bride-to-be once the women were taken hostage, the Utes apparently accepted her as a new member of their band. Josie reported that "No whites are admitted to the tents while the Utes sing their medicine songs over the sick, but I, being considered one of [Pahsone's] family, was allowed to remain. When their child was sick his family asked me to sing with them, which I did."[22]

She described the healing ceremony, in which the medicine man knelt close to the victim, his back to the family, singing in "a series of high-keyed grunts, gradually reaching a lower and solemn tone." The family members joined in the singing, and the healer would make low gurgling sounds as he pressed his lips against the breast of the sufferer. Finally, they would all take a break to smoke and talk. Then the ceremony would be repeated, perhaps throughout the night. Josie said, "The sick bed ceremonies were very strange and weird, and more interesting than anything I saw in all my captivity of twenty-three days."[23]

But her acceptance by the Utes—even to the point of receiving more lenient treatment than the other captive women—didn't mean all was easy for Josie. Shortly after the group was taken hostage, she faced a menacing Ute warrior who "rushed at [her] with a huge butcher knife" as more than twenty of his companions looked on. He threatened to kill Josie, but she didn't quiver.

> I laughed at him, though my heart was in my mouth with fear, and I exclaimed:
>
> "I'm not afraid of such as you! All the scalps you ever took you got off women's heads. You never took a scalp from any brave like these warriors here. Go be a squaw!"
>
> As I spoke I gave him a violent push and sent him head over heels. Instantly, the others joined in a chorus of jeers and groans at him, and he actually ran away into a tent to hide himself.[24]

In addition to the threats that Josie and the other hostages received from both male and female Utes, they also faced great uncertainty about the Utes' intentions. Josie said she was able to understand enough Ute words to figure out there was a division among the group. Some wanted the prisoners kept alive to be used for barter if the Utes were overtaken by the army or when peace terms were being discussed. "Others," she said, "were in favor of putting us to death by the most frightful tortures."[25]

Uncertain about the Utes' intentions and about what was being done by whites to rescue them, Josie took matters into her own hands. On October 10, 1879, she surreptitiously sent a letter to the agent at the Uintah Indian Agency in Utah, approximately 130 miles northwest of where they were then camped. She wrote:

> Grand River, 40 to 50 miles from Agency, Oct. 10, 1879
> To Uintah Agent:
> I send this by one of your Indians. If you get it do all in your power to liberate us as soon as possible. I do not think they will let us go of their own accord. You will do me a great service to inform Mary Meeker, at Greeley, Colo., that we are well and may get home some time. Yours, etc.
>
> Josephine Meeker,
> United States Indian Agent's daughter.[26]

The letter was "written with a lead pencil on the back of a piece of paper which had formerly done service as a dry goods label," according to one report at the time. But it didn't reach Washington, D.C., by way of Utah, until after the captives had been liberated.[27]

Although it arrived too late to affect the hostages' rescue, Josie's letter was acted upon. In addition to sending word to Washington, Uintah Indian agent John Critchlow did send a letter, dated October 16, 1879, to Mary Meeker in Greeley, relaying Josie's message. He also promised Mary, "I will do all that is within my power to liberate them from this captivity."[28]

Critchlow, one of the longest-serving and most trusted of any of the agents serving the various Ute bands, kept his word. He sent several Utes from his Utah reservation to Colorado, accompanied by two white men, S. B. Dillman and D. B. McLane, to attempt to free the hostages. They apparently arrived at the main Ute camp along the Grand River at Roan Creek three days after the hostages had been released. McLane wrote a letter to

Arvilla Meeker in January 1880 briefly outlining their mission. He also told how some of the Utes wanted to kill the two white men who were with them, but Nicaagat saved them from death, explaining to the other Utes that he wanted them to go to Colonel Merritt's camp to talk with the army commander on the Indians' behalf.[29]

Although Josie's clandestine letter writing did not end up winning the hostages' release, her domestic skills as a seamstress unquestionably made things easier for her and the other hostages. "The rescue party found the captives picturesquely attired in woolen blanket dresses made by themselves," Denver newsmen Thomas Dawson and F. J. V. Skiff reported. "Miss Josie's costume was the most striking. Her dress was made of an Indian blanket, plain skirt and long jacket...with tight sleeves. The blanket stuff was dark brown, the broad yellow stripes in the goods acting as a border around the bottom of the dress and the flowing waist."[30] Relations between the captives and the Utes may also have been improved by Josie's sewing. "Besides making myself some clothes, I made a lot of clothes for the young Indians, at which they were pleased."[31]

According to Josie, she and Flora Ellen both sewed as well as cooked, and though they hoped to be rescued soon, Josie was cautious enough to prepare for colder weather. "The Indians said we would be kept there all winter, and so while I expected that such would not be the case, I concluded to make some clothes for myself, especially as those I had were all banded up."[32]

Josephine Meeker's personality didn't mesh well with Victorian notions of how proper young women should act, but her independence, resolve, and resourcefulness served her and her fellow hostages well during their captivity. Their survival, however, must also be attributed, at least in part, to another woman who was willing to break with the conventions of her culture to aid the whites on the hostage trail: She-towitch.

10

SHE-TOWITCH TO THE RESCUE

THE TRIBAL COUNCIL CONCERNING THE HOSTAGES WAS CONTENTIOUS.
One group of Ute warriors viewed the three white women and two young
children taken after the attack on the White River Indian Agency as valuable items for negotiating with the army. But others—a sizeable contingent of the White River Utes—saw them as a liability. They wanted them
killed, and as quickly as possible.

Into this maelstrom stepped a woman named She-towitch (known to
the whites as "Susan"). In her mid-thirties and well known by all of the
tribal members, she was the wife of Canalla, a White River medicine man
and leader, and the sister of Ouray, the Uncompahgre chief. What she had
to say was worth listening to, even if it was unusual for a woman to address
the war council.

Josephine Meeker said the situation was precarious for the hostages
until She-towitch made her views known.

> We all owe our lives to the sister of Chief Ouray, for when the soldiers had
> engaged the savages and were defeated, there was a council called as to what

should be done with us prisoners. At that council our enemies were getting the best of it, and were clamoring to have us all burned at the stake[1] when this brave squaw did what has never been done yet by an Indian woman. She strode into the council and insisted on speaking, would be heard, and refused to be quiet. She then delivered an eloquent and convincing speech, in which she told the braves what would be the result of injuring us, and explained fully to them the advantages that would undoubtedly accrue to their own side by returning us unharmed to our friends. It was well known to all the warriors that she had great influence with Ouray. To disobey Ouray was death, and so with their natural shrewdness they saw that it would be best to accede to the good squaw's demand. We were thus saved.[2]

This council, according to Josie, occurred during the first week of their captivity, while Ute warriors still had Thornburgh's troops pinned down at Milk Creek.

Arvilla Meeker told a similar story, though she placed She-towitch's intervention on the hostages' behalf much later, after Charles Adams had arrived to secure their freedom.

We owe much to the wife of Johnson [Canalla]. She is Ouray's sister, and like him, she has a kind heart. Ouray had ordered us to be well treated and that we should be allowed to go home.

The council was a stormy one. Various opinions prevailed. The war party wanted us held until peace should be made between the Indians and the Government. They wanted to set us against the guilty murderers, so as to save them through us. After a few hours of violent speeches Mrs. Johnson burst into the lodge in a magnificent wrap and demanded that the captives be set free, war or no war. Her brother Ouray had so ordered, and she took the assembly by storm. She told the pathetic story of the captives, and advised the Indians to do as Ouray requested and trust to the mercy of the government. General Adams said he must have a decision at once or he would have to leave. That settled it and we were set free.[3]

As with so many details involving the forgotten hostage trail, there is confusion, and the hostages' stories don't entirely mesh. It is possible that She-towitch actually spoke on their behalf at two different councils, or that neither Arvilla nor Josie accurately recalled the timing of her intervention to save them. But there is little question that she did so on at least one occasion. The freed hostages were adamant about that, not only in the book written from their own accounts, but in interviews they gave to others.

One newspaper story shortly after the hostages were released gave an account similar to Arvilla Meeker's, in which She-towitch spoke at the council after Adams had arrived at the camp where they were being held. This account said She-towitch "was followed by her husband, Johnson, who also made a speech advocating the release of the prisoners."[4] In his testimony before Congress, however, Adams mentioned nothing about She-towitch speaking before the council while he was there.[5]

Even though she was Ouray's sister, little is known about She-towitch's early years. According to published accounts she was born around 1845, but her descendants say she was born at least a decade earlier, probably in northern New Mexico, where her father lived with his Jicarilla Apache wife. Two of her older brothers, Ouray and Quenche, were hired out to Hispanic ranchers in the Taos area, where they learned Spanish and a smattering of English, were baptized into the Roman Catholic faith, and mingled with people from a variety of cultures.[6]

In 1851, after She-towitch's mother died, her father, Guero, a member of the Uncompahgre, or Tabeguache, band of Utes, "decided to return to his own people with his three sons and two daughters."[7] Her life then was likely that of a typical Ute girl, moving with her family to different camps with the season and living in relative peace and tranquility in Colorado's deep mountain country. She did make occasional forays to the eastern plains, and it was on one such expedition, when She-towitch was just sixteen, that her peaceful life took a terrifying turn.

In the late summer of 1861, most of the Uncompahgre band traveled to the northeastern plains—north of the small community then known as Denver City—to hunt buffalo. "While the men were busy with the hunt and the women were processing the kill, Ouray's young sister, Tsashin [She-towitch], disappeared. Ouray, Quench and their distraught father abandoned the hunt to search, but they found no trace of her."[8] Leaving the hunt and heading west back to their mountain home, the Uncompahgre Utes "met a band of Northern Ute warriors who reported several recent battles with a band of Arapahos" just north of the area where Ouray and his band had been hunting. The Arapahos had been enemies of the Utes for centuries, and the grieving family concluded that She-towitch had been abducted by them. They could only hope that they would keep her alive.[9]

If She-towitch said much about her captivity, it was not written down. It appears that she was treated as a slave, assigned hard work and menial tasks rather than being adopted as a member of the tribe or an individual family, as many Indian captives were. Whatever her life was like, two years later she was miraculously freed. In the summer of 1863 a group of Northern Utes rode into the camp of the Uncompahgre Utes in the mountains near the Gunnison River. They "delivered a great surprise—Tsashin [She-towitch]. They had found her walking through the mountains and provided her a horse and an escort to locate Ouray's camp."[10]

Exactly how She-towitch secured her freedom is a matter of some dispute. In December 1879, following the attacks at the White River Agency, former sergeant William Carroll of the First Colorado Cavalry told a Golden, Colorado, newspaper that he and his troops had freed She-towitch. "He reported that she was found in an Arapaho camp on the Platte River near the mouth of the Cache La Poudre River [near present-day Greeley, which had not yet been founded]. The Arapahos were about to sacrifice her in vengeance for the loss of a number of their own warriors killed by a band of Utes. Sergeant Carroll with a squad of men rode into camp in the nick of time."[11]

In this version of the story, Sergeant Carroll took the freed captive home, where his wife "was able to soothe the frightened girl." Mrs. Carroll taught She-towitch some English. She sewed clothes for the Indian girl and was ready to adopt her into the family. But on the Fourth of July, when the family headed to a dance, She-towitch disappeared. "She had taken with her the clothes Mrs. Carroll had made, a piece of meat and a butcher knife."[12]

An alternate version of She-towitch's rescue was published in a book about the White River incident. The authors quoted Major Whitely, an early agent for the White River Utes, when the agency was located farther east, at Hot Sulphur Springs.

> The Major relates that while on his way to the Hot Sulphur Springs, in Middle Park, he was overtaken by a messenger from Governor Evans, who informed him of the rescue of a Ute squaw from the Arapahoes and Cheyennes by the officers of the United States Army at Fort Collins. These Indians had captured this squaw in some of their raids, and while encamped near the mouth of the Cache La Poudre, had determined to burn her at the stake. The commanding officer at Fort Collins, hearing of this, took a detachment

of troops, and by alternate threats and promises obtained her release, after she had already been tied to the stake and the fires lighted. This squaw was forwarded to Major Whitely, and after her arrival at Hot Springs was sent by him to her people...to the camp of the Indians on the Snake River, where she was received with every demonstration of joy by the tribe. Major Whitely gave this squaw the name of Susan, which she has borne ever since.[13]

A very different version was handed down through the generations by She-towitch's descendants. The family believes She-towitch managed to escape from the Arapahos on her own, without assistance from the Colorado militia or the U.S. Army.[14]

However she was freed, She-towitch didn't stay long with her Uncompahgre Ute family. Although her father had died during her captivity, he had arranged for her to marry Canalla of the White River Utes. The marriage was a way to enhance the connection between the two bands. And in contradiction of traditional Ute ways, She-towitch went to live with Canalla and his family on the White River rather than him moving to live with her and her family.[15]

The accounts of She-towitch speaking eloquently on behalf of the hostages in tribal councils were not the only reports the hostages gave of her kindness. At various times she expressed sorrow for their captivity, referred to their captors as "bad Utes," and acted on their behalf, as when she made shoes for Flora Ellen Price's young children and held and comforted the youngsters. "Johnson's wife was very kind," Flora Ellen said later. "She treated me just like a mother....She treated my little girl very kindly, made moccasins for her, and she grieved over her and my boy as if they were her own."[16]

On the day the hostages were to be released, after the long meeting between the Utes and Charles Adams, She-towitch also grew angry with her husband over his lackadaisical treatment of Arvilla, who recalled,

> Next morning, when we were about to start for the wagon, which was a day's journey to the south, Chief Johnson, who was slightly cool toward us, threw out a poor saddle for me to ride upon. His wife Susan caught sight of it and was furious. She flung it away and went to a pile of saddles and picked out the best one in the lot. She found a good blanket, and gave both to me. Then she turned to her chief and poured out her contempt with such effect that he was glad to sneak away.[17]

Several sources also say She-towitch sent word to Ouray of the Milk Creek battle and killings at the White River Indian Agency through a young Ute messenger.[18]

She-towitch's actions did not go unnoticed. In fact, her efforts, combined with confusion among whites about different Ute women, may have helped create the erroneous story that Ouray's wife, Chipeta, galloped from the Uncompahgre Valley to the Grand River to rescue the hostages. The tale apparently began with a poem written by Denver newspaperman Eugene Field in 1882.[19] The story was presented in a number of historical accounts about the White River attacks and lingered as late as the 1990s.[20] Furthermore, in at least one photograph, She-towitch was erroneously identified as Chipeta by early historians.[21]

But not everyone was confused about She-towitch or her efforts on behalf of the hostages following the attacks at the White River. In fact, those efforts attracted attention even in areas far removed from Colorado. On Wednesday, October 29, 1879, the *Chicago Tribune*'s lead, front-page headline read:

A STRATEGIC SQUAW.
How Susan, the Ute Woman, effected the Meekers' Release
By Pleading for Them in a Council of Warriors.
Such a Thing Never Before Heard Of in Indian History.[22]

She-towitch's heroism on behalf of the white hostages would lead to a brief flurry of effort on her behalf a few months later, but within six months, her efforts to protect the hostages would be largely forgotten amid the tumult of white anger toward the Utes.

NICAAGAT VERSUS NATHAN

In the aftermath of the killings at the White River Agency, two portraits of Nathan Meeker emerged. The first was popularized in much of the press, in at least one hastily prepared book, and by members of the Meeker family and politicians eager for anything that would help them rid Colorado of the Ute Indians. It painted Meeker as a saintly, paternal figure whose benevolence toward the White River Utes was rewarded with treachery.

"The annals of Indian crime do not contain mention of a darker deed than the murder of Hon. Nathan C. Meeker—Father Meeker, as he was called throughout Colorado," wrote two Denver newspaper reporters in a book published just a month after the hostages were released. "In the death of Father Meeker, a good man has passed away. He was kind and good to all, and to none more than to the Indians."[1]

While many Coloradans enthusiastically promoted that picture of the deceased Indian agent, a more realistic view of Meeker was also taking shape, primarily in the official record—but with some newspaper backing and the reluctant acknowledgment of even solid Meeker supporters. In

---

this alternative narrative, Meeker was not so perfect. The man who had tried to turn the White River Utes into farmers had been a person of indisputable honesty and integrity, according to this version, but hopelessly naive about the Indians, and more than a little arrogant in his approach to them.

This view—with differing degrees of emphasis on his integrity versus his arrogance—was endorsed by a variety of people who knew Meeker, including Clinton B. Fisk, a member of the Indian Board of Commissioners. According to Fisk, Meeker was "a most excellent gentleman, whom I had known for a great many years." But, Fisk added, he was "about as unfit for the position as a man could possibly be to go into that country, take hold of the White River Utes and manage them; destitute of that particular tact and knowledge of the Indian character which is required in an agent."[2] This is the predominant view of Nathan Meeker that has survived to this day. In books and magazine articles throughout the twentieth century, he has regularly been portrayed as an honest but arrogant man whose patronizing attitude toward the Utes and stubborn refusal to change his plans, even when they clearly weren't working, was a direct cause of many of the problems at the agency.

But there is a third picture of Nathan Meeker's character that has gotten little consideration—the view of Meeker evinced by Nicaagat and most other White River Utes. They saw Meeker as a deceitful, conniving agent, untrustworthy as well as disliked. And it was his dishonesty, as much as anything else, that caused problems at the agency.

"The great trouble with the agent was that he would tell one story one day and another the next, so that we did not know how to take him or when to believe him," Nicaagat told investigators at the Los Pinos Indian Agency in November 1879.[3] The previous spring and summer, Nicaagat had set out with near evangelical fervor to convince authorities to remove Meeker from his post. As part of that effort, he enlisted the aid of a White River Agency employee to write a letter to a Denver journalist who was a friend of Governor Frederick Pitkin to report his dissatisfaction with Meeker.[4] Nicaagat also rode 140 miles south to seek Chief Ouray's help in telling government officials about the problems Meeker was creating at the White River Agency.[5] He then galloped to Denver—nearly 260 miles away—to personally meet with Governor Pitkin to air his complaints and request the governor's assistance in getting a new agent.[6]

When Major Thornburgh and his troops were amassing at the reservation boundary, Nicaagat personally met with the commanding officer to plead with him to keep the bulk of his troops outside the reservation, but also to lay out his grievances against Meeker. He said he was preparing to do the same thing the morning of September 29 when he went out with just eight other Utes to meet with Major Thornburgh at Milk Creek, but the shooting started before he could arrange a meeting.[7]

Nicaagat was not alone in these efforts. Colorow and several other Utes also met with Thornburgh and his troops. The Utes were vocal opponents of Meeker and his policies, but less diplomatic than Nicaagat. Another group of White River Utes visited Ouray to make similar complaints about Meeker. And Sowawick and others close to Nicaagat accompanied him to Denver to meet with Pitkin.[8]

Many of the White River Utes shared Nicaagat's sentiments about Meeker and had sought ways to get rid of him without inciting violence. Nicaagat became the most prominent, in part because of his English-speaking skills, but also because he had dealt with both politicians and soldiers before. Furthermore, because he gave such lengthy testimony both at Los Pinos and in Washington, and because he is quoted most frequently by the whites involved, we know far more about what he did or tried to do than what other Utes attempted.

In the written accounts of his efforts to get authorities to understand the problems with Nathan Meeker, Nicaagat focused on several issues. Among these was Meeker's decision to kill agency beef even though the Utes maintained the cattle belonged to them and not the government; Meeker's move of the agency 15 miles downstream, in what Nicaagat saw as a clear violation of treaty requirements; Meeker's refusal to provide food and blankets to Utes from other areas of Colorado and Utah, even though Nicaagat believed he had no authority for that refusal; and the Utes' belief that Meeker was spreading lies among the whites about the Indians' actions and intentions.[9] In nearly all of these accounts, however, Nicaagat emphasized one message—vehemently and repeatedly: Meeker was dishonest in his dealings with the Utes and could not be trusted. Nicaagat believed that removing him as the White River Indian agent and replacing him with someone more trustworthy would go a long way toward reducing tensions.

The events that occurred at the White River Agency in September 1879, and the eventual removal of the Utes from their traditional homeland, were ignited to a great extent by national and regional forces. There was the westward push of the whites, driven by the inexhaustible demand for gold, silver, and agricultural land. And there was the cry, swelling louder and louder throughout Colorado, demanding that the Utes be removed from the state. Many pioneers believed that the Utes and most other Native Americans were "savages" who could never be entirely civilized and therefore should be removed to someplace like the Indian Territory, in what is now Oklahoma.

But what transpired at the White River Agency was also a direct result of the central dispute between Nathan Meeker and the Ute leaders. Although their days as free-ranging hunters who claimed most of western Colorado as their territory were undoubtedly numbered, the violence that occurred in September 1879 might have been avoided if the Utes had had any confidence that Meeker's word could be trusted—or if any of the authorities who heard Nicaagat's complaints had listened and taken action against Meeker.

Consider, for example, the affair of the wagon—a story of a promise made and broken as far as Nicaagat was concerned. Nicaagat told this story at least three times to white authorities: to Governor Pitkin in August 1879, to Major Thornburgh and his officers just days before the battle at Milk Creek, and to the official investigators at the Los Pinos Agency in November. The following account is from his testimony at Los Pinos.

> The agent then said that in a little while the Commissioner of Indian Affairs would send wagons for the Indians, so that they would have wagons of their own in which to haul poles and do their farming with. A little before the end of the month the wagons arrived.... The agent told me that the wagons were already there, and took me over to the house to see the wagons. The agent said to me that he did not like these wagons; that they were painted red, and that he knew that things that were painted red were no good....He also said the wagons were large and heavy and that the Indian horses were small, so that being heavy and painted red color, they were not fit for the Indians, but that he had a wagon that was painted green which he would give us.

That green wagon, according to Nicaagat, was not in nearly as good shape as the new red wagons. Its paint was faded, and it needed repair. But even that turned out to be more than Meeker was willing to give to the

Utes. Instead of turning the smaller, older wagon over to Nicaagat outright, "He then went back on his word again and told us we could have the green wagon for a month, use it, and return it."[10] Unfortunately, the whites who heard that story didn't understand Nicaagat's message. Instead it fed the long-held stereotype of Indians as little more than children, emotionally and intellectually. After all, here was an important leader of the Utes complaining about getting a green wagon instead of a red one.

Captain J. Scott Payne, who took command of the troops at Milk Creek after Thornburgh was killed, described the meeting with Nicaagat a few days prior to the battle.

> In this interview Jack complained very bitterly of the agent, Mr. Meeker. He stated that the agent had tried to make them farm and plow and that he had failed to fulfill a great many of his promises to them. Among other things, I recollect his principal grievance seemed to be something about a wagon. He stated that Mr. Meeker had promised him a new wagon with red paint on it, and when he had insisted upon its being given him, Mr. Meeker had offered him an old wagon from which pretty much all the paint had been rubbed off.... Jack [Nicaagat] laid more stress upon that circumstance than any other cause of complaint that he had.[11]

William Byers and Governor Frederick Pitkin were similarly unimpressed with Nicaagat's wagon complaint in their testimony before Congress. The point that Nicaagat was trying to make, however—that Meeker did not keep his word and could not be trusted—seemed lost on Payne, Byers, and Pitkin. Yet taken in the context of his other statements, it's clear that Nicaagat was using the wagon story to illustrate what he viewed as Meeker's fundamental dishonesty, not to lodge a picayune complaint about the color of the wagon. In his testimony before the White River Ute Commission, Nicaagat followed his story about the wagon immediately with the statement, "The great trouble with the agent was that he would tell one story one day and another the next, so that we did not know how to take him or when to believe him."[12]

Nathan Meeker may not have always been true to his word, but he was not a scoundrel in the manner of some Indian agents. He did not sell supplies that were meant for the Utes, or use his position to further his personal business interests.[13] When he slaughtered the Utes' cattle, it was because he believed that was the best way to ensure that they were adequately fed. As for the new wagon, he may have preferred to have it available to his white agency employees, but it may have been too large for the small Indian ponies to pull. And when it came to convincing his Ute charges to do his bidding, well…a little fibbing or stretching of the truth was just part of his patronizing method of dealing with them because he viewed the Utes as children.

After arriving at the White River Agency in May 1878, Meeker regularly wrote dispatches about his experiences that were published in the *Greeley Tribune*, the newspaper of the community he had founded eight years earlier. In one such narrative, published December 11, 1878, Meeker described his efforts to convince some reluctant Utes to work at digging an irrigation ditch by hand—the sort of manual labor that most Ute men believed was beneath them. Quinkent and his group of Utes had agreed to work on the ditch, Meeker wrote, but Sowawick, Nicaagat's right-hand-man according to Josephine, opposed doing so—that is, until Meeker threatened to write a letter about Sowawick's bad conduct to the Commissioner of Indian Affairs in Washington, D.C. Then Sowawick agreed to start digging.

Nicaagat, however, was a different matter. "Another Chief, Jack [Nicaagat], belonging to the same party, and equally violent, kept out of the way meanwhile," Meeker wrote. "But soon came around and said if the Commissioner would write him a letter telling him to dig the ditch, he would…do so." Meeker told him it would take months to get such a letter from the commissioner, and he refused Nicaagat's demand that he be paid up front for working. "So he pulled out and went to Bear [Yampa] River, where he has been camping ever since."[14]

Meeker made it sound as if he had won a victory over the Utes in convincing Sowawick to work by using the threat of a letter to the Commissioner of Indian Affairs—sort of like a mother telling a recalcitrant child, "If you don't behave, I'll tell your father." He didn't seem to realize that Nicaagat had just called his bluff. Is the Commissioner of Indian Affairs that all-powerful? Well then, just get a letter from him ordering me to work, and I will do so. When Meeker couldn't deliver on that in time to actually dig the ditch, Nicaagat demonstrated that he could leave without consequence. Even if he didn't realize it, Meeker had lost face among the remaining Utes.

Nathan Meeker miscalculated or misunderstood his relationship with other Utes as well. He believed Canavish (Johnson) had embraced Meeker's ideas for turning the Utes into farmers and would lead others to do the same. Meeker was bitterly disappointed in the summer of 1879 when that proved not to be the case.

Then there was Jane.[15] About the same age as Josie, she became one of Meeker's favorites when he arrived at the White River Agency in 1878. She worked as a household servant, and Meeker returned the favor by helping her plant a garden and tending it for her during the summer, when she left the reservation with her husband and other Utes for weeks at a time.[16] He also depended on Jane to teach him about Ute culture, particularly the lives of the women. And he believed she would provide intelligence to him about what Ute leaders such as Nicaagat and Quinkent were up to. Instead she served as a conduit of information for those Ute leaders about Meeker's activities.[17]

In the summer of 1879, Meeker and Jane had a falling out over her refusal to tend her garden the way he believed it should be worked. In the process he heightened the tension between him and all of the Utes by telling Jane that the tribe didn't really own the land of their reservation—that it belonged to the government.[18] That clearly was wrong, based on treaty language that established the reservation boundaries, but it proved to be accurate in the real world of the nineteenth-century West.

Several accounts explain that Meeker repeatedly tried to play the rivals Nicaagat (Jack) and Quinkent (Douglas) against each other. Josephine described it as "a fight between Jack and Douglas as to which would be chief. Really, Jack was the chief, but Douglas was recognized as chief by the government....Jack controlled the largest number of men. Douglas had only about forty or fifty followers, while Jack had, perhaps, a couple of hundred."[19] Thus when the dispute began with Quinkent's band about plowing near the new agency, Meeker called on Nicaagat to help mediate "because he controlled the largest number of men, and the agent thought that if he could get the consent of the majority, the rest would submit to it."[20] But Nicaagat clearly recognized that Meeker's words and actions didn't always mesh. After the agent had told him on another occasion that the Ute's words meant little, Nicaagat asked, "Why then do you send for me and get me to talk to you if it amounts to nothing except to have me abused in this manner?"[21]

One of Meeker's main conflicts with the Utes stemmed from his insistence that the White River Indian Agency be moved 15 miles downstream, away from the high mountains on the edge of what is now known as the

Flat Tops, and toward the more open valley at lower elevation, which he deemed much better for growing crops. Unfortunately, it was also in the middle of the Utes' horse pasture. Nicaagat recalled,

> I told him that the site of the old agency had been settled by treaty, and that I knew no law or treaty that made mention of the new site. Then the agent told me that we had better all move down below, and that if we did not we should be obliged to; that for that they had soldiers. I told the agent that here was the agency as under the treaty, that we had had agents here before him, among others General [Charles] Adams, who were all satisfied with the old site and that there we should stay.

Meeker's response was that Adams knew nothing of farming, otherwise he would have moved the agency. Nicaagat responded, "[I] then told him that it would be well if he farmed the piece below the agency; that I had a great many animals and wished my horses to be pastured where we had always done so, which was down on the land around the lower agency. The agent said, 'All right; we will go and see what place you like.'" In the end, however, Meeker simply ignored Nicaagat and the treaty, and moved the agency to the new location.[22]

Even one of his own employees believed that it was a mistake to move the agency to the horse pasture and then plow those lands. In a letter he wrote to his mother from the White River Agency in September 1879, Fred Shepard wrote, "I don't blame the Utes for not wanting this ground plowed up. It is a splendid place for ponies and there is better faming land, and just as near, right west of this field, but it is covered with sagebrush."[23] Shepard added that some of the Utes had offered to clear the sagebrush if Meeker would leave the pasture alone, but Meeker, he said, "is stubborn and won't have it that way and wants soldiers to carry out his plans."[24]

These incidents are further evidence of the expanding rift between Meeker and Nicaagat and the other White River Utes. In his testimony at Los Pinos, however, Nicaagat suggested that he had tried to make amends after Meeker told him that if the Utes refused to follow the orders, he would be forced to call for soldiers. "I told him that I stood in the light of a son to him, and for that reason had to come to advise with him, but I could not see why he should talk about bringing the soldiers here to enforce orders."[25]

Meeker's response was anything but conciliatory. "'Anyhow your tongue does not amount to anything,' says the agent. 'You don't know how to write, and I do; what you say amounts to nothing.' The agent continuing, 'The words you say don't go very far; my papers and what I say travels far and wide.'"[26] In response, Nicaagat said, "I asked him if he would not take back what he had said; that he had talked very badly, and in a way to cause trouble; and that we did not wish to have any trouble with our American neighbors on Bear River and elsewhere. He said 'You can stay there and talk,' and walked off. I then went to my camp."[27]

There were more confrontations between the two in the late summer and early fall of 1879. Faced with orders from E. A. Hayt, the Commissioner of Indian Affairs, to keep the Utes on the reservation, Meeker demanded that all of the White River Utes, including Nicaagat, stay close to the new agency, where he could keep an eye on them. Many of the Utes, Nicaagat especially, ignored that edict. Nicaagat kept his camp near the site of the old agency, 15 miles away.

Other Utes told Nicaagat that Meeker had accused them of stealing blankets, coats, and other items from the agency storehouse. But when Nicaagat confronted Meeker about it, and went with him to the storehouse to find out how the Utes had gotten in, Meeker only pointed to a rafter that had once held blankets but was now empty, and then suggested that the Utes had stolen or made a key to the storehouse.[28]

Additionally, according to some of the Utes who had remained near the agency, Meeker was now complaining that they were spending too much time hanging around the agency. Nicaagat recalled, "I then asked the agent why he wished to send the Indians away; that it was only a short time since he had ordered them to come and stay there, saying that he wanted to have them around him, and now he complained they were too near."[29] If Meeker responded, Nicaagat did not report it.

But the greatest source of Nicaagat's anger toward Meeker was the Ute leader's firm belief that Meeker was spreading lies about the White River Utes to people in other parts of Colorado. He had some independent confirmation for this. Nicaagat said that shortly before he traveled to Denver on August 12, 1879, to take his complaints about Meeker to Governor Pitkin, he visited Peck's trading post on the Bear (Yampa) River. Peck pulled out a piece of paper that he said contained "a notice" from Meeker advising white settlers that "the Utes wished to fight." He told Nicaagat that Meeker had been sending out similar notices and letters since early spring. It was Peck who urged Nicaagat to go to Denver to talk with the governor about the problems.[30]

After leaving Denver, on his way back to the White River, Nicaagat ran into a troop of Buffalo Soldiers in Middle Park, the same ones who would, a month later, ride to aid Major Thornburgh's beleaguered troops in the battle at Milk Creek. "I met some solders. The officer asked me how things were going on at White River; that he had heard there was trouble there....I told him what he had heard were lies. He pulled out a paper and showed me, saying that it was information received from the agent regarding the trouble." But the officer, apparently Captain Dodge, said he believed Nicaagat.[31]

These reports and Nicaagat's travels led to another confrontation between Meeker and Nicaagat. "The day after I arrived I went down to the agency, and the agent received me by asking me what business I had running around, and what business took me to Denver. I informed him that I had seen papers in which he had given information about things that were not happening. He answered, 'Is it your business to go around finding out what I have written?'"[32]

One strange episode, which the Utes also attributed to Meeker, involved crude drawings of a massacre at the White River Indian Agency—pictures made before the actual killings occurred. They purportedly showed not only Meeker and the other male employees being killed, but the women and children as well. Josie heard the stories from Nicaagat, Quinkent, and other Utes while she was being held hostage.

> They told us that pictures were found on, I think Thornburgh's body after they killed him...pictures of father, mother, me and Mrs. Price; I do not know whether any more of the employees or not; some murdered in one place and some in another; father was shot in the head, I through the heart, and all of us covered with blood, and they claimed that father sent those pictures out to stir up a sentiment against the Indians, telling them that was the way all of us would be massacred if they [the soldiers] did not hurry up and come in there.[33]

Although she did not see the drawings herself, Josie said, "They seemed to be correct pictures, because they recognized who we were. Otherwise I should have thought the soldiers drew them for their amusement."[34]

Testifying before Congress a few months later, Josephine recalled, "They were very much enraged over some pictures they had found in Major Thornburgh's pocket....He [Nicaagat] insisted that father had made those pictures, and sent them out to the soldiers so as to get them in there and to make them angry with the Utes."[35] According to both accounts, Josie was convinced that the Indians weren't making the story up because she heard it repeatedly from a number of different Utes, including Quinkent and Nicaagat. "These pictures had been drawn, I suppose, by some white person; I don't know by whom."[36]

Captain Payne offered his own evidence that drawings were found on the battlefield. He obtained one of them on the night of September 29, after the fighting broke out at Milk Creek.

> That night, after the fight was pretty well over for the day—it was nearly night, but I remember we could still see—one of Mr. Gordon's teamsters brought to me a sheet of paper about the size of letter-paper. It was dirty and rumpled. In that were the rough drafts of what were intended to be the bodies of three or four men with holes through them, as if to represent bullet holes, and underneath were tracings, horizontal, wavy lines, after the manner of a man's handwriting; and this man reported to me that he had found this paper hanging on a bush on the hill where we had passed his train.[37]

Payne offered no theories on who had made the drawings, or why. Josephine clearly didn't believe her father was the artist, and with good reason. It is difficult to believe Meeker would resort to such a poor device in an attempt to win army support. He was a man of letters, and all of his communications to Thornburgh, Pitkin, Hayt, and his family and friends in Greeley were clearly written, even when he was obviously becoming worried for his safety and that of his family and employees. There is no way of knowing who the battlefield artist was or what purpose he hoped to serve with the drawings. None of the pictures apparently survived to be examined by authorities, beyond Payne's cursory look as light faded after the first day of fighting at Milk Creek.

While Meeker's dissembling caused many problems, almost as villainous, from Nicaagat's point of view, was Meeker's refusal to do anything about the lies being told by others. Governor Pitkin was among the many whites who talked of fires being intentionally set by the Utes, especially the supposed burning of James B. Thompson's house, not far from the reservation—despite the fact that Thompson himself had not claimed his house had been burned.[38] Nicaagat's attempts to refute the governor's false charges fell on deaf ears. Although he personally attested to Pitkin during their meetings that the Thompson house was still standing in mid-August of 1879, Pitkin cited the burning of the Thompson house as fact in official correspondence. He even sent the Routt County sheriff to the White River Reservation to arrest the two Utes he had heard were responsible.[39] Quinkent refused to allow the sheriff to make an arrest, saying he had no authority to do so on the reservation.[40]

Doubting that any crimes had been committed by the Utes, Nicaagat asked Meeker's assistance in proving their innocence. Meeker's response provided one more reason to despise the agent.

> I then told the agent I thought we had better, he and I, go and see these houses that had been burned, that we might understand something about it. He answered me that it was none of his business to talk about these things, and I asked him how that could be, as he, being Indian agent, he was the man who should regulate such matters. He said the Utes were very bad men...that he had no business to be worrying himself in talking for them. I then said, "How is this? It is not well for you to talk in this way. If you take it in hand and show how it is, all would be right."[41]

Nicaagat recalled that Meeker was just as petulant in his final meeting with him, when Thornburgh's troops were on their way.

> I went to the agency to talk with the agent...and told the agent that I hoped he would do something to stop [the soldiers] coming to the agency. He said it was none of his business; he would have nothing to do with it. I then said to the agent I would like he and I to go where the soldiers were, to meet them. The agent said I was all the time molesting him; he would not go. This he told me in his office, and after finishing speaking he got up and went into another room, and shut and locked his door. That was the last time I ever saw him.[42]

In a few days, Nathan Meeker would be dead, and Nicaagat would be fighting his one-time friends in the U.S. Army.

12

TRAIL SECTION 3

T HE WOMEN HELD HOSTAGE BY THE U TES REPORTED THAT THEY SPENT
ten days along the Grand (Colorado) River—almost half of their total
captivity. But as with most of their time on the trail, the exact locations
of where they stopped and where they camped are unclear. We can only
speculate based on the women's accounts, which are far from exact and
often confusing. Nevertheless, it appears that from the top of Piceance
Creek to the Grand River, the Utes and their hostages followed the long-
used trail between the White River and Los Pinos Indian agencies—the
one identified on the Hayden Survey maps published in 1877. If so, they
would have arrived at the river about 4 miles east and upstream from where
Rifle Creek empties into it.[1] "We reached Grand River about sundown,
where we camped in the sage brush," Flora Ellen Price later recalled. "To
the south the mountains were very high and the country was bleak and
bare on the north."[2]

Modern travelers can take in the same view. Looking south from the
Colorado River about 4 miles upstream from Rifle Creek and the main
Rifle exit on Interstate 70, you can see the high peaks of the Battlements at

the east end of Grand Mesa, especially Mamm Peak. The mountains are heavily forested, and even in a dry year they might have had a dusting of snow in early October. To the north are the dull, beige-colored Book Cliffs and the Grand Hogback, much lower than the mountains to the south and sparsely covered with sagebrush and other desert vegetation.

Flora Ellen and Josie both said they spent only one night there: Tuesday, October 7, 1879. The next day they moved approximately 5 miles downstream to a place with abundant grass for the horses. That would have put them very near the mouth of Rifle Creek. Today that area is mostly developed, with businesses both north and south of the river. But the Interstate 70 rest area along the river gives you a sense of the broad, open, grassy area that existed in 1879.[3]

According to Josie, the horses weren't the only ones with plenty to eat. The Utes hadn't left the White River Indian Agency with just blankets, horses, and mules. There were also cattle. "A part of the agency herd was driven along with the procession, and a beef was killed each day. As I was requested to cook most of this time and make the bread, I did not suffer from the filth of ordinary Indian fare."[4]

While they were camped near Rifle Creek, Josie's protector and would-be husband, Pahsone, disappeared for four days. He returned with "three fine horses and a lot of lead, which he made into bullets." In fact, she said that one of the primary forms of entertainment for several of the Utes in camp was the making of bullets.[5]

It was during this time that Josephine joined Pahsone's family and a medicine man in a healing ceremony for a young Ute child. Josie also managed to write and send her secret note to the Uintah Indian agent in Utah, begging him to send help and to contact her sister, Mary, in Greeley. The note was dated October 10, the day before the cavalcade moved downriver once again, according to Josie's account.[6]

There was probably also time at this camp, and at a later camp along the Grand River, for Josie to practice her sewing and work on the woolen dress that she fashioned from one of the agency blankets.[7] In fact, the time spent on the Grand River might have been a sort of idyllic interlude in the long days of captivity and strenuous travel except for one thing: the Utes were in a constant state of agitation, believing that Colonel Wesley Merritt and his troops were marching south to attack them. Josie recalled,

On Saturday morning, the programme [*sic*] was for twenty Utes to go back to White River, scout around on the mountains and watch the soldiers, but just as they were about to depart there was a terrible commotion, for some of the scouts on the mountains had discovered the troops, ten or fifteen miles south of the agency, advancing towards our camp. The Indians ran in every direction, the horses became excited and for a time, hardly a pony could be approached.[8]

This so enraged Canalla that he "seized a whip and laid it over the shoulders" of his youngest wife. Then he turned to help his other wife, presumably She-towitch, pack items to put on horses.[9]

Flora Ellen's story deviates from Josie's in one respect. She said they stayed in the second camp on the Grand River just two days, until Friday, October 10. But her description of the pandemonium that erupted when the Utes learned how far south the soldiers had come is nearly identical to Josephine's, including the report of the frenzied horses and Canalla's anger.[10]

Both also said that during the chaos one of the Utes approached them with a gun and threatened to shoot them. "We told him to shoot away, and Mrs. Price requested him to shoot her in the forehead," Josie said. "He said we were no good squaws because we would not scare." The only difference in the two accounts of that episode was that Flora Ellen said Canalla did the threatening, while Josie attributed the threat to an unidentified young warrior.[11]

The Utes' fears about Merritt were not unwarranted. He and his troops were moving south as rapidly as they could clear trees and brush to accommodate their wagons. They had headed up Flag Creek, south from the White River, toward the summit from which Rifle Creek flowed south and Piceance Creek flowed west, about 5 miles east of Rio Blanco Summit. It was near there that M. Wilson Rankin caught up with Merritt. He had ridden rapidly from Rawlins, Wyoming, to deliver a message telegraphed from the War Department. Rankin apparently arrived sometime during the day on October 11.[12]

"The caravan had stopped. Passing by the long line of wagons and pack mules, soldiers in the lead were found working like beaver, clearing a road through the quakenasp [aspen trees] through which to move their supply train. General [actually Colonel] Merritt was at the head directing road work." Merritt was not at all pleased with the message, which directed him to halt his expedition in pursuit of the Utes so that Charles Adams could have time to attempt to secure the release of the hostages. "His first remark was, 'Oh, hell, here I am, tied hand and foot,'" Rankin recalled. "Road work was stopped. The army returned to White River the same afternoon.... Merritt's men showed as much disappointment as Merritt himself."[13] One of those men later told Rankin "that if Merritt and his men had known the contents of the message before it was delivered, they would have paid to have the courier [Rankin] hog-tied or killed before the delivery of the message could have been made."[14]

But the Utes knew nothing of the message that Rankin delivered—at least not immediately. They were aware only of what their scouts reported: that Merritt's troops were moving southward toward them. And so, on Saturday, October 11, they struck camp in a panic and moved their families and the hostages farther away from the soldiers. "We did not move until noon," Josie recalled. "We traveled until nightfall and camped on the Grand River in a nice grassy place under some trees by the water."[15]

Sunset at that location came at 5:38 p.m. on October 11, 1879.[16] If the whole entourage of nearly a hundred teepees, roughly 3,000 horses, and several hundred cattle made only 3 miles per hour, beginning about noon, and it took an hour or more to break camp, they still could have traveled five hours until nightfall and would have covered approximately 15 miles—roughly the distance from the mouth of Rifle Creek to the mouth of Parachute Creek. Halting there would have provided another ideal camping spot, with broad meadows and plenty of grass for the horses.

But they didn't stay there long. Josie said the following day was even more arduous. "The next day was the Sabbath, but alas! It was not a day of rest to us miserables. Runners were coming in every hour or so with their horses smoking and ready to drop. Each fresh one brought news of the approach of the soldiers, and of course our [captors] became more and more excited."[17] The result was another hard, forced ride on "that terrible Sunday," Josie reported. "To add to our misery, the rain fell in torrents, and yet before we halted at night we had traveled twenty-eight or thirty miles, all the way along the Grand River."[18]

Here's where things get really confusing. If the group traveled nearly 30 miles straight downriver after leaving Parachute Creek, they would have ridden much of the way through what is now known as De Beque

Canyon. But none of the hostages mentioned its very prominent steep walls and narrow passages. Since they made it a point to describe several other, smaller canyons along the trail, it seems unlikely that they would allow one as spectacular as this to go unremarked. Furthermore, according to other sources, including M. Wilson Rankin and Charles Adams, the main camp of the White River Utes at the time the hostages were released was on the broad flats at the mouth of Roan Creek, the site of the present-day town of De Beque. There is no evidence that the hostages traveled farther west along the Grand River than this camp.[19]

So what about Josie's estimate for miles traveled on that Sunday, October 12? There are several possibilities. The first is that our supposition about where the Utes and their hostages originally arrived at the Grand River is wrong. Perhaps they approached the river farther upstream than we suspect. If, however, we add together the miles they moved from camp to camp once they reached the Grand River—5 miles downstream on October 8, at least 15 miles on October 11 (my estimate), and 30 miles on October 12—that is a total of 50 miles. Backtracking 50 miles from the mouth of Roan Creek would put the site where they first reached the Grand River somewhere upstream of Elk Creek, between the present-day towns of New Castle and Glenwood Springs. But none of the contemporary reports or subsequent histories suggests they went that far east. One or more small bands of warriors may have gone as far as the Roaring Fork River above what is now Glenwood Springs while on scouting missions, but not the main caravan of the White River Utes and their hostages. Furthermore, by going so far east, the Utes would have been within 20 miles of the eastern boundary of the Ute reservation, thereby increasing the possibility that they might encounter other whites, something they most certainly wanted to avoid.

Another possible explanation is that Josie was wrong, especially about the mileage traveled on that stormy Sunday. Anybody who has ridden horseback, bicycled, or hiked in a heavy rain knows that a few miles can seem like dozens. Even in good weather, accurately estimating distance traveled over rugged terrain is difficult. And unlike military officers with experience and perhaps training in estimating distances traveled on horse-back,[20] neither Josie, Arvilla, nor Flora Ellen had such experience. If the mileage they covered in the torrent on October 12 was half of the 28 to 30 miles that Josie claimed, and they started from Parachute Creek, they would have ended up at the mouth of Roan Creek.

There are also other possible explanations. Although Josie said the group traveled "all along the Grand River," they may very well have made excursions into side canyons or climbed to mountain meadows that still overlooked the river. They might have, for instance, ridden some distance up Parachute Creek looking for a well-concealed spot to camp. They might instead have crossed the Grand River to the south and climbed the plateau we now call Battlement Mesa in search of a defensible camp site with plenty of room and grass. Either of these side trips would have added considerable time, if not a lot of distance, to the trip in that drenching downpour, and for much of the way they would still have been able to see the Grand River.

Additionally, Josie did not say that all the travel on that day was in the same direction. It's possible that they went back and forth, upriver and down. The Utes, according to both Josie and Flora Ellen, were frantic and unsure of whether to move their camp. Perhaps they were also uncertain enough about where they should establish a new one that they backtracked one or more times.

The uncertainty about what happened that day is further complicated by a statement Josie made near the end of her description of the October 12 travels: "These heavy rains continued for several days, and mother and Mrs. Price were kept traveling as hard as the horses could go. But I during the last half of the time was in camp."[21] Where were Arvilla and Flora Ellen traveling while Josie sat in camp? Were they always traveling in the same direction or were they moving here and there, generally along the river but possibly visiting different locations for possible camp sites? Was all of this traveling done on the same day, or did it occur during the several days of rain that Josie mentioned? Her account is not at all clear on these matters.

The information provided by Arvilla and Flora Ellen does little to clarify matters. Flora Ellen said only that they moved camp on the day that the Indians and their ponies were in a panic; she mentioned little more until a few days before Charles Adams arrived to rescue them.[22] Arvilla simply reported, "As the soldiers approached, the Indians moved south at intervals of two or three days."[23] Josie did say that Canalla, who had Flora Ellen with him, finally "came to a halt ahead of us." Nicaagat may have been among the other Utes who were traveling behind Josie's party since he said he was behind the hostages most of the time after he left the Milk Creek battle site—until he "also marched past us and camped with him [Canalla]."[24]

In any event, according to Josie, the hostages stayed in this final camp along the Grand River until Friday, October 17. On that day they learned that the military pursuit had been halted while a white man was attempting to reach them and secure their release. The Utes, with their scores of scouts and galloping messengers, must have realized days earlier that Merritt had halted his advance southward and returned to the White River. But they might not have known the reason for the halt, or whether it was just a temporary delay.

It was also on that Friday that Colorow made a speech telling the White River Utes that they should go no farther south because they would soon be encroaching on the territory of the Uncompahgre Utes, led by Ouray. He advised his fellow White River Utes to remain where they were and fight the soldiers there if need be.[25]

The news that the soldiers had halted their advance was "good news for us," Josie said. But it didn't mean an end to their travels. That same day they were saddled up and on the march again, this time away from the Grand River.[26]

THE WORD GETS OUT

W HEN J OE R ANKIN REACHED R AWLINS , W YOMING , AND WORD OF THE Milk Creek battle zipped across the telegraph wires, it immediately became front-page news, not only in Colorado, but throughout the country. And people were incensed. They'd had enough of Indian attacks on white settlers—and Indian wars in general.

The 1870s may have been the most troublesome decade in U.S. history when it came to what was then known as "the Indian problem." The Comanches had barely been placated in Texas and neighboring territories at the beginning of the decade before there was war with the Apaches in Arizona. After many deaths on both sides, the Apaches were finally convinced to accept peace and a farming life on their reservation—at least temporarily—but the Nez Perces in Idaho, eastern Oregon, and eastern Washington were soon balking at efforts to remove them from lands they had been promised in a series of treaties, most recently in 1873. By the time that conflict was resolved with Chief Joseph's famous declaration, "I shall fight no more, forever," the Sioux were already in the midst of an intense battle over white gold seekers' intrusions into the Black Hills of Dakota Territory. They were joined in their fight by the Cheyenne.

This led to the worst defeat for the U.S. military in all of the Indian campaigns—the annihilation of Colonel George Armstrong Custer and more than 200 troops under his command in the Seventh Cavalry at the Little Bighorn in June 1876, just as the nation was preparing to celebrate its centennial. It would take General George Crook and thousands of troops—aided by Shoshone, Crow, and Ute scouts such as Nicaagat—almost another year to bring the Sioux and their allies to heel.

There were many individual explanations for all of these battles with the Indians, but they were all ultimately related. They resulted from the continual influx of whites onto lands that had once belonged to various American Indian tribes, the efforts to push the Indian tribes from those lands, and the repeatedly broken promises the whites made to the Indians through official treaties and unofficial agreements. For many Americans, especially among those who lived near Indians, the crude statement "The only good Indian is a dead Indian" expressed their sentiments exactly. But vast numbers of other Americans, both on the frontier and back in the "civilized" East and Midwest, saw the Indians as victims of greedy whites who were after their lands and minerals, of crooked Indian agents and bureaucrats, and of poorly conceived and even more poorly executed polices for dealing with Indians.[1]

By 1879, whether they endorsed extermination of the Indians, their confinement on one vast multitribal reservation, or a reconfiguration of the government's Indian policy to treat them more humanely, most Americans were thoroughly fed up with Indian wars and news of whites again being attacked and—in the vernacular of the day—"murdered by savages." Consequently, when the news of the Milk Creek battle broke—with no word initially of what had happened to Indian agent Nathan Meeker, his employees, or family—it sent shock waves through the country.

The *Chicago Tribune*—then, as now, one of the Midwest's leading papers—offers a glimpse of how the news was treated outside of Colorado and of the public schizophrenia related to "the Indian problem." From October 2, 1879, when the *Tribune* published its first story about the battle at Milk Creek, until November 9, after the hostages had returned safely to their homes in Greeley, the *Chicago Tribune* published stories about the Ute uprising in Colorado every day but two. In the coming months, it would continue to run stories, editorials, letters, and interviews with key people involved while it covered the two official investigations regarding the events at Milk Creek and the White River Agency, and congressional efforts to forge a treaty that would remove most of the Utes from Colorado. Even two years later there were stories about what was happening with the Utes.[2]

The first story in the *Tribune* on Thursday, October 2—three days after the fighting broke out at Milk Creek—took up nearly the entire news hole on the front page. It included dispatches from Captain J. Scott Payne and Lieutenant Samuel Cherry that Rankin had carried with him to Wyoming. One story stated that the battle must have resulted from a Ute ambush because "Thornburgh did not blunder." An editorial that same day proclaimed, "The end should be, so far as the hostile Utes are concerned, extermination, and after that, some change in the Indian policy of the Government that shall render impossible a repetition of this massacre."[3]

Over the next month there would be more editorials and letters from Chicago-area residents, some arguing for better treatment of the Indians, others for their elimination from Colorado, if not the planet. Some articles conflicted with earlier news stories. For instance, on October 2 it was reported that the "Southern" Utes (newspapers of the time frequently and incorrectly referred to the Uncompahgre Utes, led by Chief Ouray, as the Southern Utes) were preparing for war. But on October 4 the *Tribune* declared, "Most Southern Utes are peaceable. No trouble expected on their reservation."

There would be frequent reports from Secretary of Interior Carl Schurz regarding his views on the events and whether there would be a much more widespread uprising than just the White River Utes (he thought not), as well as reports from Colorado politicians predicting all manner of mayhem from numerous tribes and demanding immediate and strong military response.

After the hostages were freed, interviews were conducted with them and other members of the Meeker family, notably Josie's sister Rozene and her brother Ralph. And there was a lengthy interview with Charles Adams, the man who rescued them. There were also exclusive interviews with retired military men in the Midwest who knew the region where the Utes lived, and with former Indian agents who were familiar with the Utes.[4]

Newspapers in Colorado reported the White River events blow by blow, as might be expected since what occurred there was critical to the state and its future. At least two newspapers in New York also had reasons to cover the story in depth: the *New York Tribune*—formerly owned by Horace Greeley, for whom Nathan Meeker once worked—and the *New York Herald*, for which Ralph Meeker worked at the time of the uprising. Even the *New York Times* chimed in with an editorial arguing against attempts to force the Utes off their Colorado reservation, to which they had as much legal right, the paper said, "as any home-owner in New York."[5]

The *Chicago Tribune* covered the White River events and subsequent political battles not because of a direct connection with anyone involved, but because it was one of the important national news stories of the day. *Tribune* readers and writers alike—people who, for the most part, were ardent abolitionists before the Civil War and solid supporters of local heroes Abraham Lincoln and Ulysses S. Grant—struggled to find answers to "the Indian question." On some days the *Tribune* editorials were critical of the Department of the Interior and the cautious, nonmilitary solutions that Secretary Schurz proposed for dealing with the Utes. At other times they supported his plans as the best ideas available.[6]

But activity in response to the White River outbreak was not confined to the pages of newspapers. Colorado citizens moved away from isolated ranches and communities that were close to the Ute reservation, and leading citizens of those communities reported their willingness to gather their fellow citizens to fight the Utes and drive them from Colorado. Governor Frederick Pitkin ordered segments of the Colorado militia, especially in mining communities, to be prepared to engage in battle against the Utes.[7] The army mobilized around Colorado, with units from New Mexico, southern Colorado, Nebraska, and Wyoming moving to within striking distance of the Utes. At one point fully a third of the country's active-duty army units were in the state or near the Colorado border.[8]

But the massing of troops wasn't enough for Colorado politicians such as Pitkin. They wanted the army to take immediate and decisive action against the Utes. In one exchange of letters in late October, published in the *Chicago Tribune*, Governor Pitkin claimed that he had received information that "satisfies me that most of Ouray's warriors were in the Thornburgh fight." Whether or not Pitkin actually believed that statement is unclear, but it wasn't true. Nevertheless, Pitkin said it was reason enough to call in more troops and wage an all-out war against the "barbarians."

Interior Secretary Schurz disputed Pitkin's claim with his own letter, published in the *Tribune* the same day. He noted that Pitkin had recommended Charles Adams to Schurz as the man to attempt the rescue of the hostages, calling Adams "a gentleman of excellent character, uncommon ability [who was] intimately acquainted with the Utes." Schurz wrote that this man, who was so highly touted by Pitkin, said in his last report to Schurz "that none of the Southern and only part of the White River Utes have been engaged in the trouble."[9] It didn't matter. Pitkin would continue libeling Ouray's Uncompahgre Utes at least into the following spring.[10]

The most important action taken during this time, at least so far as the hostages were concerned, was Schurz's recruiting—with the support of Pitkin and others—of Charles Adams to ride to the White River Ute territory and secure their release. There is little question why Adams was everyone's first choice for the job. He had been an Indian agent at both the White River and Los Pinos agencies and was widely respected by nearly all of the Utes, as well as Colorado residents. Ouray and he were friends, and Nicaagat cited Adams's actions appreciatively when arguing with Nathan Meeker over moving the White River Agency 15 miles downstream.[11] Adams also knew the leaders of both the Uncompahgre and White River Ute bands, and he knew their territory. He was respected by government officials as well. At the time of the White River Ute uprising, he was a special agent for the U.S. Post Office.[12]

North on the White River, meanwhile, Colonel Wesley Merritt and his relief forces had left the Milk Creek battle site. Those who had fought under Major Thomas Thornburgh—and Captain J. Scott Payne, following Thornburgh's death—were sent back to Fort Steele to be treated for their wounds and to rest from their long ordeal. Thornburgh's body was sent first to Fort Steele and then to Omaha, Nebraska, where his funeral was held on October 22, 1879.[13]

Merritt's forces moved south to the White River, then south and west down the river until they came to the site of the White River Indian Agency. There they found the burned remnants of the buildings and the disarray of hastily rummaged materials—some taken and some left behind. And they found the bodies of the agency employees.

Most gruesome was that of Nathan C. Meeker. Its posture was very different than when Arvilla had knelt beside her dead husband more than a week earlier. She had described him as clothed only in a shirt, with a gunshot wound to his head as the only evidence of his violent end.[14] But when Merritt's troops found Meeker, one side of his head was smashed in, his naked body had reportedly been dragged by a large chain around his neck—and a barrel stave had been driven through his mouth.[15] The last act was believed to have been done to prevent Meeker from telling more lies in the afterlife.[16]

The discovery of the bodies further inflamed the already steaming hostility of the whites—especially those in Colorado—toward the Utes. The demand that "The Utes Must Go!" reverberated throughout the state and in many other parts of the country as well.[17]

Colonel Merritt wisely decided that the site of the agency, where Meeker and his employees had been killed, was no place to bivouac his troops. Instead he pulled them a couple miles upstream to a broad, flat area along the White River. Some of the log buildings that he and his troops began constructing for their winter quarters would, a few years later, become the first permanent structures in the newly designated town of Meeker.[18]

Merritt also began preparations to head south in pursuit of the White River Utes—not to rescue the hostages, but to punish the Indians responsible for the agency killings and the military deaths at Milk Creek. Following the well-used Ute horse trail that headed south toward the Grand River, he had his troops engaged in cutting trees, removing rocks, and smoothing out sections of the trail south from the White River along Flag Creek so that his wagons and infantry could traverse the route.[19]

But officials working on a resolution to the Ute uprising, and the successful release of the hostages, had other plans. It was near the head of Flag Creek—not far from the headwaters of Piceance Creek, where the hostages had been held for nearly a week—that Wilson Rankin caught up with Merritt and his troops. And it was there, on October 11, that Rankin delivered the telegram ordering Merritt to halt his pursuit of the Utes, much to Merritt's disgust, so that Special Agent Charles Adams could try to peaceably win the hostages' release.[20]

 **14**

TRAIL SECTION 4

When Colonel Merritt and his troops moved, so did the Utes. And so did their hostages. They had been moving steadily south, beginning with that horrible evening nearly three weeks earlier when they had left the burning remains of the White River Indian Agency behind. Now Josephine and Arvilla Meeker, along with Flora Ellen Price and her two children, were headed southward once more at the insistence of their Ute captors.

There had been a few diversions, mostly during the week they spent along the banks of the Grand River, but most of their movements had followed the direction of the winter sun. So it came as little surprise to the white women when, on October 17, they mounted their Ute ponies and headed south once more. "At last news was received that the soldiers were on the White River, moving south," Flora Ellen reported. After considerable excitement, "We started for another camping place south of the Grand River."[1]

But there were limits to how far south they could go—constraints imposed not by geography but by Ute territorial divisions and by Chief

Ouray's anger over what had transpired with the White River Utes. Josie recalled that "The Utes were now close upon the Uncompahgre District," where Ouray was the undisputed Ute leader, "and for that reason could not retreat much further."[2]

Josie noted that in addition to moving camp, there was another important change that day—one that meant the hostages would all be in closer proximity. "Johnson [Canalla] held a long talk with Douglas [Quinkent] and as a result, took mother to his tent."[3] Canalla then led a small band of Utes—ten to fifteen teepees—away from the Grand River and away from the main group, who were camped at the mouth of Roan Creek.[4]

Josie said they rode the whole day, south and west, and camped that night "on a small stream called Plateau Creek." But that wasn't their final destination. "The next day we were marched 12 or 15 miles still further off."[5] That journey, on October 18, put them on the banks of an even smaller stream known as Mesa Creek, on the north flank of Grand Mesa, just a few miles south of the present-day community of Mesa, Colorado. It was here that Charles Adams would find the hostages and arrange for their release three days later. Standing in the modern-day pasture that is believed to be the site of the women's final camping place during their captivity, it's easy to picture the meadow as Adams and his small band of rescuers first spied it: "Four tents were all we could see at first, but after a little, more were visible and finally our eyes were greeted with a valley of at least 5,000 acres sloping towards the creek with numerous flocks and herds of Indian stock grazing upon its luxuriant grasses."[6] Even the old juniper tree, which was identified in a 1924 photo as the central feature at the "Meeker Massacre Captive Release Site," still stood in a cow pasture on private land when we visited in early 2006. But, as is typical with information about the hostage trail, the precise route that was ridden by the Utes and their hostages to reach this site is unknown.

The main body of Utes under Nicaagat, Quinkent, and Colorow was encamped at the mouth of Roan Creek. There may have been as many as 200 tepees and 800 Utes, including men, women, and children.[7] But the hostages, with the likely exception of Arvilla, may not have been there. Until the morning of October 17, when Josie said the discussion occurred between Canalla and Quinkent, Arvilla was still with Quinkent in the main camp. It's not clear where Canalla, who had Flora Ellen with him, was camped. But Josie's statements give little indication she was in that main camp. In fact, she reported that the main body of Utes went past where she was camped on that stormy Sunday, October 12, when they traveled some 30 miles along the Grand River.

It is likely that Josie and Pahsone—her Ute captor, protector, and would-be husband—and his family were about 5 miles upstream. Today the Una Bridge crosses the Colorado (Grand) River near that site. And near the bridge is a place where crossing the river on horseback would not have been difficult in late autumn of a very dry year. Also, from that location, they would have had easy access to Wallace Creek, the route that both oral tradition in western Colorado and some historians say the Utes and their hostages took to reach the final camp on Mesa Creek.[8]

But why Wallace Creek? From the mouth of Roan Creek to the spot on Mesa Creek where the hostages were held the final few days there is a much easier route. It leads directly across the Colorado River near the present-day town of De Beque, up what is known as the Sunnyside Trail, then eventually drops down a canyon to reach Plateau Creek. From there it would have been a relatively easy ride of perhaps 10 miles to the final campsite.

In the fall of 2005, Alan Moore and I rode our horses south from De Beque on the old Sunnyside Trail, which was once used as a wagon trail and later a rough automobile route. After just a couple hours, we reached a high point overlooking Plateau Creek—and a canyon with a trail winding down to the Plateau Valley. We also found a large, rusted mule shoe, evidence of the use of this route by wagon freighters in the decades following the events recorded in this book. Sunnyside Trail is a much more direct route toward Mesa Creek, with substantially less climbing, than following Wallace Creek.

But the Utes weren't necessarily looking for the fastest or most direct route this time. They were seeking to keep the hostages hidden as soldiers approached. In another account she gave of her time as a hostage, Josie put it this way: "They took us off some 10 or 15 miles to a little creek they called Plateau Creek where, if they meant to fight or have any trouble, the soldiers would not find us at all. They meant to have us secure."[9] In still another report of the twenty-three days on the trail, Josie made it clear that keeping the hostages away from the soldiers was one of the Utes' primary considerations. Another was halting Merritt's troops as they moved south. "They wanted to keep us away back where the solders could not reach us. They intended to fight the soldiers. Only a few of them went with us, away from the rest. They said if the soldiers advanced, they were going to kill them. They were preparing for war. They dared not go south, for Ouray sent word for them not to come further south, and they were going to stand their ground."[10]

Wallace Creek would have taken the Utes and their hostages farther into hard-to-reach territory in the foothills on the northern edge of Grand Mesa, but the area was not unknown to them. In fact, the Hayden Survey maps of Colorado published two years earlier show what appears to be a trail heading south from the Grand River and climbing one branch of Wallace Creek. Furthermore, the trail had probably been used by the Utes for generations. One report said Wallace Creek is believed to be the route used by Fathers Domínguez and Escalante when they descended from Grand Mesa, escorted by Ute guides, during their excursion of 1776.[11]

In October 2007, Alan Moore and I rode a portion of the trail up the main branch of Wallace Creek. Once we got beyond the lower country of ranches and roads servicing natural gas wells, we were on a narrow trail leading through thick stands of Gambel oak, taller than a man on horseback in many places. The trail winds into higher country of juniper and pinyon pine, and eventually into aspen and evergreens. Josie's report of their trip on October 17, 1879, fits well with our experience. Even though we began our trip roughly 5 miles south of the Colorado River, on the Wallace Creek drainage, it became apparent it would require the better part of the day to climb over the Battlements on the northeast edge of Grand Mesa, drop into Kimball Creek, then follow that to Plateau Creek. If the area in 1879 was much like it is today, it is not difficult to imagine that the small group of Utes and their hostages, who had left the main band, would have been all but invisible to any army scouts that the Utes feared might be watching.

 15

OUTRAGE!

WHAT LITTLE PUBLIC SYMPATHY EXISTED FOR THE UTES FOLLOWING the battle at Milk Creek and the killings at the White River Indian Agency all but evaporated after December 30, 1879. That's when the *Colorado Chieftain* newspaper in Pueblo published a letter from Arvilla Meeker.

In the letter, Arvilla recalled being interviewed by "officers of the government"—referring to Charles Adams and a stenographer who met with her and the other white women in Greeley after they had been released from captivity. And she told these government officials that she, her daughter Josephine, and Flora Ellen Price had suffered "the sickening and most humiliating misfortune that can befall a woman." She also chastised the government for "suppressing" this information, even though she and the other women had begged them to do that very thing more than a month earlier.[1] Although she used vague words, everyone understood her meaning. It was the horrific confirmation of what many people had suspected since they had first heard of the events at the White River Agency: the women hostages had been raped!

Author Marshall Sprague described the reaction to the letter: "For all its mild tone and colorless presentation, Arvilla's letter rocked the nation. The worst suspicions of Coloradans were now confirmed."[2] The *Chicago Tribune* first mentioned the letter on January 7, 1880, with an article headlined, "THE INDIANS: A SHOCKING STORY." It described "a letter published recently from Mrs. N. C. Meeker, disclosing the fact that each and all of the women who were held as captives after the massacre at White River suffered the violation of their person through fear of worse treatment at the hands of these red devils."[3]

The *Greeley Tribune* was more restrained, but indignant nonetheless. "To us the saddest thing in the whole affair is that Mrs. Meeker, whom one would suppose had already suffered enough, should be forced to the additional humiliation of writing a letter to the newspapers on such a subject," it said, also on January 7. "Let us hope that the indignation aroused by the publication of this letter, may lead to the adoption of measures against these Indians more in accord with common sense."[4]

In most respects, the white women said they were treated well by the Utes during their captivity on the hostage trail. But this allegation was incendiary, and not everyone believed it. The Utes led by Ouray insistently denied claims that the white women had been raped—or "outraged," to use the vague Victorian term that could mean anything from inappropriate sexual contact to rape. A variety of evidence lends credence to the Utes' claims, including an official report a year later which argued that one of the supposed perpetrators was innocent.[5]

Even today, descendants of the White River Utes say the reports handed down through generations of their families clearly state that no rapes occurred.[6] And from Ouray's time to this day, Utes have pointed out that the women changed their stories, a fact that is undeniable.

When Charles Adams arrived at the camp on Mesa Creek to arrange the release of the hostages, he questioned each of the women briefly, beginning with Josie. "I then asked her how the Indians had treated her," he recalled a few months later. "She said, 'Well, better than she had expected.' I asked her whether they had offered her any indignity to her person. She made the off-hand remark, 'Oh, no, Mr. Adams, nothing of that kind.'"[7]

Adams noted that they were in a tenuous situation. When he first met Arvilla a short time later, "Chief Douglas [Quinkent] and other chiefs stood around her so close that with her I could not possibly speak about the murders because if they had thought that I was making any investigation there, I considered my life and others in danger too."[8] But not long afterward, Adams found himself alone with Flora Ellen—with no Utes to overhear their conversation. "I asked her the question whether any indignity had been offered to her. She said, 'No.' I thereupon wrote the dispatch to the Secretary [of Interior] that the women had been given up and no indignities had been offered to them."[9] Interior Secretary Carl Schurz quickly released a statement based on Adams's dispatch saying that the women were safe and on their way home, with their honor intact.[10]

It wasn't until November 4, two weeks after the women were released and Adams was able to meet with them in Greeley, that an entirely different story emerged. Adams recalled,

> After Mrs. Price had given her story I approached the subject of their personal treatment, and I saw at once that there was something more behind it, that so far had not come out. I told her I must have the full facts. She said no; she would not tell; that that was none of my business. I said it was; that she was under oath and she must tell the whole truth. Finally she said, "O, as soon as I tell you, you will go and tell some newspaper man, and they will have it all over the country, and I will be dishonored forever." I said, "No, Mrs. Price, I am no newspaper man; I am not in the habit of going to newspaper men and telling them everything. But," said I, "as soon as this report is submitted to the Secretary and by him to Congress, of course this matter will come out; there is no help for that." Well, she cried, and was very anxious not to be obliged to tell. Finally she admitted that this man that had captured her the first day had outraged her person and had finally given her away or sold her, she did not know which, to the Chief Johnson [Canalla], and that he, the same morning that I came to camp, had made an attack upon her, but that those were the only two instances of her being outraged.[11]
>
> I then went to see Miss Josephine. She told her story the same as she had told it before, but, having learned from Mrs. Price that she had also been subjected to the same treatment, I asked her to state all the particulars about it. She did not want to testify; she thought that she ought not to be made to tell all these matters. Finally, she testified, and afterwards Mrs. Meeker also testified. I then returned, met General Hatch at Alamosa, and we went to the [Los Pinos] agency.[12]

At the Los Pinos Agency, the home of Ouray and the Uncompahgre Utes, the first official investigation into the White River events would be held, with Charles Adams, Ouray, and Major General Edward Hatch jointly presiding. Hatch, an active military officer, was named president of the commission. During that investigation, although the women who were held hostage did not testify in person, Adams entered into the record the statements that he had taken from each of them in Greeley. Newspaper reporters who lingered around the hearings were not allowed into the log building in which the special commission met, so as Adams had promised, the details of those statements did not become public knowledge immediately.

First to be introduced was Flora Ellen Price's testimony, read into the official record on November 14, 1879, the second day the commission met. Like the two Meeker women, she recalled what happened in the days leading up to the killings at the White River Agency, and the events of that day, their capture by the Indians, and some of what happened during their twenty-three days as hostages. Then, faced with insistent probing by Adams, the young woman said she had been "outraged" twice during her captivity. One attack, she said, came on the first day by an unknown Uncompahgre Ute, and the second one—on the very morning that Adams arrived to rescue them—was committed by Canalla.[13]

But Canalla was a well-known Ute healer and leader, brother-in-law of Ouray. He and his wife, She-towitch, had done more than any of the other Utes to protect the white women during their captivity. Would he, on the very morning when he knew Charles Adams would be arriving—in the company of a protective entourage of Utes specifically appointed by Ouray—decide to take one of the women out in the willows along Mesa Creek and rape her? As his great-great-grandson Jonas Grant said, "It doesn't make sense."[14]

Arvilla Meeker's statement to Charles Adams in Greeley was read into the record next, on November 17, 1879. When Adams had asked Mrs. Meeker about the "outrages," she responded, "It was made known to me that if I did not submit I would be killed or subjected to something of that kind, and after I gave up, nothing was said about it. Douglas [Quinkent], I had connection with him once, and no more. I was afraid he had disease." But she also talked of the security Quinkent offered. "One great advantage in it was that he was protection for me from the other Indians. More than a dozen wanted me to go and sit down in their tents, and I said I was Douglas's squaw and that kept them from me."[15] She did not explain, however, why one of the most senior leaders of the White River Utes, who clearly had the power of life and death over her, and who held her captive in his lodge for nearly three weeks, demanded sex with her on only one occasion.

Finally, on November 19, Josephine Meeker's statement was read into the record. Asked whether Pahsone—the Ute who guarded her and held her hostage—treated her well, Josie responded, "No better than what I expected when I was first captured, because I know the Utes and I know their natures pretty well." Asked to elaborate, she said, "Of course we were insulted a good many times; we expected to be."

"What do you mean by insult, and what did it consist of?" Adams asked. "Of outrageous treatment at night," Josie responded.

"Am I to understand that they outraged you several times at night?"

"Yes, sir."

"Forced you against your will?"

"Yes, sir."

"Did they threaten to kill you if you did not comply?"

"He did not threaten to kill—Pahsone did not," Josie said. Then she added, "Only on one occasion."[16]

It's at this point that Josie begins to reveal the nature of her relationship with Pahsone, which suggests something other than captor and powerless captive. "I asked him if he wanted to kill me. He said, 'Yes.' I said, 'Get up and shoot me, and let me alone.' He turned over, and did not say anything more that night."

In fact, Josie said, she refused Pahsone's advances on several occasions. "A good many times I pushed him off, and made a fuss, and raised a difficulty."[17] If this sounds like something other than a captor-slave arrangement, that is quite evidently how Pahsone viewed it. When Adams asked Josie whether any other Utes attempted to molest her, she replied, "No, sir; not to me. He [Pahsone] took me as his squaw, and of course the rest dared not to come around."[18]

In fact, Josie said that Pahsone faced down one of the Ute leaders to keep her from being taken by another. "Douglas [Quinkent] came and tried to take me away from Pahsone when we were going to the river. He tried to push Pahsone away and tried to take me away by the arm, but Pahsone pushed him away and they had it pretty hot in Ute. I thought they were going to quarrel, but Douglas turned away and went off."[19] That struggle between Quinkent and Pahsone was recounted by Josie on at least one other occasion, as evidenced by Flora Ellen's mention of it in her own statement to Adams.[20] The story is, however, more evidence of Pahsone's determination to protect Josie at all cost, given that Quinkent was a Ute leader with a substantial group of followers, whereas Pahsone was, according to Josie, "just a common Indian."[21]

But if Pahsone was just a commoner in the Ute hierarchy, he treated Josie as royalty. On the first day of her captivity, Pahsone demonstrated respect for her in an unusual way. "Pahsone in the morning led my horse up to the tent and knelt down on his hands and knees in order that I might mount," she said. "This he always did when he was present, and when he was away fighting our soldiers his squaw did it for me. This was a mark of special favor, and was done for none of the rest, nor did I see it done among the Indians at all."[22]

Josie may never have witnessed this act of respect performed by Utes before, but her father had, more than a year earlier. Nathan Meeker described it in a dispatch from the White River to the *Greeley Tribune*, published on June 26, 1878. He told of watching a chief's wife pack all of her family goods on a horse, including the lodge poles for the family teepee, as the family was preparing to move to a new campsite. Then she mounted the same horse. Meeker reported that "The manner of mounting was as follows: The chieftain got down on his hands and knees, she stepped on his back, when he rose gradually and the thing was done."[23]

Josie also reported a quarrel over who would control her, offering this assessment of Pahsone: "I must add in justice, that this Indian became, I may say, almost devoted to me after this incident, and treated me with respect and considerable kindness."[24] Not only did Josie offer favorable assessments of Pahsone and his family, but she also recounted her participation in a healing ceremony for one of Pahsone's children (see chapter 9). No whites were admitted to such ceremonies, she said, "But I, being considered one of Pahsone's family, was allowed to remain."[25] It was another important indication that Pahsone and the other Utes considered Josie his wife, or at least his wife to be—a part of his family, not just a captive. Later in the same account, Josie said, "I felt sure that the rescuers had come, and that Pahsone wanted to keep me out of the road until they had gone away. His object in this was to induce me to marry him and live among the Ute tribe."[26]

One contemporary source said Pahsone had been attracted to Josie long before the outbreak of fighting at the White River Agency and the capture of the women. Many Utes, including Quinkent, had tried to court her as soon as she arrived at the White River Agency in the summer of

1878. "Pahsone, a younger and handsomer, and withal a better Indian, had also avowed his passion and his desire to possess 'the white lily.'"[27]

All of this points to an inescapable conclusion regarding the "outrages" inflicted on Josie. Although she may have viewed her sexual relations with Pahsone as rape after she had been freed from captivity, he viewed her as his mate. He treated her with respect and kindness, and as a member of his family. Other Utes on the trail, such as the English-speaking Jane, clearly accepted Pahsone as Josie's protector.[28] And on the single occasion when he threatened her with violence and she rebuffed him, he turned away and left her alone. Josephine accepted this familial status, and Pahsone's intimacy, as a way to protect her from other Utes.

Josie's relationship with Pahsone is just one example of incidents related to the White River uprising that seem contradictory or confusing regarding the supposed "outrages." Another was the questioning of both Quinkent and Canalla during the White River Ute Commission investigation at Los Pinos. The two leaders appeared before the commission during the first two days of the investigation, and both were asked in detail about the killings of Meeker and the other employees at the White River Agency. Both denied any personal involvement in the killings or even much knowledge of the events that had occurred there. But when the two men appeared before the commission, Adams already had the statements taken in Greeley from the three women accusing them of sexually assaulting them. Why, then, was neither Quinkent nor Canalla asked a single question about the alleged assaults? (Pahsone didn't testify before the commission.)[29]

Furthermore, as the commission was wrapping up its work on December 6, 1879, Adams delivered an impassioned speech to the Ute leaders gathered there, urging them to bring in for trial the twelve Utes accused by the white women of having participated in the killings at the White River Agency on September 29. "I cannot excuse the action of those cowardly dogs who went to the agency and shot from the roofs of the houses, like birds from trees, the white men who were not dreaming of danger, and who certainly had given the Indians no cause to be killed," he declared.[30]

It was a bold statement to make in a building where the Utes far outnumbered the whites. It suggests that Adams did not fear retaliation, and it demonstrates his deep anger over what had occurred at the agency. But he mentioned not a word about the alleged rapes. In fact, although Quinkent, Canalla, and Pahsone were among the twelve Utes who were supposed to be turned over to the whites, in the official comments before the commission demanding that they be handed over for trial, none of the three was accused of sexually assaulting the women. There was no mention of the alleged "outrages."[31]

Then there was Ralph Meeker's reaction.

On January 19, 1880, a few weeks after Arvilla's letter hinting at the alleged assaults appeared in the *Chieftain* newspaper of Pueblo, the *Denver Tribune* published a letter from Ralph castigating his journalistic colleagues for allowing their industry to become "a sewer for the distribution of every species of nastiness" by printing reports of the sexual assaults. "I ask if the slaughter of nine or ten innocent people at White River does not warrant the hanging of every Indian seen there at the time?" he wrote. "The White River Utes are responsible for that atrocity. That crime is hideous enough and black enough for vengeance and justice without dragging out personal matters."[32]

He took the Pueblo paper to task in particular for hinting that Josie had lied in her public statements and presentations since her release from captivity by not mentioning the alleged sexual assaults. "Josephine Meeker never denied, never prevaricated, and never flinched," he said. "She simply said, considering what she had expected when she left the Agency, she was well treated, but at best her experiences were a horror that she could never forget. A gentleman of honor could have pressed his inquiries no further."[33]

Josie also made statements around this time that seem to cast doubt on the claims of sexual assault. On January 30, 1880, just after Adams had testified before Congress about his involvement in securing the women's release and traveling to Greeley to take their statements, including information about the alleged assaults, Josie wrote a letter to Ralph. "I wrote home as soon as Gen. Adams had given his testimony, telling them it was all right and that newspaper reports were false. But you see, they are wild out there and will not believe the truth, nothing but newspaper reports."[34]

In his letter to the *Denver Tribune*, Ralph mentioned nothing about the alleged assaults suffered by Flora Ellen, and made only a fleeting reference at the conclusion of his letter to the possibility that his mother had been assaulted. "If murderers and incendiaries cannot be punished without grinding up a family, and torturing a venerable and bed-ridden mother into a confession that no decent white man outside of a penitentiary would listen to, then justice should die," he wrote.[35]

By the time Ralph wrote his letter, there had been a definite split in the Meeker family. Josie was then in Washington, D.C., working for the Interior Department. Ralph was back in New York. Arvilla had remained in Greeley with daughter Rozene, who was engaged in her own speaking tour about the White River events, during which she attacked not only the Utes, but the government's reaction to them. And she pushed her mother to go public about the alleged outrages.[36]

That infuriated Josie. In the January 30 letter to Ralph, she said that Adams blamed Rozene for word of the outrages getting out, "and so do all the Colorado people here that I have seen." She added, "If [Rozene] could only learn to keep still! But she never will."[37]

Three weeks later, in another letter to Ralph, Josie said she had just sent a letter to Rozene. "You do not understand my feelings toward her," she told her brother. "I am ready to look over anything from anybody, though you do not know—and it is not worthwhile for me to tell you— anything what we have had to endure because of her foolishness—lack of common sense—and it would seem as if she has less judgment now than she had years ago, and she despises whoever dares criticize her."[38]

Josie was the only one of the three women to testify before Congress in early 1880, and she made no mention of the alleged sexual assaults. The allegations did, however, come up in other testimony. Adams briefly told the House Committee on Indian Affairs about his November 4 visit to Greeley, when he obtained statements from the three women. He also mentioned the twelve Utes who were supposed to be given up and sent east for trial, adding, "Four of these men are the persons that maltreated these women and who were also engaged in this massacre."[39]

Contradicting the women's stories was another witness before the House Committee who testified that Ouray was certain that no sexual assaults had occurred. "Ouray tells me that it is simply impossible that the women should have been outraged, as it is reported they were; that he has looked into the matter thoroughly," said Clinton Fisk, a member of the Board of Indian Commissioners. Ouray also said, "'How could an Indian do that with his own wife alongside of him?'" Fisk reported. "He says that it is an afterthought on the part of somebody to increase the feeling against the Utes."[40]

Many years later, when Arvilla recalled her days as a hostage, she didn't mention the supposed "outrages." In a letter to her surviving children written on March 5, 1897—her eighty-second birthday—Arvilla told them about her life, particularly the events of 1879. She recounted several incidents, not mentioned in her earlier accounts, from the days when she, Josie, and Flora Ellen were captives of the Utes. There was the time she was threatened with knives by one unidentified "old Indian," but she stood her ground and called his bluff. There was also the occasion when, she said, her life depended on her ability to cure a sickly Ute child, which she did. She also recalled better treatment by many Utes. "When dangers threatened me, some Indian with a smile and look of kindness would come to my rescue, telling me what to do."[41] She didn't offer the slightest hint at any sexual assaults.

Perhaps most important of all, by early 1881 several leading Colorado citizens who had spent months traveling among the Utes in Colorado to persuade them to sign the agreement approved by Congress in 1880 were proclaiming Quinkent's innocence and asking that he be released from federal prison in Fort Leavenworth. The five-member Ute Commission had been appointed by the secretary of the interior to obtain the Ute signatures, examine potential areas for a new Uncompahgre Ute reservation, and report on the condition of the Utes. Not all of them were from Colorado, but two of them—Otto Mears and Judge Thomas McMorris—were well-respected Coloradans and were among those who helped ensure that most of the Utes were moved from Colorado to Utah.

In its final report the commission wrote, regarding Quinkent, that all of the Utes they had talked to affirmed that he "did not participate in the murders and outrages." The commission reached the same conclusion. "The Indians appealed to the Commission to use their influence to have Douglas [Quinkent] released from confinement and sent home," the group reported, "and believing as we do that he is not guilty, we respectfully recommend that he be released and sent to his people."[42]

The commission did not discuss the guilt or innocence of another prominent Ute leader accused by the hostages of sexual assault—Canalla. But it appears that he was hiding in plain sight when the commission determined that it was impossible to find the guilty Utes during the summer and fall of 1880. From July 29 to July 31, the commission obtained the signatures of 110 Utes in the Uncompahgre Valley on the agreement requiring them to abandon the bulk of their reservation in Colorado. Signature number 21 was listed in the commission report as "Johnson—his x mark," and signature number 103 was "Johnson No. 2—his x mark"; Canalla was known to the whites by both names.[43] It's difficult to believe that an

old western Colorado hand such as Otto Mears didn't recognize Canalla—
or Johnson 2—as one of the Utes wanted by the authorities.

What reason might the women have had to exaggerate or fabricate
stories about sexual assault? One possibility is money. Arvilla and Rozene
were both eager to get reparations from Congress for the death of Nathan
Meeker and their combined suffering. In fact, on the day that Arvilla's letter appeared in the Pueblo newspaper, legislation was supposed to be
introduced in Congress that would provide $10,000 each for Arvilla, Flora
Ellen Price, and the widow of Frank Dresser, one of the White River
Indian Agency employees killed on September 29. Did Arvilla believe
support for that funding would be stronger if the public learned of the
alleged sexual assaults?[44]

Ralph hinted that money was involved with his mother's efforts in an
angry note he wrote to Arvilla a week after her letter appeared in the
Pueblo paper. "You should have kept still and kept out of the papers—or at
least have asked my advice," Ralph admonished his mother. "I know what
I am about. Our family needs money and I am trying to help them and
preserve their good name."[45]

There is no independent record of Adams's meetings with the three
women in Greeley on November 4. There is no indication he talked to
them about obtaining money from Congress for their suffering. But we do
know that he was aware of the Meeker family's eagerness to receive money
from Congress. In a letter to Arvilla dated December 31, 1879—the day
after her letter appeared in the Pueblo paper, shortly after the White River
Commission had wrapped up its investigation at Los Pinos, and just
before Congress began its hearings on the White River events—Adams
wrote: "I shall go to Washington and what little I can do with our national
Legislators to have the nation acknowledge substantially your claims, I
shall certainly do."[46] Shortly thereafter, Adams either forgot his promise
not to talk to newsmen about the alleged sexual assaults, or an imaginative
reporter concocted words for him. On January 11, the *Chicago Tribune* published a lengthy interview with Adams in which he talked freely of the
purported outrages and how shocked he was to learn of them. Adams also
offered information that clearly wasn't true, based on the statements of the
women themselves—that all three of them were "continually outraged."
Additionally, he gave the name of the Uncompahgre Ute who had reportedly assaulted Flora Ellen on the first night—Ouch-Ta-Pit. The man's
actual name, according to the official record, was Ahu-u-tu-pu-wit.

Although Flora Ellen did not identify him, Colorow had said he was the man who took her captive that first evening. But Colorow didn't accuse him of "outraging" or otherwise attacking her.[47]

About this time Adams also wrote a letter to Secretary of Interior Schurz, explaining why keeping news of the alleged outrages secret was important—because of "the furious excitement this would raise in this State," which might also lead to unfairly implicating the Southern Utes in the crimes. But, he said, he had told Governor Frederick Pitkin about the women's testimony, "in order that it never can be said that I or yourself had endeavored to hush up the crimes of the Indians."[48]

Adams's precautions had little effect. Arvilla claimed that government officials had attempted to keep it secret, and newspapers and others in Colorado picked up the claim. Governor Pitkin became one of the harshest critics of the Interior Department.

The legislation to provide money to the women didn't pass immediately. In fact, it would be several months before Congress finally approved a bill, in June 1880, setting aside money not only for Arvilla and Flora Ellen, but for Josie and the relatives of others killed at the White River Agency in September of 1879. The money was deducted directly from funds that were supposed to go to the Utes under treaty agreements to pay for food and other goods.[49]

Beyond financial issues, the former hostages were under a great deal of pressure to confirm the widely held belief in American society that all Indians were "savages," and that the males could not control their primitive urges when around white women. Newspapers grew testy when the women failed to meet those expectations, as Ralph Meeker's letter to the *Denver Tribune* revealed.

The criticism of Josie became more intense in January 1880, when she visited cordially with Ouray, Nicaagat, and other Utes who had traveled to Washington to testify before Congress. None of the twelve Utes alleged to have been involved in the killings at the White River Agency, including the four alleged rapists, was among those she visited, but it was still unforgivable to some people in Colorado. "It is reported from Washington that when the Utes arrived there, the only visitor admitted to see them was Josie Meeker, and that she remained for half an hour talking freely with all the Utes," the *Colorado Miner* newspaper of Georgetown stated on January 17, 1880. The paper added, "If she can so soon forget the massacre of her father and the personal indignities that she was forced to undergo, the sympathies of Coloradans will be narrowed down to the poor old widow of the butchered agent."[50]

A week later the same paper was even more vehement and insulting: "Poor Josie Meeker is still making a fool of herself in Washington," it declared. "Her latest exhibition of folly was her statement to Ouray that she 'doesn't hate the Utes.' She perhaps regrets having left the teepee of Pahsone."[51]

In the end, we can never be certain about what happened with the Utes and their female hostages along the hostage trail. We have only the women's statements—taken several weeks after their release, and in contradiction of their original statements—that they were assaulted or "outraged." And we have the Utes, beginning with Ouray and on through successive generations, arguing that no such "outrages" occurred. There are also the official documents that raised questions about the guilt of Quinkent and Canalla. At the time, however, the women's claims and whites' preconceived notions of how American Indians behave were all that mattered. Once the accusations became public, it was the same as if a black man had been accused of assaulting a white woman in the Old South. The women's statements were evidence enough, and denial from the suspects was given no credence whatsoever.

In the wake of the battle at Milk Creek and the killings at the White River Agency, the Utes had little chance of holding on to their large reservation in western Colorado. But the allegations that some of the Indians had committed sexual assaults on the white women they held captive were like adding kerosene to the already burning demand of a majority of people in Colorado that "The Utes must go!"

Plate 1. "Ruins after White River massacre." *Frank Leslie's Illustrated Newspaper*, December 6, 1879. Denver Public Library, Western History Collection, X-30699. Illustration by Lt. C. A. H. McCauley

Plate 2. "The Ute scare in Colorado. Settlers abandoning their ranches and flying to Meeker for safety." The information in the Denver Public Library file says that this sketch is from *Frank Leslie's Illustrated Newspaper*, September 3, possibly 1867, but that's impossible. There was no community of Meeker then—nor in 1879. This is probably from 1887, from what was known as Colorow's War. Denver Public Library, Western History Collection, X-30701.

Plate 3. "An achievement of a Medal of Honor. Sgt. Edward P. Grimes runs with ammunition at battle at Milk Creek." *Harper's Weekly*, July 13, 1912. Denver Public Library, Western History Collection, Z-3257.

Plate 4. "Illustrated interview of our lady artist." *Frank Leslie's Illustrated Newspaper*, April 3, 1880. Chipeta is standing on the left, and Ouray is seated, reading. The man leaning over his shoulder, pointing, may be Nicaagat. Denver Public Library, Western History Collection, X-30709.

THE UTE WAR.

AMONG the losses sustained by our troops in the recent fight with the Ute Indians, one of the most serious was the death of that veteran Indian fighter Major THOMAS T. THORNBURGH, of the Fourth Infantry. This gallant officer was born in Tennessee, from which State he was appointed a cadet in the West Point Military Academy, July 1, 1863. Four years later he was graduated, and was commissioned Second Lieutenant in the Second Artillery, June 17, 1867. After three years' service upon the Pacific and Atlantic coasts, he was regularly promoted, April 21, 1870, and as First Lieutenant of Artillery was appointed Major and Paymaster, April 26, 1873. In this capacity he served upon the staff of Brigadier-General GEORGE CROOK, with station at Omaha; but tiring of the inactivity of the life, he sought and effected an exchange with Major G. H. THOMAS, Fourth Infantry, May 23, 1878. By this transfer Major THORNBURGH stepped above no less than two hundred and fifty captains of infantry and many lieutenants of that corps, whose original commissions antedated his, and procured his command of Fort Fred Steele, in Wyoming Territory.

In the fall of 1878 he was placed in charge of the troops assembled at Sidney, Nebraska, to intercept the Cheyennes. The latter crossed the Union Pacific Railroad near Julesburg, and a few hours later, having been conveyed to this point by a special train, THORNBURGH's column was in hot pursuit. The Cheyennes forded the treacherous Platte, with whose shifting quicksands they were familiar, and took refuge for the night in an adjacent cañon. THORNBURGH followed, but his preparations for an immediate attack were foiled by a dense fog, which rose from the river and enveloped it. In the early morning smouldering fires revealed their late proximity, but the Cheyennes had dispersed. Their trail led fan-shaped into and through the dreaded sand-hills. THORNBURGH followed, and during the day accomplished not less than eighty miles. For forty-eight hours he wandered through this terrible waste, and was only relieved from extreme hunger and thirst by the timely arrival of Major C. H. CARLTON, Third Cavalry, a battalion of that regiment. By many his failure was attributed to excess of caution, but perhaps he only avoided then the disaster that has so recently overwhelmed his command.

Major THORNBURGH was shot in the breast and instantly killed while gallantly leading his men in a counter-charge. He was a man of splendid physique, and if not a brilliant soldier, a very earnest, brave, ambitious, and conscientious officer, and a genial, whole-souled gentleman. An excellent horseman, he was the finest shot in the army. He hunted prairie-chickens and grouse with an ordinary Springfield rifle. When Dr. CARVER made his superb score with glass balls at Omaha, Major THORNBURGH, at the solicitation of his numerous friends, followed and almost equalled

MAJOR THOMAS T. THORNBURGH.—PHOTOGRAPHED BY HORDAY, NORFOLK, VIRGINIA.

it. Immediately subsequent to the fruitless chase after the Cheyennes, a council was held with RED CLOUD, YOUNG-MAN-AFRAID-OF-HIS-HORSES, and other prominent Sioux chiefs at Fort Sheridan. At its termination the Indians were in an unusually amiable mood, and facetiously compared the battered carbines in the hands of our cavalrymen to their own handsomely mounted Winchesters. Major THORNBURGH, seizing at random one of the former arms from a soldier, challenged the group of dusky boasters to a trial of their vaunted weapons. Silver half and quarter dollars thrown into

the air, or even nickels, were rarely missed; and the coins being too soon exhausted, they insisted on tempting his unerring aim with potatoes, which, although they grow particularly small in the rugged Northwest, he invariably cleft in their flight. The braves stood aghast at such wonderful dexterity, and conferred upon him a euphonious sobriquet in their own language, meaning "The-chief-who-shoots-the-stars."

Major THORNBURGH was a brother of the ex-Congressman of that name from Tennessee. He leaves a wife (daughter of Major R. D. CLARK, Paymaster, and niece of Paymaster-General ALVORD, U.S.A.) and two children, a boy and a girl, who are now at Fort Fred Steele.

The Ute Indians as a tribe are well known to travellers and scientists as the Rocky Mountain Indians, and occupy the range for several hundred miles. They have always been peaceable and well inclined toward the whites, although being native-born savages. Three or four years ago a hunter or tourist was as safe in a Ute camp as in any Eastern village, while they heartily enjoyed it if they could give their white guests a little scare. They are truly mountain Indians, knowing every crook and cranny for hundreds of miles. They make frequent forays on the plains during the buffalo season, and on such expeditions go well armed, and equipped with camp fixtures. The Sioux, or Plain Indians, have always been their inveterate enemies, and when they meet, a fight is certain; but the Sioux have never dared follow them to the foot-hills or mountain fastnesses, where their resources are such that they could favorably compete with a powerful army.

The Utes as a nation have never sought war with the whites, or advance of civilization, but have always submitted to many indignities, that could be related, rather than resent them and incur the ill-will of the great white father. As a specimen of the confidence reposed in them, it can be said that when Major THOMSON was Indian Agent, with head-quarters at Denver, he always gave the Indians full range of the government offices, and let them sleep on the floor at night when belated. Also, CARLOS GORE, the largest dealer in fire-arms, ammunition, and general outfits, including beads, vermilion, etc., would frequently lock his store in the evening, leaving a dozen or more Indians sleeping on robes on the floor, which they preferred to any bed. Very few of the Utes can speak any English, and it was conical enough to see a big buck Indian, followed by his squaw laden with buffalo-robes, come in. The buck would hold up five fingers. Mr. GORE would say, "What you want?" Answer: "Winchester." That would be all cash; the robes, worth eight dollars each—forty dollars, price of Winchester rifle. The next deal would be for ammunition, made by signs in the same manner, and to-day there is hardly a Ute buck or warrior but has a good Winchester rifle and a Colt or Smith & Wesson revolver, with plenty of ammunition stored in the mountains. They are very careful about using fire-arms on

PROSPECTING ON THE UTE RESERVATION—AN OMINOUS MEETING.—DRAWN BY W. A. ROGERS.

Plate 5. Major Thomas T. Thornburgh (*top*). The sketch below depicts a Ute confronting a prospector on the reservation. *Harper's Weekly*, October 25, 1879. Denver Public Library, Western History Collection, Z-4087. Illustration by W. A. Rogers.

(A) Residence.   (B) Store-houses.   (C) Dwelling and Mess Houses of Mexican Employés.   (D) Underground Store-rooms for Vegetables.   (E) Carriage presented by Governor McCook.   (F) Farm and Freight Wagons.

RESIDENCE OF OURAY, CHIEF OF THE TABEQUACHE UTES, AND HEAD-MAN OF THE UTE NATION.

UTE "JOE," A GOVERNMENT SCOUT AND DETECTIVE.   GENERAL WESLEY MERRITT, COLONEL OF THE FIFTH U. S. CAVALRY.   THE HERALD "SPECIAL" EN ROUTE TO THE FRONT.

THE HOUSE OF JOHNSON, SUB-CHIEF OF THE UTES ON THE AGENCY FARM.

COLORADO.—THE LATE UTE OUTBREAK AND MASSACRE AT THE WHITE RIVER AGENCY.—From Sketches by Lieutenant C. A. H. McCauley, Third U. S. Cavalry.—See Page 238.

Plate 6. Colonel Wesley Merritt (*center*); Ouray's home (*top*); Canalla's house (*bottom*). *Frank Leslie's Illustrated Newspaper*, December 6, 1879. Denver Public Library, Western History Collection, Z-4088. Illustration by Lt. C. A. H. McCauley.

COLORADO.—IGNATIO, CHIEF OF THE SOUTHERN UTES, ESCORTING THE WOMEN, CHILDREN AND STOCK IN THE ANIMAS VALLEY TO A PLACE OF SAFETY.
FROM A SKETCH BY J. J. REILLY.—SEE PAGE 271.

Plate 7. "Ignacio, Chief of the Southern Utes escorting the women, children and stock in the Animas Valley to a place of safety." *Frank Leslie's Illustrated Newspaper*, June 18, 1881. Used by permission of Fort Lewis College, Center of Southwest Studies.

JACK, WAR CHIEF OF THE WHITE RIVER UTES.   SARAH, SISTER OF OURAY.   PIAH, CHIEF OF THE MIDDLE PARK UTES.

DOUGLASS, HEAD CHIEF OF THE WHITE RIVER UTES.   OURAY, HEAD CHIEF OF THE UTE TRIBE.

A UTE SQUAW SADDLE.   UTE SQUAWS AND PAPPOOSES.   A UTE NECKLACE AND GUN-CAP BOX.

COLORADO.— THE LATE UTE OUTBREAK AND MASSACRE AT THE WHITE RIVER AGENCY.— FROM PHOTOGRAPHS FURNISHED BY E. A. BARBER AND LIEUTENANT C. A. H. McCAULEY.
See Page 179.

Plate 8. (*top, left to right*) Nicaagat (Jack), She-towitch (Susan), and Piah; (*center*) Quinkent (Douglas) and Ouray. *Frank Leslie's Illustrated Newspaper*, November 15, 1879. Used by permission of Fort Lewis College, Center of Southwest Studies.

OU-RA, HEAD CHIEF.

COLORAL.

BILL, SUB-CHIEF OF MIDDLE PARK UTES.

passionately fond of beads, wampum, vermilion, brass buttons, etc., and their long black hair, parted in the middle, will frequently have a row of brass buttons or knobs from the forehead to the crown of the skull, and the long hair of the scalp, which they are so proud of, is braided into strips of skin from the mountain lion; and no young buck is recognized until he has killed his lion, tanned the skin, and worn it braided in his hair.

One of our portraits is that of OU-RA, head chief of all the Ute tribes. He appears here in Indian costume, but he can appear in civilized dress when he pleases. He is very favorable to the whites, speaks English fluently, and is said to be a very kind-hearted man, and one that has worked hard to secure discipline among his tribes. He endeavored, without success, to prevent the recent outbreak of hostilities.

UN-CA, chief of the White River Utes, was in all probability the author of the recent outrage, and JACK, his sub-chief, was in command of the Indians who did the merciless work. JACK's face fully expresses what he is capable of, while his brother BILL, who is a sub-chief of the Middle Park Utes (successor to COLORAL, who was degraded for bad behavior), looks like an inoffensive Indian, but he has plenty of Indian fire in his brain. At one time he boasted that no lead could kill him, and when one of the tribe said he would like to try, BILL stood up, folded his arms, and said, "Fire!" The bullet went through his left side below the ribs. BILL laughed, and said, "I told you lead no kill me." He was laid up about two weeks, and came out all right. PIAH is the chief of the Middle Park Utes. He is a clever fellow enough, but very deceitful. He has been to Washington, New York, and Boston, as have some of the others. PIAH says he got shaved in Washington, which accounts for the few hairs on his chin, of which he is very proud. In conversation with him, he said, "Washington

game, and prefer using the bow and arrow to burning powder or wasting lead.

Ute chiefs are usually very shy, and dislike to sit for a photograph, but when they do, they want to make a display of the cartridge belt well laden with ammunition, and feel a pride in being the owner of a vest, but never wear a coat. They are

UN-CA, CHIEF OF WHITE RIVER UTES.

DOUGLAS.

UTE PAPPOOSE.

heap big, heap big houses; New York heap big, big houses, big boats, plenty white men;" and so of other Eastern cities; but at the end he says, "White man heap no good, heap lie, Indian no lie." Upon being asked what the great white father said to him, his answer was: "White father at Washington said Indian must make potato, cabbage, and work. I tell white father no make potato, cabbage, no work; Indian hunt, fish. No hunt, no fish, Indian fight and die."

ANTELOPE, OU-RA's runner, is quite a feature, as he is always ready to carry messages to the most distant tribes, and never takes any undue rest until his return.

TAB-E-NASH is a son of the old chief WASHINGTON, and as bad a boy as can be ordinarily brought forward, being treacherous, and devoid of principle in many respects, which is an exception to the rest of the tribe.

DOUGLAS, or QUINCOR-BUCK-UNT, a leading chief of the White River or Yampa band, is also inclined to be peaceable, but being a man possessed of little force of character, has not been able to restrain his followers from deeds of violence.

The relief of the remnant of Major THORNBURGH's command, who after his death intrenched themselves, under Captain PAYNE's orders, behind their wagons and dead horses, was accomplished in the most gallant manner by the troops under General MERRITT. Their march across a difficult country was a marvel of endurance. During the twenty-four hours before they reached the beleaguered band they marched seventy miles. The conduct of Captain DODGE's company of colored cavalry was heroic. On hearing of the peril of their comrades they instantly set out for their relief, and on reaching the spot made a gallant charge through the surrounding Indian lines, losing nearly all their horses and several of their number in killed and wounded. Their brave conduct should set at rest forever the silly

sneers against colored soldiers, in which some people still persist. Their valor was proven during the late civil war on many memorable occasions. The brave fellows who were holding out against fearful odds, with every prospect of annihilation, will always bear emphatic testimony to the fighting qualities of their colored comrades.

JACK, SUB-CHIEF.

TAB-E-NASH, WHITE RIVER UTE.

ANTELOPE, OU-RA's RUNNER.

BEADED TOBACCO POUCH AND NECKLACE.   INDIAN DRAWINGS.

CLAY TOY HORSE AND BONE WHISTLE.

THE UTE WAR—PORTRAITS OF CHIEFS—TOYS, DRAWINGS, ETC.—FROM PHOTOGRAPHS.

Plate 9. Ouray (*top, left*) and other Ute leaders, including Nicaagat (Jack) (*top, right*), Colorow (*middle, left*), and Quinkent (Douglas) (*middle, center*). *Harper's Weekly*, October 25, 1879. Used by permission of Fort Lewis College, Center of Southwest Studies.

Plate 10. Nicaagat, late 1860s or early 1870s. Denver Public Library, Western History Collection, WHJ-10333. Photo by William Henry Jackson.

Plate 11. She-towitch (incorrectly identified as "Chipeta"), date unknown. Denver Public Library, Western History Collection, X-30460.

Plate 12. Colorow (*seated, far right*) and other Utes in Colorado Springs, sometime in the 1870s. Denver Public Library, Western History Collection, Z-2727. Photo by B. H. Gurnsey.

Plate 13. Canalla (*standing*) and unidentified Utes, date unknown. Denver Public Library, Western History Collection, X-30714. Photo by A. Zeese and Co.

Plate 14. A group of Ute leaders and whites gathered in 1874, about the time of the Brunot Agreement: (*back, left to right*) Washington, She-towitch (Susan), Canalla (Johnson 2), Nicaagat (Captain Jack), John; (*middle*) Uriah Curtis, J. B. Thompson, Charles Adams, Otto Mears; (*front*) Guero, Chipeta, Ouray, Piah. W. G. Chamberlain photo. Denver Public Library, Western History Collection, X-19251. Photo by W.G. Chamberlain.

Plate 15. Governor Frederick
Pitkin, date unknown.
Denver Public Library,
Western History Collection,
H-77. Photo by Rose and
Hopkins.

Plate 16. Josephine Meeker,
August 20, 1881. She was then
living in Washington, D.C.
City of Greeley Museums,
Permanent Collection.

Plate 17. Josephine Meeker in
the dress that she sewed on
the hostage trail, 1879.
William Henry Jackson
photo. City of Greeley
Museums, Permanent
Collection.

Plate 18. Josephine
Meeker, Johnny Price,
Flora Ellen Price, and
May Price, 1879. William
Henry Jackson photo. City
of Greeley Museums,
Permanent Collection.

Plate 19. Flora Ellen Price,
date unknown. City of
Greeley Museums,
Permanent Collection.

Plate 20. Arvilla Meeker,
1881. William Henry
Jackson photo. City of
Greeley Museums,
Permanent Collection.

Plate 21. Ralph Meeker (*right*) and Alfred Wheeler in Odessa, Russia, June 1877, en route to the Russo-Turkish War to work as correspondents for the *New York Herald*. City of Greeley Museums, Permanent Collection.

Plate 22. Nathan Meeker, 1876. City of Greeley Museums, Permanent Collection.

Plate 23. Rozene Meeker, date unknown. B. F. Marsh photo. City of Greeley Museums, Permanent Collection.

Plate 24. The Meeker house in Greeley, Colorado, circa 1900. Arvilla and Rozene Meeker are standing out front. City of Greeley Museums, Permanent Collection.

16

THE RESCUE TRAIL

It's too bad Charles Adams was so concerned about his duties as special agent for the U.S. Post Office. If he hadn't been, he might have arrived at the White River Indian Agency prior to September 29, 1879—before the battle at Milk Creek and the killings at the agency. He might have been in time—armed with his understanding of the Utes—to soothe the animosity between Nathan Meeker and the White River Utes, and prevent the violence that occurred.

Adams was summoned to Denver on September 24 for a meeting with Governor Frederick Pitkin and Secretary of Interior Carl Schurz. When Adams was asked to make a hasty trip to the White River to try to ease the escalating tensions there, he initially agreed to go. Then he suddenly recalled important court cases pending in New Mexico that he was pursuing for the Post Office. Those cases took precedence over the conflict brewing at the White River Agency.[1]

If he had decided to go to the agency immediately, Adams would have had to travel rapidly to reach the White River before violence erupted. But it wouldn't have been impossible. A train trip could have taken him to Cheyenne, Wyoming, then west to Rawlins. From there, as Joe Rankin demonstrated after the battle began at Milk Creek, with hard riding on multiple horses one could make the estimated 140 miles in less than 30 hours. From Milk Creek, it was another 25 miles to the White River Indian Agency. But on September 24, no one had any idea what would transpire in northwestern Colorado five days later. Even Nathan Meeker sounded guardedly optimistic when, on that day, he wrote a note to Governor Pitkin saying all was quiet at the White River Indian Agency since he had acceded to most of the Utes' wishes.[2] So, instead of making a full-speed dash to the White River, Adams headed south to New Mexico on Post Office business. But he would make an even more impressive journey a few weeks later.

"I returned to Colorado on the 7th of October, and then first heard of the fight with the soldiers and also the massacre of the agent," Adams told members of Congress in early 1880. "On the 14th of October, I received a telegram from the Secretary, and also a telegram from my department, the latter detailing me temporarily to the Interior Department."[3] By then stories had filtered out from western Colorado that the women were alive and being held hostage by the Utes. Adams was asked by Schurz to go into the mountains of Colorado's Western Slope and determine if the women were still all right. If so, he was to try to arrange their release and ask the Utes to cease fighting.[4]

To do this, Adams would need the aid of his friend Ouray. And meeting with Ouray meant a very long and roundabout trip to reach the hostages. First Adams went by train to Alamosa, presumably from his home near Colorado Springs, a trip of roughly 180 miles that would have taken him on the Denver and Rio Grande Railroad's new tracks over La Veta Pass. The route had just been constructed in 1877 and was at the time the highest railroad pass in the world.[5]

On his rail trip he encountered the German diplomat Count August Donhoff, who amazingly persuaded Adams to let him go with him on his mission to rescue the women. Neither man offered an explanation in later interviews for this decision. Both apparently thought it unremarkable that a secretary assigned to the German delegation in Washington, D.C., should join Adams on this difficult and sensitive mission into the Colorado mountain wilderness.[6] Adams had actually met Donhoff a few weeks earlier, when he had visited Adams's home in Manitou Springs—just west of Colorado Springs—in the company of Secretary of Interior Shurz and Governor Pitkin.

Perhaps because Adams himself was a German native, he felt comfortable in Donhoff's company. Adams was born Carl Schwanbeck in 1844 in Pomerania, a region that straddles the modern border of Germany and Poland. Like Schurz, he had fled Germany as a college student after getting involved in student riots over the policies of King William I. He lived briefly in Boston and served with a Massachusetts regiment during the Civil War, suffering a lung injury during the fighting. He arrived in Denver in the late 1860s and before long asked the territorial governor, Edward McCook, for a job dealing with the increasing numbers of German immigrants arriving in Colorado.

Instead of offering him that position, McCook hired the tall young man as a bodyguard, especially to deal with the Utes who frequented Denver and often barged into McCook's office unannounced. He also put Adams in charge of a portion of the Colorado militia, allowing him to earn the title "General," which he carried the rest of his life. McCook also introduced him to his widowed sister-in-law, Margaret, and they were married not long afterward. It was she who insisted he change his German name to the all-American-sounding "Charles Adams."[7]

By 1870 Adams had been assigned as agent at the White River Indian Agency—no doubt with the political assistance of his brother-in-law, the governor. At the time, the agency was in its original location, high on the White River. Nathan Meeker detested that spot, and he would move the agency approximately 15 miles downstream nine years later.

It was at the White River Agency that Adams first became acquainted with Quinkent, Nicaagat, Colorow, and other White River Utes. He also met and became friends with Ouray and Chipeta when the Uncompahgre Ute leader visited the White River.

By 1872 Adams and his wife were back on Colorado's Front Range, trying to establish a cattle ranch near Colorado Springs. Ouray is said to have visited him there to ask him to take over the Los Pinos Agency because the agent then in charge had proved to be a disaster. Adams agreed to seek the post, and Governor McCook heeded Ouray's concerns. He finagled with his friends in Washington, D.C., to have Adams appointed the new agent at Los Pinos.

In 1872 the Los Pinos Indian Agency was not in the balmy Uncompahgre Valley, but in an inhospitable high-mountain location some 80 miles to the east, near Cochetope Pass. There, in the spring of 1874, a lone traveler wandered in from the west with a strange tale of being lost in the snowbound mountains with his five companions, all of whom had died but him. His name was Alferd Packer, and he would become famous as Colorado's cannibal. Adams didn't believe Packer's convoluted story of what had happened. As a result, he has the distinction of being the first person to incarcerate Packer. Packer would eventually stand trial for murder and go to prison, although he was later pardoned.[8]

In 1875, Charles and Margaret Adams were once more living in the Colorado Springs area, and he was working as a special agent for the U.S. Post Office. He had also developed significant political skills, helping to organize German immigrants to vote for several Republican candidates, including, in 1878, gubernatorial candidate and mining magnate Frederick Pitkin. By 1879, Adams was well known both in Colorado political circles and in the lodges of Colorado's Ute Indians. Thus it was no surprise that he was the man chosen by Pitkin and Schurz to attempt to rescue the hostages.[9]

From Alamosa, it was horseback and wagon only for Adams and Donhoff. There were no more trains, and no scheduled stage service to the Los Pinos Agency on the Uncompahgre River. Adams and Donhoff were probably on good horses, because they covered the 230 miles over rugged mountain terrain with remarkable haste. Although it is not clear from his testimony before Congress exactly when Adams left home, some sources say he left October 15, the day after he received the telegram with his assignment. A long day and night train trip would have gotten him to Alamosa early on October 16. According to a clerk at the Los Pinos Agency, Adams and Donhoff arrived there about noon on October 18, meaning he and Donhoff had covered the 230 miles from Alamosa in less than three days. They left the agency headquarters about 7:30 that evening, but they traveled only about 10 miles down the Uncompahgre Valley, to Ouray's house.[10]

When they headed toward the camp on Mesa Creek where the women were held hostage, they didn't go blindly. Horseback messengers had been traveling regularly between Ouray's headquarters and the camps of the White River Utes. Ouray knew exactly where the women were being held. Adams and Donhoff also didn't go alone. Some thirteen Uncompahgre Utes—led by Ouray's brother-in-law Sapivanero—accompanied the pair as guides and protectors. In addition, at least three other white men joined them on the journey: George Sherman, a clerk at the Los Pinos Agency; Captain W. M. Cline, a former Civil War officer and friend of Adams's who by 1879 was operating a small trading post on the Cimarron River, 15 miles east of the Los Pinos Agency; and a reporter from the *Denver Tribune* named Saunders.[11]

This small group also brought a buckboard and wagon packed with canned foods, blankets, and other goods that might be helpful for the hostages upon their release. The wagon was apparently pulled by a mismatched pair—a horse and a very balky mule. When the mule refused to pull up one steep grade along the way, despite repeated whipping and some spirited cursing on the part of the news reporter, Captain Cline solved the problem by putting his own horse in the traces and joining the buckboard gang.[12]

From Ouray's home near the Los Pinos Agency to the spot on Mesa Creek where the women were held is roughly 100 miles. Sherman said that their party covered 40 of those miles on October 19 and camped along the Gunnison River that night. The following day,

> We broke camp on the Gunnison at an early hour and pushed on without stopping for dinner until about 5 o'clock p.m. when we came to a creek, one of the affluents of the Gunnison, about 80 miles from Ouray's. Up to this time we had been traveling on what is known as the old Mormon road [a wagon road leading to Salt Lake City] but here Gen. Adams informed us he would have to leave the wagons behind and take a mountain trail. And that as soon as supper was over we should start immediately for the Indian camp.

Before they could depart, however, a pair of Utes named Coho and Henry Jim arrived from the camp where the women were being held. Coho's "reception by our escort was decidedly cool and it was some little time before anyone even spoke to him," Sherman reported. That may have been due to the tension between the Uncompahgre and White River Ute bands that had developed as a result of the violence on the White River, or it may be that, as Sherman said, Coho was not well liked personally by the Uncompahgre Utes. In any event, the newcomers joined the Ute escort, and the rescue party prepared to leave.[13]

Sherman recalled that "Just as the dazzling sun began to decline behind the mountain range, stealing away our daylight and its genial warmth, we started on our night ride of twenty miles." Dramatically, he added, "The night ride of Paul Revere saved a nation, and the night ride of

Gen. Adams saved three helpless women and two still more helpless children." If Adams and his group had arrived ten hours later, Sherman contended, news of an accidental confrontation between a few of Colonel Merritt's troops and several Utes—in which two whites and two Utes were killed—would have reached the camp where the women were being held and might have prompted the Utes to kill the women in revenge.

Sherman was speculating for the benefit of readers of the mining camp newspaper who were already inflamed by the White River events and ready to believe only the worst about the Utes. Certainly, the Utes were angered when they learned of the skirmish involving Merritt's men and the Ute lookouts. But they were also eager to reach an agreement that would halt Merritt's march toward them. They knew killing the women was not the means to achieve that goal.[14]

How exactly Adams and his escort arrived at the camp where the hostages were held is a matter of some debate. One twentieth-century author has suggested that from Whitewater Creek they climbed a narrow, winding trail to the top of Grand Mesa, an elevation of more than 10,000 feet, and then dropped down to Mesa Creek. But that would have taken them on a steep climb over the top of the mountain—which was unnecessary since a slight diversion westward would have led them toward Mesa Creek with far less climbing.[15] Sherman reported they followed the latter route, going into lower country, not higher.

"Sometime in the night, we reached Grand River near the mouth of Plateau Creek and went into camp for a few hours sleep." But even that lower-elevation route had not been an easy ride. "Mile after mile was passed over at that never ceasing gait for which the Ute Indians are so noted," Sherman wrote. "At first the Indians as well as the whites indulged in many a joke, but as the trail grew more narrow and difficult we dropped into single file and as the darkness increased, conversation ceased."[16]

Sherman's firsthand account of the route is more plausible, based on the terrain in the area. A group on horseback heading north and west from Whitewater Creek would find it far easier to reach the Grand River near Plateau Creek, then head up to Mesa Creek to the camp where the women were, than to climb the steep cliffs to the top of the mesa and then drop down the other side.

The party arrived at a hillside overlooking that camp early on the morning of October 21. "At 10 o'clock we came in sight of the Indian camp," Sherman said.[17] The Utes recognized that the rescue party had arrived, and at least one woman attempted to delay the inevitable. Josie recalled,

> A big squaw came to the tent and hung a blanket over the opening so that I could not see out. In a moment I was on my feet, and peeping over the top edge of it I beheld General Adams and his escort mounted on their horses at a little distance. The sight made me tremble with hope and expectation, and for a few moments I could not move. But quickly, very quickly, I recovered myself, and the strength of Hercules seemed to possess me. Taking hold of the blanket I ripped it down as though it had been paper, and sprang outside the tent, where the squaw, a powerful-looking woman, confronted me. An instant more and I seized her and flung her away like she had been a child, and then bounded to General Adams with the glad cry: "Oh, sir, God bless you for saving us!"[18]

Adams's recollection of the scene is similar, but not quite as dramatic. "I went to the lower end first, and by inquiring, I saw Miss Meeker peeping out of a tent. I dismounted and asked her who she was, not knowing her personally at that time, and told her that I had come to release her, and asked her where her mother and the other woman were. I then mounted again and told Miss Meeker to be ready to leave, if possible, that afternoon."[19]

From there Adams went to the other end of the camp, where he found thirty or so Ute men "talking very boisterously." Although he knew most of them, they refused to talk to him, except to tell him to wait until Quinkent arrived. The Ute leader showed up about an hour later. He told Adams that Merritt and his troops were advancing southward from the White River, and the Utes would not release the hostages until the soldiers were halted. Adams told Quinkent he would go to Merritt's camp to try to halt his advance "after you give up the women."[20]

Back into conference the Utes went, with Adams primarily an observer, but occasionally a participant.

> I believe they talked there until about four or five o'clock in the afternoon, some in a very hostile manner, and others in a peaceful manner. One of the Indians that I had taken with me could speak Spanish, and through him, as interpreter, I had several remarks to make to them, but always to the effect

that they must first give up these prisoners without conditions, and then I might perhaps be able to do something for them.[21]

Finally, the Utes at this gathering agreed to free the women. "They said, 'We don't want to have anything more to do with the government. All that we want is that the soldiers shall not pursue us in our own country. We can live on game, as we have lived before, and do not desire to have anything to do with the government, but we give these women to you, and if you can do anything for us afterwards, all right.'"[22]

Sometime during this meeting—the exact chronology is not clear—Adams left the gathering and met Arvilla Meeker and Flora Ellen Price. He arranged for all three women and Flora Ellen's two children to be placed together in one teepee. They were to get ready to ride to Whitewater Creek at the Gunnison River the next morning, where the wagon awaited them. From there they would make the trek to Los Pinos and beyond.

Shortly after finishing the conference with the thirty-plus Utes at Mesa Creek, Adams and his escorts saddled up and rode with Quinkent to the main Ute camp on Roan Creek, approximately 20 miles away. There an even longer conference awaited him.

The group arrived about 11 p.m., he said. "All the chiefs had assembled. One had gone ahead and told them that I was coming....The Indians were all in the tent of a chief called Sowawick, and in this tent we sat up all night, and they told me their story, and asked me to report that story to Washington. Chief Jack [Nicaagat] was the spokesman that night."[23] Nicaagat recounted his story of the fight at Milk Creek to Adams, as well as the Utes' grievances against Nathan Meeker and the killings at the agency by unnamed Utes.

Sometime around dawn, this group broke up. Adams and his party rested until roughly 10 that morning, when they saddled up again and headed up the Grand River, planning to eventually reach the White River and meet with Merritt.[24] As they embarked, Adams discovered that his entourage of accompanying Utes had changed, both in number and purpose. "I had asked for an escort of four or five Indians to go with me," he said. "But when I started out the crowd kept increasing until there were about twenty-five with me, and they kept so very close around me and from their whole movements I saw that I was more of a prisoner than anything else."[25]

They moved on, but they had been on the trail only a couple of hours when they received distressing news.

About noon that day, just after crossing Grand River, away ahead, I saw an Indian coming towards us at a very fast gait. Some of the Indians also saw him at the same time, and they galloped up ahead very fast. I then saw several loose ponies with saddles on, coming over the trail following the first one, and pretty soon two more Indians, mounted.

When I came up I found them gesticulating and talking very loudly, and from some words that I understood in Ute, and the motions they made, I saw at once that they had had another fight.

All of them looked very morose and hostile; but finally, after talking among themselves awhile, Sapivanero turned around and said, "It is all right; the Indians and the soldiers have had another fight, and two Indians were killed and two white men; so it is all right."[26]

The party camped on the Grand River that night, October 22, Adams said. The next morning, as they were heading north toward the White River, they encountered more Utes, who also told of the recent skirmish. "Very soon afterwards, about the place where this fight had occurred, one of the Indians told me that he had seen the head of a horse some two or three miles in advance on the road, and he did not want to go any farther, and he asked me to go on alone."[27]

It was near this point that Adams made his first contact with Merritt's troops, and it proved to be a dicey situation.

So we took our handkerchiefs out and tied them to poles, and Count Donhoff and myself went ahead to his place where the Indian had seen the horse, and found two or three loose horses only. I then said to Count Donhoff, "I will go on slowly, and you ride back and tell the Indians to come; that there are no soldiers here," and he did so. I rode ahead quietly, and just as the count and these Indians, some twenty-five in number, were riding pretty fast to overtake me, I saw the soldiers ahead; in fact they were all around us at once.

My Indians also saw them in a moment and ran off to the mountains, leaving me and Count Donhoff alone. We kept on but the soldiers did not seem to recognize us; at any rate they kept skirmishers all deployed, and kept coming closer around us, and some of them were even dismounted and were ready to fire, but fortunately an officer, who was a little ahead, saw me and came and conducted me to the commanding officer [Lieutenant E. V. Sumner].[28]

The party of soldiers they encountered had been sent out to recover the bodies of the two white men killed in the unexpected skirmish the day before. And they weren't happy about finding Utes in the area. "There were some threatening remarks made by some of the scouts to the effect that it would be a good thing to shoot us, but nothing of that kind happened. I went back to get the Indians to come, Colonel [actually Lieutenant] Sumner promising to take in his lines. He said he had been informed that there were more than 300 Indians in front. I told him that there were not more than twenty-five, and that they would come with me."

Adams signaled to his Ute companions to come down and join him, but only Sapivanero did so. As the two talked, he saw "another company [of soldiers] come right behind us, cutting us off from the road and from the other Indians on the mountain. The Indians on the mountain hallooed to the chief who was with me and he looked around and saw the soldiers and at once accused me of betraying him. He hadn't time to get his gun out or I think he would have fired at me." Instead, Sapivanero galloped through the ring of soldiers back up the mountain where his companions waited. Adams followed and assured the Utes that he was not guilty of treachery. Then he returned to Sumner, who said it was all a misunderstanding, that one company of soldiers had not heard the bugle call to halt.[29]

The soldiers pulled back, and the Utes quickly found the bodies of the white men about 25 miles south of the White River "on the divide between Grand River and White River," probably near the top of Rio Blanco Hill. The Utes then returned to their mountain overlook. Adams went on with Donhoff, but without his Ute escort, to meet Merritt.

Adams's meeting with the military commander did not occur until the following morning, October 24. Adams told Merritt that the Utes had agreed to free their captives. Merritt responded, "under such circumstances he would have to stay where he was" until Adams had ample time to return to where the women were held and escort them to the Los Pinos Agency.[30]

Adams had promised the Utes he would return and tell them what Merritt intended to do.

I went back and met the Indians at the same place; in fact before that they had been on the mountains watching to see whether I would come back or not. I went back with them to their camp.... We arrived back at the camp [on Roan Creek] about noon the next day, stayed there all night; rode back about daylight towards the small camp; found that the Indians had kept their word, and that the women had gone.[31]

The women had in fact left the camp on Mesa Creek the same morning that Adams and Donhoff had departed the main Ute camp on Roan Creek on their way to meet with Merritt. That morning "we left for Uncompahgre in charge of Captain Cline and Mr. Sherman," Josie said. "To these gentlemen we were indebted for a safe and rapid journey to Chief Ouray's house on the Uncompahgre River near Los Pinos."[32]

There was a brief confrontation when Captain Cline reached the wagon and discovered a number of Utes already there, eating canned fruit that was meant for the women and dividing among themselves the blankets that were also for the women. Angrily, Cline jumped from his horse, grabbed an axe, and declared, "Chief Ouray shall hear of this, and will settle with you!" The Utes fell back and allowed Cline to gather up the canned goods and blankets just as George Sherman rode up with the hostages. Later they would learn from Ouray that he had chosen several Utes to observe the scene, and they were prepared to help if the women appeared to be in any danger.[33]

The small party departed, with the women riding in the buckboard, and after two days' travel they arrived at Ouray's house on the Uncompahgre River, where they were greeted warmly and fed well by Ouray and his wife, Chipeta. Ralph Meeker was waiting for his mother and sister at the Los Pinos Agency. He accompanied them, as well as Flora Ellen Price and her two children, on the slow but uneventful journey to Alamosa, and from there by train to Denver. After a few days' rest, they finally made it home to Greeley.[34] Their long ordeal on the hostage trail was over.

CHICAGO RALLIES FOR SHE-TOWITCH

ON NOVEMBER 4, 1879, THE *CHICAGO TRIBUNE* PRINTED SOMETHING DIFferent from anything it had previously published regarding the Utes and the events at the White River Agency: a lengthy editorial titled "A Plea for Susan," urging "the women of America" to recognize what She-towitch had done on behalf of the white women and children held hostage by the Utes.

By the time this editorial appeared, the *Tribune* had been alternately critical and cautiously supportive of the Indian policies of Secretary of Interior Carl Schurz. It had not been as vehement in its denunciation of the Utes as many of the newspapers in Colorado, but it had condemned them, and had reached the conclusion that the best solution to the conflict would be for the Utes to leave the state. When it came to She-towitch, however, the *Tribune* offered nothing but accolades. "The women of America have an opportunity to pay a tribute of gratitude to one of their own sex such as never before has been accorded to them," the article said. "As this woman is not in a position to make an appeal for gratitude, and probably is not aware that she has done anything calling for gratitude, The Chicago Tribune makes the appeal for her."

The *Tribune* also said it was "confident that her whiter sisters who are doing so much for others not half so worthy will move in her behalf, and by some fitting testimonial express to her their appreciation of her human-ity, kindness, and bravery; and that they will do this all the more heartily when they realize that the heroism of this woman is unprecedented in the annals of her race."[1]

The newspaper recounted stories of She-towitch's kindness toward the hostages: how she made sure they had adequate food and how she pro-tected them from the taunting or threats of other Utes. It took special note of the incident in which Ouray's sister spoke up on the captives' behalf during a tense meeting of tribal leaders, when some of the White River Utes reportedly urged killing the hostages. Not only were these acts by She-towitch important to the captives on the hostage trail, but the *Tri-bune* foresaw much broader impacts from the Ute woman's heroism. "It will be very far-reaching in its influences. It marks a new phase in the pol-icy of the Indians towards the whites. It will serve in the future to make them more kindly disposed towards helpless prisoners."[2]

The *Tribune* compared She-towitch to Pocahontas, but said She-tow-itch's acts of bravery were greater. It also gave her a place in the highest rankings of what was then a fledgling feminist movement.

> For the cause of women's rights, Susan has done more than a thousand like the Susan whose last name is Anthony. She has saved these captive women the right to a woman's honor and a woman's life....
>
> The large-hearted women of this country will prove themselves ungrate-ful if they fail to recognize the bravery and humanity of this Indian squaw in defense of her pale-faced sisters. It was a noble deed that will take the place in history it deserves among the instances of personal heroism displayed by woman. It does not lower the deed because it was done by a squaw.[3]

The response to this editorial was neither overwhelming nor immedi-ate. In fact, it was more than a month before a very unusual woman then living in Chicago publicly accepted the *Tribune*'s challenge. She did so with a very specific idea to protect She-towitch and her family for years to come.[4]

The woman's name was Jane Grey Swisshelm, and on December 15, 1879, she responded to the *Tribune* editorial with a letter in which she proposed a petition to Congress that would guarantee She-towitch, her family, and their descendants ownership of property in Colorado for generations to come. "Also, her tribe, for her sake, should be left in Colorado," Swisshelm wrote.[5]

It was not her first letter to the newspaper about the White River Utes, and it was far from her first venture into controversial political issues. In fact, by 1879, Swisshelm was among the most well-known women in the United States. She had been an ardent abolitionist for more than twenty years before the Civil War and had become a critic of President Lincoln during the war because, in her view, he had moved too slowly to end slavery. As a woman who had suffered a tyrannical husband, whom she eventually divorced, she was also a staunch advocate for women's rights. She had written for a number of different newspapers and published at least three of her own in Pennsylvania and Minnesota. She had written at length about atrocities committed by the Sioux in western Minnesota in 1863, and it was then she apparently developed disgust toward religious groups that sought to intercede on behalf of Indians.[6]

By 1879, Swisshelm was dividing her time between her home outside of Pittsburgh and Chicago, where her daughter lived. The confrontation with the White River Utes provided her an opportunity to reprise a favorite theme: The Indian problems in the United States were due in large part to the soft-hearted policies of Christian do-gooders, especially Quakers.

Her first essay in the wake of the White River events appeared in the *Chicago Tribune* on October 4, 1879, under the title "Indians and Christians: Where Miss Swisshelm Locates the Responsibility of the Thornburgh Slaughter." The opening sentence let readers know exactly what Swisshelm thought: "So it seems that the Utes have found use for the scalping knives so considerately furnished them by the Peace Commission, representing the Christianity of this Nation!"[7]

That was quickly followed by this line: "You may talk about the Utes— I say that American Christians butchered Maj. Thornburgh and his gallant command!" Christians were to blame, she said, because

It is the Church which maintains the tribal system and insists upon treating with every few hundred of these lousy loafers as if they were an independent nation, the equal of the United States! It is the Church which undertakes to feed and clothe them in idleness; which deprives them of the ordinary incentives to industry; which undertakes to coddle them into civilization and so removes them from God's highway to improvement.[8]

Swisshelm's sentiments, although more virulently anti-Christian than most people's, represented a growing belief in the United States—shared by Secretary of Interior Schurz—that the answer to "the Indian problem" was to eliminate the reservation system, give each Native American family a plot of ground of 160 acres or so, and allow them to rise and fall as any other landowners in the nation.[9]

Swisshelm wrote at least a half dozen other letters to the *Chicago Tribune* over the next few months regarding the Utes. On November 7, 1879, she asked, "Why Must the Utes Go?" In that letter she suggested giving individual plots of land in Colorado to each Ute family, and she reiterated her complaints about the Christians, whose policies, she believed, had led to a corrupt Department of Indian Affairs and a disgraced reservation system. "Savages we found them, and savages we keep them, that the most corrupt political ring which ever disgraced a Government may make money by their savagery."[10]

When, in mid-December, Swisshelm proposed her petition on behalf of She-towitch, she returned to the idea of individual plots of land for each of the Ute families. The Ute reservation should be surveyed, she said, "and each alternate section reserved one year for pre-emption by the heads of Ute families." The other sections would be opened to white homesteaders under her plan. The legislation for this should include a provision that the land claimed by the Utes could not be transferred by the original Utes or their descendants for at least fifty years, Swisshelm suggested, "so that he may not be defrauded, and may not defraud himself, so as to be homeless."[11]

Swisshelm's proposal apparently won support from a number of people in the Chicago area, but not in Colorado, where the predominant view was to force the Utes out—or exterminate them. One Colorado newspaper wrote: "Mrs. Jane G. Swisshelm is trotting around with a petition praying that every family Ute be assigned a quarter section of land. That is better than holding three thousand acres, or more, apiece, as is now the case. Jane should next get up a petition to the Ute requesting him to remain on his quarter section. The best way to keep him on it would be to bury him in it."[12]

By the time that Colorado newspaper article was written, January of 1880, Swisshelm had decided on two separate petitions: one for all members of the Ute tribe, and one just for She-towitch and her family. Addressed to the U.S. Senate and House of Representatives, the She-towitch petition said:

> Your petitioners, citizens of the United States, do respectfully entreat you to recognize the services of Susan [She-towitch], wife of the Ute Chief Johnson [Canalla], in protecting the captives, taken in the White River massacre of 1879, by securing to her, one section of land, to be by her selected on the present Ute Reservation in Colorado, and that you would make the title inalienable, in her and her heirs, until July Fourth, 1976. [13]

Why she chose the date of the U.S. bicentennial as the end date for that "inalienable" title is not clear.

In addition to signing her own name, Swisshelm rounded up twenty-seven others to attach their signatures to the petition. They included some of Chicago's leading figures. The signature of "J. Medill" is almost certainly that of Joseph Medill, owner and publisher of the *Chicago Tribune*, although his newspaper didn't report his involvement with the petition. Reverend David Swing was a well-known minister in the Windy City whose sermons were often published in the *Tribune*. C. B. Farwell was a local politician who would eventually be elected senator from Illinois. Their petition on She-towitch's behalf was presented to Congress and referred to the Senate Committee on Indian Affairs on January 6, 1880. And there it apparently died. It is not clear whether Swisshelm ever presented the second petition she wrote about, to give each Ute family a quarter section of land.[14]

Neither She-towitch nor any of her family members were given land in Colorado. After the brief flurry of newspaper articles and Swisshelm's petition, She-towitch was largely forgotten in the white world. History replaced her with another Ute heroine a few years later, under a mistaken premise. An 1882 poem by Denver newspaperman Eugene Field incorrectly portrayed Ouray's wife, Chipeta, as the heroine of the 1879 events. That tale would hang around for more than a century, eclipsing the story of She-towitch's actual deeds.[15]

The oral history of She-towitch's family says the once-renowned woman survived the forced removal of the Utes to the reservation in northeastern Utah. Unlike her famous sister-in-law, Chipeta, who remained a celebrity among whites in Colorado until her death in 1924, She-towitch lived in obscurity and died that way, in 1934. She was more than 100 years old, according to her descendants, but about 90 based on published accounts of her birth date. Her family doesn't know exactly where she was buried.[16]

She-towitch's actions on behalf of the hostages were heroic and compassionate, but history has largely forgotten her. In that regard, Jane Grey Swisshelm proved a poor prophet. On December 29, 1879, she wrote about She-towitch in a letter to the *Chicago Tribune*: "That squaw will live in history when we are all forgotten."[17]

18

INVESTIGATION, FRUSTRATION, AND FARCE

On December 6, 1879, in a crowded meeting room at the Los Pinos Indian Agency, General Edward Hatch and Charles Adams delivered the government's demands to the twenty-five Ute leaders gathered before them: Surrender the twelve White River Utes believed to be responsible for killing Nathan Meeker and his employees at the White River Indian Agency and allow them to stand trial for these crimes.

The Ute response was dramatic. First there was silence. Then Colorow, the massive Ute who had been a leader at the Milk Creek battle, passed a pipe among the Utes. When it had made its way around the group, he stood and pulled his knife from his belt. He then flung it, point first, to the wooden floor, where it stood quivering. "Instantly every Indian present dropped his hand to his belt and laid his hand on his knife or pistol. The whites did the same, and the two parties stood fronting and defying each other for some moments, each waiting for the other to make a forward move."[1]

If other Utes stabbed their knives to the floor, as Colorow had done, it would represent a rebuke of the whites' demands and a vote for war. Chief Ouray broke the tension, telling the whites that the accused Utes would be delivered, but only if they could be taken to Washington for trial. "The Colorado people are all our enemies," he said. "And to give them up to be tried in this state would be to surrender them to be hanged."[2] Hatch agreed to send a telegram to Washington with Ouray's response. The Indians chose peace, not war, so the climactic moment of the White River Ute Commission's hearings ended without violence.

The commission had been meeting for nearly a month at the Los Pinos Agency on the Uncompahgre River, south of where the city of Montrose now sits. Ten witnesses had testified in person, nine of them Utes. The statements of the three women who had been held hostage by the Utes—statements taken by Charles Adams in Greeley on November 4—were read into the record. So were numerous telegrams from Nathan Meeker, Major Thomas T. Thornburgh, and Interior Department officials.[3]

The White River Ute Commission, sometimes called the Peace Commission, would technically remain in force until early January 1880. But little would be accomplished in the final month. The bulk of its work and its important conclusions had all been reached by the morning of December 6, when Colorow stabbed the floor with his knife.[4] By the time the commission finally adjourned on January 9, the House Committee on Indian Affairs was preparing to open hearings in Washington, D.C., regarding what it termed "the Ute Indian outbreak." But the Washington hearings would be far more political in nature than those held in the low log building along the banks of the Uncompahgre River.

The White River Ute Commission acted more like a grand jury, attempting to determine who was responsible for the killings at the White River Indian Agency, then decreeing that they be held for trial. It wasn't a court exactly, or an entity with official judicial standing, but it had authority granted by Secretary of Interior Carl Schurz. That authority was given even before Charles Adams had returned from his expedition to arrange the release of the Utes' hostages.

"All these things together induced me to telegraph to the Secretary to have an investigation, and stop the advance of the soldiers at that time," Adams said later. "The mail going east had hardly left with that dispatch when I received a dispatch in answer to mine from White River, saying that such a commission had been already appointed by him, naming me as one of the members."[5]

The commission opened its hearing at 2:30 p.m. on November 12, 1879, with General Hatch, Charles Adams, and Ouray presiding. The only other person listed as present at that first meeting was First Lieutenant Gustavaus Valois of the Ninth Cavalry, who served as both recorder and legal adviser. He would be present and keep a record of the proceedings every day the commission met.[6] Over nearly two months the commission officially convened on forty days, but on fifteen of those days it did nothing but read and approve the minutes of the previous meeting. Ouray, who had been suffering for five years from Bright's disease, a kidney ailment, missed several meetings when he felt poorly. Charles Adams announced on December 12 he was returning to his home in Colorado Springs, and he was not present for any of the meetings after that.[7]

The only business conducted on the first day was to hear Adams's suggestion that all meetings be conducted behind closed doors—with the milling newspaper reporters kept outside. Even so, a number of papers carried almost word-for-word reports of commission hearings based on interviews with participants afterward.[8]

On November 13, the commission was ready to get down to business. The same four people were present, and a stenographer, clerk, and interpreter were appointed. General Hatch was elected president of the three-member commission and then the first witness was called. Quinkent (Douglas) was sworn in by Ouray. The oath that he took was not typical courtroom fare. "Douglas, sworn by Ouray according to custom of Utes," the official transcript reads. "In taking the oath Douglas said: 'There is one spirit governing the heaven and the earth; he looks down upon me, and sees upon earth as well as in heaven. Therefore, I cannot speak anything but the truth.'"[9]

Subsequent Ute witnesses would be sworn in "according to the form of the Utes."[10] And like Quinkent, most of them would have faulty memories about what occurred on September 29. For instance, Quinkent recalled for the commission some of the events preceding that day, and even drew a rough sketch of the White River Indian Agency and surrounding buildings. But when it came to questions about the Milk Creek battle or the killings at the agency, he offered little but variations of the following response: "I know nothing about that."[11]

Other Utes followed with equally limited knowledge of the events—or equally faulty memories. Sowawick even forgot the all-night meeting in his teepee at the camp on Roan Creek and the Grand River after Adams came to negotiate the release of the women and the end to hostilities. His forgetfulness angered Adams. "Was I ever in your tent on Grand River?"

Adams asked after Sowawick had been unresponsive to virtually every question put to him by the commission. When Sowawick answered "No," he was dismissed as a witness. Then Adams lashed out.

> The answer to the last question was not true. I was in his tent, and in his tent we held a council which lasted from eleven o'clock at night until six o'clock in the morning. Sowawick was present, and agreed with the others about what was done; and today he comes here and says he does not know anything. For that reason I believe that he has not spoken the truth, and does not want to speak the truth. I believe also that none of them want to speak the truth, and it is, therefore, almost unnecessary to go any further. They have refused to mention a single name, while they well know the names of all of them.[12]

Adams then asked Ouray for his advice on how to get his fellow Utes to provide more information. But Ouray demurred. "I cannot force them to say what they do not wish to," he said. A short time later, when Adams and General Hatch continued to press him on getting the Utes to testify about who was involved in the killings, Ouray displayed a lawyerly knowledge of legal rules. "Show me any act of law by which a man is compelled to criminate [*sic*] himself," he declared. He would later demand a change of venue to Washington, D.C., because he believed it would be impossible for the accused Utes to obtain a fair trial in Colorado.[13]

It would be two weeks before the commission heard from a Ute witness who was more forthcoming. The first would be Colorow, listed as "Colorado" in the commission transcripts. "What I have seen I will tell you, whether for or against my people," he said to the commissioners. "I will not lie."[14] Colorow then spoke at length of the events leading up to the battle at Milk Creek, of his efforts and those of Nicaagat to persuade the soldiers not to enter the reservation in the days prior to the battle, of Nicaagat's attempts to keep the Ute warriors from firing at the soldiers. Colorow also named the Ute who had first taken Flora Ellen Price prisoner, and some of those who were present around the battlefield. But since he was not at the White River Indian Agency when Meeker and the other employees were killed, or when the women were taken hostage, he could plausibly deny knowledge of those events.[15]

Two days later, on December 3, Nicaagat began testifying. He would continue into the following day. In length and detail, his testimony would be second only to Josephine Meeker's statement. Nicaagat reiterated his complaints about Nathan Meeker. He described his encounters with Governor Pitkin and Major Thornburgh, as well as the military maneuvers leading up to the Milk Creek battle. But, like Colorow, he had spent all his time at the battle site and therefore could offer no information about what had occurred at the White River Indian Agency, 25 miles away.[16]

For Nicaagat, Colorow, and the other Utes who participated in the Milk Creek battle, the White River Ute Commission reached a critical conclusion. While it didn't exactly exonerate the Utes involved in the battle, it didn't accuse them of any crime. Charles Adams explained it on December 6, as the commission was describing its conclusions to the Utes. The commission, he said, had "heard all the particulars of the fight with the soldiers; and while I think that if the chiefs had exerted their influence better the fight and the subsequent murders might have been averted, still I consider this part more the action of a lot of crazy and hot-headed young men than the result of a preconcerted plan." The actions of the Utes involved in the battle "could be overlooked by the government," he added.[17] In other words, despite what the soldiers had claimed, and what most reports since then have argued, the commission found no evidence that the Utes had intentionally set out to ambush Thornburgh and his troops.

The government could not, however, overlook the actions of those accused of murdering Meeker and his employees, whom Adams termed "cowardly dogs." "If I or any other white man commit a crime against the laws, we expect to be followed and captured and tried by a jury of twelve men, who shall say whether we are guilty or not," Adams declared.

> If we defy arrest, the whole power of the State or government will be turned against us.
> In that position some of your people are today, and as we have been unable to learn from you the names of those that are guilty, we have been obliged to accept the testimony of the captive women.[18]

General Hatch then offered his own statement to the Ute leaders, telling them that they would have to comply with the government demands or there would be a "final struggle with the Indians, which must end in their utter destruction, forfeiture of all their treaty rights, and loss of their lands." Hatch read the list of the Utes believed to be involved in the agency killings and demanded that they all be turned over for trial. The two most prominent names on the list were Douglas (Quinkent) and Johnson (Canalla). It included Josie's protector and would-be husband, Pahsone, as well as Canalla's son, Tim Johnson, and Quinkent's son-in-law, Johnny. Others identified by the women as being present during the killings—and therefore on Hatch's list—were Wausitz (also identified as "Antelope"), Ebenezer, Ahu-u-tu-pu-wit, Serio, Cre-pah, Thomas (identified as a Uintah Ute from Utah), and Parvitz.[19]

It was after Hatch read the list of wanted Utes that Colorow threw his knife, and the Utes wavered between war and peace. Shortly after they opted for peace, Nicaagat and Colorow headed to the White River, reportedly to find the designated Utes and surrender them to the government, although there was soon confusion about exactly what they were doing. Newspapers reported frequently on Nicaagat's actions. First they said he had abandoned the search and fled to Wyoming, only to report later he was on his way back to Los Pinos.[20] Even Ouray wasn't sure. He reported to General Hatch on December 20 that other White River Utes had told him Nicaagat was gathering his people to leave Colorado and head to Wyoming, then east to meet up with Sitting Bull.[21] There seems to have been little truth to the story. Three days later Ouray announced that Nicaagat had arrived at Ouray's house near the Los Pinos Agency along with several other White River Utes. But he had brought none of the twelve accused Utes with him.[22]

Nicaagat, Ouray, and other Ute leaders may have intended to bring in some or all of the Utes accused of the killings at the White River Agency, but by late December they appeared more interested in arranging a trip to Washington, D.C., to plead their case to officials in the nation's capital than in actually rounding up the suspected killers.

One of the accused, Johnny—Quinkent's son-in-law—actually surrendered and was turned over to Hatch and his small military escort on December 9.[23] But the other accused Utes played a cat-and-mouse game, not only with the whites, but evidently with the Utes who sought to bring them in. And all this led to a colossal mix-up—or perhaps an intentional deception—that infuriated General Hatch but left him powerless to effect a change.

On December 12, Ouray told Adams and Hatch that he expected the prisoners would be brought in within a few days. He also said he thought it best if he rode to the White River to "bring in those who should go to

Washington." He reported it would take him ten days *"to return with the chiefs"* (emphasis added).[24]

Ouray made his trip to the White River and back in eight days. On December 20, after Adams had already left for Colorado Springs, Ouray told Hatch and Valois he had given the White River chiefs an ultimatum: They had five days to come to Los Pinos Agency "with the prisoners." "If not," he said, "I would have nothing more to do with them."[25] By December 23, Ouray was able to announce that Nicaagat, Colorow, Sowawick, and other White River Utes were at his house and ready to travel to Washington. But when General Hatch asked him whether the accused Utes would also be arriving, Ouray gave a stunning response.

"No!" he declared. "They are in their camps. *I thought you did not want them anymore"* (emphasis added). Hatch was bewildered and exasperated. "I cannot see how such a mistake could have been made," he cried. "You must have understood that the Secretary's dispatch said that no chiefs can be taken to Washington unless the guilty demanded by the Commission were surrendered." Ouray responded weakly, "I must have misunderstood the interpreter."[26]

Ouray was fluent in Spanish but did not speak English as well. Most of the official testimony during the commission hearings, along with the statements from the women hostages and telegrams from various officials, were translated for him. It's possible there was miscommunication.[27] His statement from December 12 suggests he planned to travel to the White River only to contact the chiefs whom he wanted to go to Washington. But based on his December 20 statement, it seems obvious he expected some of the Utes to bring in the suspected killers. It's hard to square that with his statement three days later that "I thought you didn't want them anymore."

In frustration, Hatch announced at the December 23 meeting that he was going to leave Los Pinos for a ranch on the Cimarron River owned by Captain Cline—the same man who had accompanied Charles Adams from Los Pinos to Mesa Creek to arrange the release of the hostages. The following day, when the commission met again, General Hatch was more amicable toward Ouray. The Uncompahgre leader announced that runners had been sent to the White River, but he could not say for sure whether the accused Utes would be brought in. If they weren't, he asked Hatch, "Will you take me, with two or three of my friends, to Washington?"

Hatch responded, "You are a member of the commission. I will take you and a few friends, under any circumstances."

Then Ouray revealed one possible reason why he and the White River leaders had been unable to bring in the accused. He asked that news of the planned trip to Washington be kept secret, explaining, "I don't wish the Indians to know it as I have a great many enemies, even among my own tribe. I am charged with working for the white man, against the interest of the Indians."[28] It may have been that while Ouray, Nicaagat, Sowawick, and other leaders had agreed to surrender the accused Utes, the majority of Utes disagreed with that decision and with the effort by these leaders to go to Washington to negotiate further.

The commission did not meet Christmas Day, and the following few days involved more waiting, with little accomplished. On December 27, Ouray said the White River chiefs were still at his house, but there was no new word on the prisoners. Hatch announced that the commission would reconvene December 29 at Cline's ranch.

When that meeting occurred, Ouray had another surprise. Instead of bringing "two or three of my friends" to accompany him to Washington, he had arrived with ten, including Nicaagat and Sowawick. Hatch, somewhat pleadingly, asked whether there was any chance of securing the surrender of the accused Utes if he were to return to the Los Pinos Agency. "I believe there is no chance," Ouray responded. "Some have gone hunting toward the Sierra Las Sals [in Utah] and the others won't come in." Even if Hatch returned to the agency and waited until February, it would do no good because the snow would be too deep by then to allow wagons to travel out with the prisoners, equipment, and rations, Ouray said. An exasperated Hatch said Ouray and the other Utes should be ready to leave for Alamosa, en route to Washington, the following day.[29]

The White River Ute Commission met officially three more times: On December 31 it convened on Indian Creek (about 20 miles southeast of the Cimarron River) but conducted no business. Then, on January 6, 1880, it met in Alamosa with Hatch, Ouray, and Valois present, but it conducted no business. Hatch told Ouray to have all the Indians ready to head for Washington the next morning. The following day only Hatch and Valois were present, and the White River Ute Commission adjourned for good.[30]

Nearly a month earlier, in a December 11 telegram to Hatch, Secretary of Interior Schurz had offered his congratulations to the commission for its success. But with none of the accused Utes brought to trial, few people in Colorado agreed with that assessment. The *Greeley Tribune* expressed the Colorado viewpoint on December 31, 1879: "The investigation at Los Pinos has ended as everyone expected it would, by the Indians refusing to surrender the most guilty," it said. "This investigation has been a farce since its commencement."[31]

THE TRAIL TO WASHINGTON

WHEN THE TRAIN CARRYING THE UTE LEADERS TO WASHINGTON steamed into Pueblo, Colorado, early in January 1880, angry whites surrounded the Utes' coach, threatening to hang the Indians and pelting their passenger car with lumps of coal. A security guard of army troops riding with the Utes prevented any serious violence.[1]

As the group of Indians moved eastward with their escorts, they were treated more and more as celebrities and less like criminals. At Joliet, Illinois, an estimated 1,500 to 2,000 people turned out to see the notorious Utes. When the train stopped to take on water, some gawkers climbed into the coach itself, stood on cushions and seat backs, and hooted at the Indians. They disembarked quickly when the train began rolling on.[2]

In Chicago, where the Utes briefly left the train for dinner at a local hotel, the crowd was even larger—there may have been as many as 8,000 people. But here the crowd seemed more curious than vengeful.[3] When the Utes left the train and boarded a horse-drawn bus, much of the crowd followed peaceably. When the Utes disembarked, the fascinated onlookers allowed Nicaagat to lead the other Utes single file along the city streets and even stop to comment on Chicago's size. "The Indians rather relished the notoriety, and Jack, the White River Chief, was led to remark, 'That big village; heap wigwam; much people.'"[4] The other Utes were more reticent about sharing their thoughts, "but looked on and wondered." Even so, they impressed the *Chicago Tribune* reporter sent out to greet them. "The Utes, apparently, are not quite as stoical as other Indians, and they are much cleaner and better dressed than any savages that have yet shown themselves in this city."[5]

The Utes remained at the Grand Pacific Hotel for several hours and "were visited by a large number of people," according to the *Tribune*. They left for the train depot about 8:30 p.m., and large crowds continued to watch them until the train departed for Fort Wayne, Indiana, and then Washington, about 9:10 p.m.[6]

There was reportedly some prearranged sightseeing in Washington designed to impress the Utes with the majesty and power of U.S. society.[7] Then the Utes quickly settled down in a hotel room under guard, where they were held more as prisoners than guests. During the first days of their stay in Washington they had only one visitor: Josephine Meeker.

"I have been today to see the Utes whom they keep locked up at the hotel," Josie wrote to her brother Ralph on January 11, 1880. "Ouray and his wife were friendly, but Jack [Nicaagat] at first seemed afraid of me, but when I told him I was 'no mad' he shook hands warmly and told all the men over and over that I was his 'sister' and that he all the time liked me. They are all sick and seemed to feel better. I was told that it was the first they had talked."[8]

It was an unusual gathering, to say the least—a former hostage meeting cordially with some of those who had once held her prisoner, people who were by then little more than prisoners themselves. Newspapers took note, and it was this meeting that provoked the first denunciation of Josie in the Georgetown, Colorado, newspaper, suggesting she was far too friendly with the Utes.[9]

Three days after Josie wrote that letter, the House Committee on Indian Affairs convened to take testimony on what it titled "the Ute Indian outbreak." Charles Adams, who had accompanied the Utes to Washington, was the first to testify. He recounted the story of his trip to arrange the release of the hostages and relayed what the Utes had told him about the reasons for the outbreak.

He was followed in a couple days by far more political witnesses. There was William Leeds, a former chief clerk for the Indian Office, who had little good to say about Commissioner of Indian Affairs E. A. Hayt. Leeds was followed by Hayt himself, who made it clear that it was the previous administration that had created the root of the problem with the Utes. Next up was Clinton B. Fisk, a New York banker and member of the Board of Indian Affairs, who had his own dispute with Hayt and made no secret of that fact in the press.[10]

Hayt's defense of himself and his administration before the House committee might have sufficed to protect him had not other problems surfaced. Hayt testified twice before the House committee, on January 19, 1880, and again on January 22. But a week later, as Fisk continued to raise questions about Hayt with the press, Hayt's boss, Secretary of Interior Carl Schurz, "summarily dismissed" him. Schurz explained that Hayt's reports to Schurz concealed irregularities about his mine speculation on Indian lands in Arizona, which amounted to an abuse of his office.[11] The following day Schurz said the only reason Hayt was fired was that he was withholding information from him, but an editorial in the *Chicago Tribune* called Hayt's Indian department among the most corrupt branches of government services.[12]

Before all this happened, Nicaagat, Sowawick, Wass (a White River Ute also known as "Washington"), Charles Adams, and Otto Mears—a Colorado trader, road builder, and friend of Ouray's who had also accompanied the Utes to Washington—were off on another long trip. Less than two weeks after they arrived in the nation's capital, they were sent back to Colorado—once again assigned to bring in the Utes accused of killing Nathan Meeker and his employees.[13] That mission—at least Nicaagat's part in it—annoyed Josie. Despite her warm greeting of the Ute leader a few weeks earlier and her assurance that she wasn't mad at him, Josie revealed a different view of Nicaagat in a letter she sent to her brother on January 25, two days before she would testify before the House committee.

"We think when our testimony comes out it will change things considerably," she wrote, "as we shall lean heavily against Jack [Nicaagat] as being the chief criminal whom the government has not only allowed to return to his tribe but has acknowledged his power to be greater than that of Ouray's, inasmuch as they have sent him to do that which Ouray confesses he cannot do [bring in the accused killers]." She continued, "We shall show that if anyone ought to be punished, it is Jack, but the government has not only promised to protect him, but has showed him great honor."[14]

Josie did refer repeatedly to Nicaagat during her testimony before the House committee beginning two days later, but most of her statements refer to Nicaagat's anger with Nathan Meeker's attempts to turn the Utes into farmers, and his role as the leader of the Ute faction that most strongly resisted Meeker's efforts. She offered no information that painted Nicaagat as a criminal. In fact, she noted that, despite their differences, her father called on Nicaagat several times to help him resolve disputes involving other Utes. And while she accused him of planning the battle with Thornburgh's troops, she presented no evidence to back up that claim. Her testimony reinforces the image of Nicaagat as a rational leader, worried and angered about the possibility of troops coming onto the reservation, but attempting to work with both Nathan Meeker and Major Thornburgh until the very day of the Milk Creek battle to peacefully prevent the bulk of the troops from entering the reservation.[15]

Josie was not the only one upset that Nicaagat had been allowed to return to Colorado. Governor Pitkin, also in Washington to testify before the House committee, told the *Chicago Tribune* that "Jack was just using the mission as a ruse to escape from Schurz's hands." And members of the House Committee on Indian Affairs complained that all of the Utes except Ouray had returned to Colorado, and the committee couldn't get them back to Washington to testify.[16]

Neither complaint proved to be accurate. Nicaagat and Sowawick would both return to Washington and testify before the committee. They would also be partially successful in their mission to bring in the wanted Utes. But to achieve success, they had to make another journey—one more in a remarkable record of expeditions related to the events at the White River in 1879.

By train they returned from Washington, D.C., to Alamosa, Colorado, accompanied by Charles Adams and Otto Mears. Then, by horse-drawn sleigh in the dead of winter, they retraced Adams's route from Alamosa to the Los Pinos Agency—approximately 230 miles. Based on Mears's description of the return trip on the same route two weeks later, it was not a pleasant excursion.

The ride was an exceedingly cold and dreary one, over a wide waste of snow, which was anywhere from five to six and seven feet deep. The cold at times was intense, and sleep for the travelers was almost one of the impossibilities. Gen. Adams' sled was upset at one time, and he disappeared under the horses and in the snow, which was so deep that no sight could be caught of him. After a little while, he came up, his head peering from out the snow, and he was hauled back into the sled. This ride…was about as mean a trip as a man could well imagine.[17]

And that was only part of the long trek made by the Utes. After leaving Adams and Mears at the Los Pinos Agency, the Utes headed north, toward the Grand and White rivers, to seek the accused killers. According to Adams, "Jack [Nicaagat] made no promises, and refused to set a time for his return," saying only, "I will do my best to effect a surrender of the prisoners." An earlier dispatch said Nicaagat had the authority to bring in the guilty "dead or alive."[18]

What difficulties Nicaagat, Sowawick, and the other Utes encountered on their journey of at least 250 miles round-trip are unknown. It's also unclear what methods they employed as they attempted to get the accused Utes to surrender themselves. We know only that they returned to the Los Pinos Agency ten days after they had left Adams and Mears, accompanied by three of the twelve accused killers—Quinkent, Tim Johnson, and Thomas.[19]

Despite the antagonism that Governor Pitkin, Josie Meeker, and others had expressed toward Nicaagat when he left on his journey, this trip boosted public opinion of him. The *Chicago Tribune* wrote, "Of Captain Jack it may be said that he fought Thornburgh in a fair, open fight, and it was he who brought in the three Indian prisoners."[20] Charles Adams sent a telegram to Secretary of Interior Schurz on February 15 informing him of their partial success. "Chiefs Jack, Sowawick and Wash returned here yesterday with Douglas, Thomas and Tim Johnson. Will start with these and three additional Uncompahgres tomorrow on sleighs, hoping to reach Fort Garland [just outside of Alamosa] next Thursday and will proceed to Washington without delay."[21]

According to one article, Nicaagat explained to Adams that only three of the accused were brought in because, "owing to the depth of the snow in the mountains and scattered locations of the camps, it would take at least three weeks to capture the remaining nine prisoners." The Ute leader was said to be "very reticent and declines to state how or in what manner the capture was effected."[22] The same news account revealed that not all of the nine accused Utes still at large were in locations where they couldn't be reached. One of them simply declined—albeit politely—because he had other pressing business. "Chief Johnson [Canalla], one of the prisoners demanded by the Commission, sent his regrets at being unable to accompany the party to Washington, giving as the reason that he was a Medicine Man and had a very sick patient whom he could not leave."[23]

There was also another piece of important information that day: "Jack [Nicaagat] insists that the women are mistaken in the names of certain Indians who they testified were present at the time of the outrages."[24] That appears to have been confirmed after Nicaagat and the others returned to Washington with two of the three prisoners—Tim Johnson and Thomas— and Josie again visited. "Miss Meeker has called upon them, but was unable to identify them as Indians concerned in the White River outrages."[25]

There is confusion about the use of the word "outrages" in this account. If the newspaper meant that Josie was unable to identify the two as being involved in the alleged sexual assaults, that's no surprise. Tim Johnson and Thomas were never accused of that. However, if the paper was using "outrages" to describe the killings and everything else that occurred at the White River Agency—as seems to be the case when it said Nicaagat insisted that the women were mistaken about who was present "at the time of the outrages"—then Josie's failure to identify Tim Johnson and Thomas lends credence to Nicaagat's statement.

Quinkent, the only one of the three prisoners accused of sexually assaulting any of the white women, didn't make it all the way to Washington, D.C. He was left at Fort Leavenworth, Kansas, as the *Chicago Tribune* noted when the train carrying Adams, Mears, and the Utes on its way to the nation's capital once again stopped in Chicago.[26]

Douglas [Quinkent] did not come on to Chicago with the party. He was left in Fort Leavenworth, Kansas. It came very nearly being the case that neither Tim Johnson nor Thomas were of the party to go to Washington. Orders came from Washington Wednesday to have Douglas, Thomas and Johnson left at Fort Leavenworth, but Gen. Adams thought it advisable not to place all three there, and so telegraphed to Washington, but recommended that Douglas be incarcerated in the fort, and that the other two be imprisoned in Fortress Monroe [near Hampton, Virginia, south of Washington, D.C.]. After a few moments a telegram came to take all three prisoners to Washington, but it was too late, as Douglas had already been left in charge of Gen. Adams for his prison.[27]

Another account says that Adams planned to leave Tim Johnson at Fort Leavenworth with Douglas, but the teenage Ute broke into tears, and Adams had so much pity for the young man that he kept him out of prison and took him to Washington to join the other Utes at the hotel. However, this account doesn't jibe with newspaper reports that he and Thomas were incarcerated at Fort Monroe, or with oral history from Tim Johnson's family that recounts he definitely spent time in federal prison before being released and returning to Colorado.[28]

The *Tribune*'s editors weren't happy about how Quinkent was being treated. "Some of the Ute prisoners who have been brought here will probably be sent to Fortress Monroe. Douglas will remain at Fort Leavenworth, and will be comfortably housed and fed at Government expense, while poor Rose Meeker is obliged to work hard for her bread in the Interior Department." (The paper apparently confused Rozene Meeker, who was still in Colorado, with Josie, who was working for the Interior Department in Washington.)[29]

After stopping at Fort Leavenworth to drop off Quinkent, the group proceeded to Washington, which they reached on February 28. They had traveled by train more than 4,000 miles and another 460 miles round-trip by horse-drawn sleigh. The Utes—Nicaagat, Sowawick, and Wass—had covered another 230 miles or more on horseback, through the mountains in the winter, and had brought back with them prisoners who were not eager to accompany them. All of this in little more than a month.

It was an amazing journey, to say the least. But the Utes' efforts to accomplish what the whites demanded would prove to have minimal benefit for them. Political and legislative efforts were underway that would result in their removal from Colorado, no matter what they did.

20

THE COLORADO PLAN

BEFORE NICAAGAT AND HIS PARTY RETURNED TO WASHINGTON, D.C., IN February 1880 with the White River prisoners in tow; before the gavel sounded in January for the congressional hearings on the White River Ute uprising; even before Charles Adams, General Hatch, and Ouray wrapped up their investigation of the White River killings—the legislative wheels were turning to rid Colorado of the Utes.

On December 2, 1879, Colorado congressman James Belford introduced legislation in the House of Representatives "ordering the removal of the Utes from the state." Belford's bill attempted to implement a plan long-sought by whites in Colorado, particularly political leaders, to rid their state of American Indians. By the late 1870s, this meant the Utes residing in the western third of the state, since the Plains Indians of eastern Colorado had already been defeated and forced onto reservations in other territories. As the *Chicago Tribune* noted in mentioning Belford's legislation, the Utes, "besides being a constant menace to the peace and security of settlers, are a bar to the settlement and development of the young State."[1] Politicians in Colorado began stumping for this removal even before their territory became a state. In early 1876, the year Colorado finally achieved statehood, "the territorial Legislature sent a memorial to Congress calling for the removal of all Utes to Indian Territory in Oklahoma."[2]

The core of the Colorado plan was articulated by Governor Frederick Pitkin well before the battle at Milk Creek and the killings at the White River Agency. "Along the western borders of the State, and on the Pacific Slope [the western side of the Continental Divide in Colorado] lies a vast tract occupied by the tribe of Ute Indians," he said. "It is watered by large streams and rivers, and contains many rich valleys and a large number of fertile plains...and nearly every kind of grain and vegetable can be raised without difficulty. No portion of the state is better adapted for agricultural and grazing purposes." But this agricultural Eden was blocked from white settlement by the Utes and their treaty-defined reservation, which Pitkin saw as an unnecessary hindrance to progress. "If this reservation could be extinguished, and the land opened to settlers, it will furnish homes to thousands of the people of the state."[3]

That declaration employed mild language, however, compared to the notorious statement Pitkin made shortly after the Milk Creek battle: "My idea is that, unless removed by the government, they [the Utes] must be exterminated. I could raise 25,000 men to protect the settlers in twenty-four hours. The State would be willing to settle the Indian problem at its own expense. The advantages that would accrue from the throwing open of twelve million acres of land to miners and settlers would more than compensate all the expenses incurred."[4] In his testimony before Congress, beginning in late January 1880, Pitkin was more restrained, but he still expressed his view that the western third of Colorado would be best utilized by whites, not Utes.[5]

He was not alone. In December, an even more powerful Colorado politician, Senator Henry Teller—the man who had done more than anyone to secure the position of White River Indian agent for Nathan Meeker—had declared that Colorado wanted all of the Utes removed. If they couldn't be taken to the Indian Territory, he said, then they should all be placed on the Uintah Reservation in northeastern Utah.[6] And on December 11, 1879, Colorado's lesser-known senator, Nathaniel Hill, had won passage of a resolution in the Senate demanding that Secretary of Interior Carl Schurz negotiate with the Utes to get them removed from Colorado.[7]

In fact, Schurz was pursuing an agreement along those lines. By late January 1880, the broad outlines of an agreement had been hammered out between the Department of the Interior and the Utes who had come to Washington earlier that month, with Charles Adams acting as a mediator. The agreement would require the White River Utes to be moved out of Colorado entirely and relocated on the Uintah Reservation in northeastern Utah. Other Utes, including Ouray's Uncompahgre band, along with the Muache, Weminuche, and Capote bands who lived along the New Mexico–Colorado border, were to be relocated to a new reservation straddling the Colorado-Utah border in the Grand River valley—near the present-day city of Grand Junction, Colorado.[8]

Ouray accepted the proposal, despite the fact that a few days earlier he had publicly questioned why all of the Utes should be punished and forced to move from their lands when only a handful of White River Utes were accused of crimes. He noted during a conversation with Secretary Schurz that "were a white man in Washington to commit murder, the officials would not make the entire population of the country suffer for it."[9] But to Colorado's political delegation, the agreement Shurz was developing was unacceptable. Both Congressman Belford and Senator Teller were quick to denounce it.[10]

Governor Pitkin again carried the banner for the Colorado plan when he proclaimed to the House Committee on Indian Affairs in February 1880 that any agreement that allowed some of the Utes to remain in Colorado was not in the best interest of the Utes themselves. "While it would be a great benefit to the people of the State and to the people that are coming to the State from all parts of the Union if the Indians were removed entirely out of the State," he said, "it would at the same time be for the highest interest of the Indians themselves, because, in case of a conflict, the Indians, being the weaker party, of course would suffer most."[11] It should also be noted that just before he left Colorado for Washington, Pitkin had received reports of gold being found in the Grand River in the area proposed for a new Ute reservation. No significant amounts of gold would ever be recovered there, but even the hint of a possibility of gold was one more reason to prevent the Utes from calling it home.[12]

Pitkin countered Ouray's complaint that not all of the Utes deserved punishment by claiming Ouray's Uncompahgre Utes were deeply involved in the Milk Creek battle. "I believe that a considerable number of Ouray's warriors, the younger portion of his tribe, were in the fight," he said. His proof? A member of the state militia had relayed third-hand information to Pitkin that some of the Uncompahgres had returned to the Los Pinos Agency ten days after the Milk Creek battle "with their horses tired out as though they had been ridden hard, and that they brought back no game." That would hardly be surprising, since riders were continually coming and going to give Ouray updates on what was happening with the White River Utes and the U.S. Army troops. But Pitkin made it sound as though it was clear proof that they were involved in the fighting.[13]

Pitkin also cited a newspaper report that said Ouray's nephew and cousin were killed by Thornburgh's troops as an indication that Uncompahgre Utes had been involved in the fighting. It's not clear who these were, but we do know that one of Canalla's brothers (or perhaps a son) was killed at Milk Creek. And since Canalla was Ouray's brother-in-law, and because the Utes' understanding of familial relations was generally much broader than whites, Ouray might very well have considered Canalla's brother a cousin. Even so, the man killed was a White River Ute, not an Uncompahgre.[14]

If Pitkin depended on hearsay and speculation to link the Uncompahgre Utes with the Milk Creek battle, his attempt to list the number of white citizens killed by Utes over the twenty years preceding 1879 was even more fanciful. He estimated that forty-five to fifty whites in Colorado had been killed by Utes dating back to 1859. But that included some for whom bodies had never been found, or who were found but the cause of death was unclear: "The people of the State generally believe that these are the bodies of persons who have gone out prospecting and never returned, having been murdered by the Indians," he said.[15] It is possible that some of those listed were killed in confrontations with Utes, but others may just as well have been killed by whites or died of accidental causes in the rough terrain of Colorado's mountains. In any event, Pitkin had personal knowledge of only a few of the deaths.

A few weeks later, when Henry C. Olney, publisher of the *Silver World* newspaper in Lake City, Colorado, offered similar testimony about alleged Ute killings of white men based on third-hand evidence, the House committee decided he had gone too far. Committee members agreed to strike all of Olney's testimony that wasn't based on his personal knowledge of what had occurred. They moved to strike some of Pitkin's earlier testimony as well.[16]

A few Coloradans and former residents of the state attempted to counter the descriptions of the Utes as savage, brutal, and untrustworthy. They included people who, unlike Pitkin, had actually lived among the Utes. One of them was Edward F. Danforth, who had been agent at the White River Indian Agency prior to Nathan Meeker. "Mr. Danforth said that during the four years that he had lived among the Utes, he felt that he was in no danger from them," the *Chicago Tribune* reported. "His wife had often been left alone on the reservation without fear or danger.... It is entirely wrong, Mr. Danforth thinks, to hold the Utes, as a tribe, responsible for the acts of a few desperate men."[17]

Another such voice was Reverend Sheldon Jackson of Colorado. On the day the Milk Creek battle began, Jackson and a companion were riding across the Ute reservation and traveled unmolested by them, he said. There were also hundreds of miners scattered across the reservation that day, individually or in small groups, illegally intruding on the Utes' land. Yet the Utes "molested no one," said Jackson, "except the troops and the persons whom they held responsible for bringing the troops to the Agency. Now the civilized white people want to butcher or drive from their home a whole tribe for the acts of a few of its members."[18] "Both Dr. Jackson and Mr. Danforth, who know the Utes intimately, insist that the character of the latter is wickedly misrepresented by the press and people of Colorado generally," the *Tribune* said.[19]

But public defenders of the Utes were rare in early 1880, and their voices were barely heard among the clamor to get the Utes removed from Colorado. They stood little chance of slowing the legislative juggernaut that was gathering steam against the Utes. By March 1, a bill was drafted by Secretary Schurz's office, based on his agreement with the Utes, and sent to Congress. It was trumpeted as a historic document because it marked "the first time in the history of this country that a tribe of wild Indians has agreed to take lands in severality"—meaning they would accept individual plots of lands for each family rather than one communal reservation. Although that was viewed at the time as a most progressive development, it had the effect of significantly reducing the amount of land that whites needed to set aside for the Utes.[20]

The agreement also set aside allotment money for all of the Utes. It directed the White River Utes to go to the Uintah Reservation in Utah, while the Uncompahgres, along with the three smaller southern bands—the Muaches, Weminuches, and Capotes—were to be settled on the new reservation near the junction of the Grand and Gunnison rivers.[21]

The bill rolled through the Senate and House in March and early April, although Senator Teller added a highly significant amendment giving the secretary of Interior discretion to move the Uncompahgre Utes out of Colorado entirely if it was determined that the land in the Grand River valley was not suitable for them.[22] That sealed the Uncompahgres' fate as far as their future in Colorado was concerned. Teller continued to oppose the bill, however, arguing that giving the Utes individual plots of land was a mistake. In this he was at odds with his fellow Coloradan, Senator Hill, who supported Secretary Schurz's plan. Hill's view won out, and the bill passed in the Senate on April 13. It was approved in the House a few days later, although it had been changed to allow the southern bands a small reservation along the Colorado–New Mexico border.

The task of getting the Utes to sign the agreement would prove difficult.[23] Even though the Ute leaders in Washington had agreed to the measure put forth by Secretary Schurz, some had been reluctant to sign it. They were not sure how ceding their tribal lands to the whites would be viewed by their fellow Utes back in Colorado.[24] They signed it nonetheless—or at least most of them did. But not Nicaagat. One report listed the nine Utes who signed the agreement on March 6, including Ouray and Shavano representing the Uncompahgres; Ignacio, Alhandro, and others from the southern bands; as well as Wass (Washington) and Sowawick for the White River Utes. Although Nicaagat had returned to the nation's capital with Sowawick and the others a week earlier, his name was not included among the signatories to the agreement.[25]

The signed agreement was given final approval by Congress, with amendments, by mid-June. The terms required the White River Utes to move to Utah and settle on farms within the Uintah Reservation. The Uncompahgre Utes were to move to allotted "agricultural lands on Grand River, near the mouth of the Gunnison River, in Colorado, if a sufficient quantity of agricultural land shall be found there." The southern bands of Utes, who were not at all involved in the events at White River, were to move to allotted farms on unoccupied land on the La Plata River in Colorado or, if not possible there, along the same river in New Mexico. Upon their removal, the Uncompahgre and White River Utes were to receive annuities from a $50,000 trust. Compensation was to be paid to the families of those killed at the White River Indian Agency from White River Utes' annuities for a period of twenty years.[26]

The agreement adopted by Congress also required the approval of three-fourths of the adult male Utes by October 15, 1880. Despite Ouray's urging of his people to sign, obtaining the signatures proved difficult. A five-member commission appointed by Secretary Schurz was sent to Colorado to obtain the signatures—or marks from those who couldn't write. It included people supportive of Schurz's views, one friend of Senator Teller, and eventually, the indefatigable road builder, entrepreneur, and purported friend of the Utes, Otto Mears.[27]

Even so, most of the Utes refused to sign the agreement, so Mears decided to make the signing a business transaction. He agreed to pay each Ute who signed the document two dollars of his own money.[28] The scheme worked, and eventually sufficient signatures were obtained to ratify the agreement, although people then—and now—dispute whether the purchased signatures were valid. In fact, George W. Manypenny, chairman of the five-member commission, refused to endorse the agreement when he learned what Mears had done and demanded an investigation of Mears by Secretary Schurz.[29]

Manypenny wasn't the only one raising such questions. A. B. Meacham, another member of the commission, sent a telegraph to Secretary Schurz in late 1880 expressing his frustration with Mears's tactics. Although the Uncompahgre Utes were ready to have their lands in the Uncompahgre Valley allotted to individual Ute families, he reported, "They say Mears represented to them last summer that they were not selling Uncompahgre Valley, but only the mountains. In my opinion, there can be no peaceable removal of the Utes until the misunderstanding is corrected.[30]

Mears was ordered to go to Washington to answer questions about his dealings with the Utes, but the 1880 election changed the administration. President Rutherford B. Hayes had not sought re-election, and he was followed in the White House by fellow Republican James Garfield, who replaced Carl Schurz with Samuel S. Kirkwood as secretary of Interior. Kirkwood not only dropped the investigation against Mears, but also publicly commended him and reimbursed him for the $2,800 he had spent obtaining signatures from the Utes.[31]

The Utes had suffered another blow late in the summer of 1880, when Chief Ouray succumbed to Bright's disease on August 24. He was buried in a hidden cave in southern Colorado, but was later reburied in the town of Ignacio on what became the Southern Ute Reservation. Many of the Utes, especially from the White River, had come to distrust Ouray's willingness to reach agreement with the whites, but he remained until the end a strong voice for his people and a shrewd negotiator with the whites.[32]

THE TRAIL TO UTAH

"Don't play in the gullies and washes," Jonas Grant was told by his great-grandmother when he was growing up in Utah. "That's where they left the People who couldn't keep up."[1] Grant's ancestors—Canalla and She-towitch—belonged to both the White River and Uncompahgre Ute bands, and in 1881 they were among the Utes who were forcibly moved from western Colorado to new homes in northeastern Utah. Many of the people walked, Grant said, because there were few horses, even though these bands of Utes had once had thousands of them.[2]

Official reports of the move provide few details of the actual journey and offer only sanitized versions of what occurred. Los Pinos Indian agent W. H. Berry even claimed that the Uncompahgres were "cheerful and happy" when they left Colorado.[3] But that account doesn't jibe with reports made by military officers and others present at the time of the removal, much less the stories handed down by the Utes themselves. Grant's family history tells of people dying along the way, some even being shot by soldiers if they fell behind during the trek.

We will never know exactly what happened during the six weeks or more that it took the Uncompahgre Utes to move roughly 160 miles from Colorado to the new reservation in Utah. We do know that the family stories handed down by the Utes are far different than what white officials reported. None of the official accounts lists the deaths of any Utes on the trek, but the statistics included in the annual reports for the secretary of Interior include one hint that there may have been problems with the move. In 1878, before the events at the White River stirred up public opposition to the Indians and arguments for the forced removal of most Utes from Colorado, the population of the Uncompahgre Utes was listed as 2,000. In autumn 1881, when the trip occurred, the population was listed as 1,500. In 1882, after the trek was completed, the population was reported to be 1,400.[4]

There is no 1881 estimate of the White River Ute population in the official records of the Interior Department, but according to Josephine Meeker, there were approximately 800 White River Utes in late 1879, when the battle occurred at Milk Creek.[5] The 1878 statistics compiled by her father during his first few months as agent for the White River Indian Agency listed 890 White River Utes.[6] By 1882, after the White River Utes had been settled on the Uintah Reservation, the official report from the Interior Department listed only 541 White River Utes.[7] During the same time period, the recorded populations of the Southern and Uintah Utes remained essentially stable, declining from 934 to 925 for the Southern Utes and remaining at 430 for the Uintahs.[8]

Loya Arrum, a direct descendant of Colorow, recalled stories from her great-grandmother about women and children huddling by large rocks at night to keep warm—this from people who had lived for centuries in the Colorado mountains and were used to dealing with the cold. But as one army officer noted, they had been forced to abandon their blankets and other belongings.[9]

Francis McKinley, an Uncompahgre Ute and Navajo who was born on the Uintah Reservation in 1920, described the journey as similar to the terrible treks that other tribes had been forced to make. "We've had examples of that in U.S. history, the Cherokee group, the Trail of Tears," he said in a 1988 interview. McKinley relayed stories handed down from his grandfather, Charlie Shavano, one of the leaders of the Uncompahgre Utes after Ouray died. McKinley said the Utes were "broken down, spiritually, emotionally and everything else."[10]

One group of Utes moving to the Utah reservation took pains to keep an injured infant hidden from whites who may have been following them. "My mother was small," recounted Uncompahgre Ute Marietta Reed in a 1969 interview. "She was just a baby in a cradle.… My grandmother had threw her into a dried up beaver pond. And at that time, the little ones knew when they were bleeding that they couldn't cry or anything. They were taught this when they were young." A day later, perhaps two, "when they got to a safe place and my grandmother…my great-grandmother had told my grandmother…to go back and get the baby. So when she went back, the baby was safe and nothing had harmed her or anything."[11]

The legislative seeds of the Ute exodus were sown in 1880. It took time, however, for those efforts to culminate with action in Colorado. Until that occurred, the army was charged with keeping the peace between the Utes and whites on both the Los Pinos (Uncompahgre) Reservation and at the White River. Colonel Wesley Merritt's troops and their replacements remained on the White River to keep the peace, although Merritt relinquished command and returned to his post in Wyoming. Secretary of Interior Carl Schurz requested that troops also be sent to the Uncompahgre Valley, ostensibly to protect the Utes from white interlopers.[12] But that was not how the assignment was viewed by the soldiers involved. One young officer who went to the Uncompahgre Valley in the summer of 1880 recorded that the "Indians angrily opposed" the pending move to Utah. "A bloody fight was expected," recalled James Parker, then a first lieutenant with the Fourth Cavalry under Colonel Ranald Mackenzie.[13]

Parker's belief that the Utes were spoiling for a fight is backed up by Francis McKinley. "Many of them didn't want to come. Many of them were depressed, anxious, frustrated, maybe even asking for some more violent action.…They weren't in a peaceful mood."[14] When he arrived in the Uncompahgre Valley, Parker found the attitude of the Utes toward the troops "sullen, but not hostile." He added, "They were a fine-looking tribe, rich in herds of horses, cattle and sheep, well provided with property, many richly clad in garments lined with the fur of the beaver and other animals, and armed to the teeth. It was easy to see they would make dangerous fighters."[15]

The troops knew that Schurz's specially appointed Ute Commission was negotiating with the Utes for their removal. But Parker said, "Of the progress of the negotiations we knew nothing and we were rarely brought into contact with the Indians." He recalled only one potentially dangerous confrontation with a Ute during that summer of 1880, and he dismissed its importance. "I could even say we never heard a hostile shot, if one day, returning from a hunting expedition, I had not heard a bullet whiz by me. Looking around I saw that it had been fired at a very long range by a small Indian boy high up on the slope of the mountain," he wrote. "The boy, in great trepidation, decamped. I did not follow him nor did I think it worth while to report the incident."[16]

By October 1880, Parker's cavalry unit was no longer needed in the Uncompahgre Valley, although an infantry detachment remained. He and his troops returned to Fort Garland, near Alamosa, Colorado, and then moved on to Fort Riley, Kansas, where they spent the winter. But by May of the following year, they were on their way back to Colorado and the Uncompahgre Valley, where the situation was even more tense than the year before. One reason was that Otto Mears and others had worked hard to ensure that none of the Uncompahgre Utes would remain in Colorado. Mears and two other members of Schurz's Ute Commission, Judge Thomas McMorris and J. J. Russell, were assigned to scout the area around the confluence of the Grand and Gunnison rivers—the site of the present-day city of Grand Junction. They were to determine if it would be suitable as a new reservation for the Uncompahgre Utes in Colorado, one much smaller in size than their existing home.

Mears, McMorris, and Russell, accompanied by a cavalry escort and two Uncompahgre Ute leaders, Sapivanero and Guero, along with Los Pinos agent W. H. Berry, made the trip to the Grand and Gunnison region in June of 1881. "We examined the land on the Grand River near the mouth of the Gunnison and found it to be, in our opinion, unsuitable for the Indians for agricultural or grazing purposes," the three reported to George Manypenny, the chairman of their commission. It would take irrigation to grow anything, they said, and canals would be difficult to construct. Also, there wasn't sufficient land suitable for grazing the Ute livestock. The Utes who accompanied them supposedly agreed wholeheartedly.[17]

Their assessment of the land's agricultural potential was wildly off the mark, however. Within a little more than a decade after the Utes were forced to leave, white settlers had constructed miles of irrigation ditches and turned the area into one of the most promising agricultural regions in the state.[18] But that probably was the idea all along, as one of Mears's literary boosters made evident. "Mr. Mears and Judge McMorris being Colorado men, with Mr. Russell coinciding, they made up their minds that the Indians had to go," wrote Sidney Jocknick, a one-time Los Pinos Agency employee and a friend of Mears's. "They at once saw that, for the benefit of the state, it would be better to keep the Indians somewhere else, and out of Colorado, as the land on the Uncompahgre and at Grand Junction would become very valuable if settled by the whites."[19]

Having found the lands of the Grand-Gunnison region wanting, Mears and his companions headed north and west into Utah, to the confluence of the Green and White rivers. There they found land that they decided was far more suitable for the Uncompahgre Utes. "Along the Green River there is an abundance of…timber for the wants of the Indians for fencing and fire-wood," Mears and fellow commission members reported. "The bottom lands are rich and can be easily irrigated and made available by inexperienced men."[20] The commission members claimed that the only reason this supposed paradise hadn't been already populated, either by Indians or whites, was that it was situated along the trail that connected the old White River Ute Agency and the Uintah Reservation. There was "danger in living between these two bands of Indians and along their trail from one agency to the other," the commissioners reported.[21]

Mears and his companions did acknowledge concern about there being suitable pasture there for Ute livestock, but they suggested some arrangement could be made to pasture the animals on lands along the White River, not actually on the proposed reservation. Regardless, they, like Nathan Meeker, believed the Utes had far too many horses—ten times as many as they needed, the commissioners claimed—and the smaller amount of pasture would force them to get rid of most of their ponies.[22]

The new reservation never would develop anything close to the agricultural capacity of the Grand Valley, which includes Grand Junction. But when Mears and his fellow commission members hustled back to Colorado and informed Colonel Mackenzie that they had found a much better place for the Utes, few people disputed them.

One who did was George Manypenny, the chairman of the Ute Commission and the same man who had forced Mears to go to Washington to answer bribery charges in 1880. The proposed new reservation was nearly 150 miles north and east of the Grand and Gunnison country, which violated the terms of the 1880 agreement, Manypenny argued. But Mears noted that language added to the agreement by Congress said land for the reservation must be at the confluence of the Grand and Gunnison rivers or *adjacent* territory. "As Utah was then a territory, [and] it was self-evident

that it was adjacent, consequently in an equivocal sense, the commissioners obeyed *the letter* of the law," Mears's friend Sidney Jocknick wrote years
later.²³

Not surprisingly, since he had the support of Pitkin, Teller, and other
leading Colorado citizens, Mears's parsing of the 1880 agreement prevailed. As Mackenzie and his troops prepared to move the Uncompahgre
Utes to Utah, Mears hurried to make the arrangements he had proposed.
According to Jocknick,

> [He] proceeded at once to Denver and from there to Salt Lake, so that he
> would arrive at the place selected for an agency before the Indians could get
> there overland, and also have the necessary provisions and temporary ac-
> commodations ready for the use of the agent, William H. Berry, as soon as
> he should arrive. For a distance of 150 miles between Heber City and Green
> River, Mears found no settlement. He immediately contracted for buildings
> and mill work, the specifications for which, on Berry's arrival, were turned
> over to him.²⁴

There is some independent indication that the Uncompahgre Utes
were not thrilled about the prospect of moving to the confluence of the
Grand and Gunnison rivers in Colorado, nor about moving to Utah. One
man who traveled among the Utes that summer, Arvis Gilson, wrote a letter to Colonel Mackenzie on June 21, 1881, informing the military commander that he had recently visited with "various Utes" in the area around
the San Miguel River, west of the Uncompahgre Valley but still considered Uncompahgre Ute territory. "All say they would rather die than go to
the Grand River country because it is worthless."²⁵

And there is no question that the Utes opposed the idea of leaving
Colorado for the desolate canyons of east-central Utah. The same Arvis
Gilson sent a second letter to Mackenzie on July 25, 1881, this time from
the Uncompahgres' main camp. He said the Utes were worried because
they didn't know what they would do with their thousands of head of cattle, sheep, goats, and horses if they were forced to move to Utah. "They say
it's impossible to find unoccupied country west of here and northwest of
the Grand River with sufficient grass to keep one tenth of their sheep, not
speaking of their other stock."²⁶

Others also told of the Utes' fears and anger at the proposed move. "In
very truth, they did not take to the prospect of being exiled from the valleys

of their forefathers, either pleasantly or seriously," Jocknick wrote, "for they made all kinds of excuses against it, professing injured pride because they could not remain where their forefathers were buried, and contumaciously pleaded for more time in which to gather up their stock."[27]

James Parker, the young lieutenant who served with Mackenzie, recalled a more nail-biting scene in the late summer of 1881. "All was excitement on the Uncompahgre; the Indians, some two thousand in number, were evidently preparing for a fight and had intrenched [*sic*] themselves on the summit of a lofty mountain, where they evidently proposed to defend their wives and children while the main force raided the settlements."[28]

Mackenzie, who by that time had left Fort Garland to attend to the Ute situation in person, had traded a series of telegrams with Secretary of Interior Samuel J. Kirkwood and Secretary of War Robert Lincoln, informing them that the situation was getting dire, and that it was necessary to get the Utes moved to the new reservation before winter or they would likely lose many of their sheep and goats, which they depended on for subsistence. He received authority to use force if necessary to get the Utes on the trail to Utah.[29]

Up on the White River, things appeared to be going more smoothly. On June 18, 1881, Colonel A. B. Meacham (a member of the Ute Commission with Otto Mears, George Manypenny, and the others), wrote to Assistant Secretary of Interior A. Dill to inform him that "All White River cattle will go to Uintah," and that agreement appeared "to remove all obstacles to the peaceful removal of the White River Band to the Uintah Agency."[30] A letter from the White River military headquarters to General John Pope on June 23 reported, "The White River Utes are coming into camp in squads of about 40. Col. Meacham says he is certain they will go to the reservation and there will be no trouble."[31]

On June 27, Major Orlando H. Moore, stationed at the White River with the Sixth Infantry, said in a letter to the army's Department of the Missouri headquarters that members of the White River band had accepted the terms of the agreement "and don't appear to be hostile." But Moore also offered an unhappy appraisal of the White River Utes' situation. They would comply with the terms of the agreement, he said, "more as a heartbroken people than a band of warriors."[32]

In an August 20 letter to Secretary of War Robert Lincoln, Secretary of Interior Kirkwood told of reports from the Uintah Indian Agency that said some White River Utes had already arrived at that post.[33] Back in the

Uncompahgre Valley, Colonel Mackenzie was nearly ready to move the Utes from that area to the new reservation at the Green and White rivers in Utah. In an August 28 telegram to army headquarters, the colonel reported that after consultation with the Ute leaders, they had finally agreed to move to the new agency peaceably.[34]

The move did not occur, however, until after one final confrontation in which Mackenzie's resolute manner overcame the Utes' reticence. Both Sidney Jocknick and James Parker were in the area when that confrontation occurred, and both describe it in their books, but in very different terms. "There was trouble brewing, but Mackenzie was ready for it when the psychological moment arrived," Jocknick wrote. Mackenzie's troops set off rockets as signals, sounded bugles, and deployed quickly into battle formation.

> Not a ripple of excitement was there to mar the perfect line of front that now faced the enemy, who presently came into view around a bend of the river, yelling like so many demons let loose, and riding cowboy fashion, all in a bunch. Evidently the sight that now met their gaze was their first intimation of the military reception that was awaiting them. Its effect was instantaneous, for they at once slackened their mad ride and came to a halt to engage in a parley among themselves. Then, in no longer time than it takes to tell it, they sized up the situation and decided that they wanted no more of "war's grim-visaged front" in theirs, so they quickly turned "about face" and beat a hasty and ignominious retreat back to camp.[35]

Parker recorded a less dramatic, but nonetheless tense, encounter. Mackenzie, after receiving authorization from Washington to use force if necessary, quickly deployed "about ten companies of infantry and cavalry, some 300 to 400 men" into battle formations, Parker said. "This done, Mackenzie sent word to the chiefs to come in for a conference."

> It took place the following morning [August 28]. Mackenzie informed the chiefs that the matter had been turned over to him for settlement; they had promised to move to Utah, and he wished to know whether or not they were going. Somewhat daunted by his cool, determined manner, the leading chief commenced an oration in which he denounced the whites for wanting to deprive the Indians of their land, and was proceeding to more violent expressions when Mackenzie, with his hat in his hand stood up.

"It is not necessary for me to stay here any longer," he said. "You can settle this matter by discussion among yourselves. All I want to know is whether you will go or not. If you will not go of your own accord, I will make you go. When you have sufficiently discussed this matter and have arrived at a conclusion, send for me. Remember, you are to go, at once."

The Indians were full of consternation. They expected a long parley, lasting weeks. In the meantime, they would have time to finish their preparations, which were not nearly complete, should the war become necessary. And they had thought the white man was afraid.

After a debate lasting several hours, they sent for Mackenzie. They proposed a compromise. They said they had concluded they must go, but first they wished to go back to their camp and talk with their old men. "No," said Mackenzie. "If you have not moved by nine o'clock tomorrow morning, I will be at your camp and *make* you move."

"The next morning, shortly after sunrise, we saw a thrilling and pitiful sight," Parker wrote.

> The whole Ute nation on horseback and on foot was streaming by. As they passed our camps their gait broke into a run. Sheep were abandoned, blankets and personal possessions strewn along the road, women and children were loudly wailing. Poor things! They were leaving the land which had been theirs for centuries, their home, their country, for an unknown destination hundreds of miles away.[36]

That's a far cry from the "cheerful and happy" mood described by Los Pinos agent W. H. Berry, but Parker's account is backed up by General John Pope, who wasn't present for the removal but received reports from Mackenzie. He recorded that following their confrontation with Mackenzie, the Uncompahgre Utes had finally agreed to leave Colorado, "manifesting the greatest grief and regret."[37]

As the army pushed the Utes westward toward the new reservation in Utah, impatient white settlers "hurried after us," Parker said, "taking up the land and at once commencing the erection of their houses. As we pushed the Indians onward, we permitted the whites to follow, and in three days the rich lands of the Uncompahgre were all occupied, towns were being laid out and lots being sold at high prices."

Parker would not accompany the Utes very far on their trek. A new Indian crisis had developed with the Apaches in Arizona, and Parker and his Fourth Cavalry Unit had been called up. They left the Uncompahgre country on September 5, headed for Fort Apache, Arizona.[38] Sidney Jocknick did not accompany the Utes to Utah either. He gave only a brief, matter-of-fact report of their trip. "September 1st 1881 was the date when the last band (Colorow's) left Colorado, and September 13th that of their arrival at their destination."[39]

It is clear, however, that the Utes did not make the 160-mile trip nearly as quickly as Jocknick claimed. An October 3 telegram from General George Crook to the army's Department of the Missouri headquarters reported that "no Ute Indians have arrived yet at the junction of the Green and White Rivers" where the Uncompahgre Utes' new home was to be.[40] In fact, it appears that the army officially lost track of the Utes for a brief time. General Pope, in his annual report dated September 22, 1881, said, "The last [we] heard of the Indians, they were far down on the Grand River, moving quietly along the north side of the river to Utah."[41]

In November, Otto Mears and his fellow members of the Ute Commission reported that most of the Uncompahgre Utes had not arrived at the new reservation on the Green and White rivers until late October. But that delay had nothing to do with difficulties or deprivation for the Utes, they assured commission chairman George Manypenny. "Finally, on the 28th [of August] they all started, and by slow and easy marches, some of them reached Green River on the 25th of September; others lingered along, hunting in the mountains, and did not arrive until late October," Mears, McMorris, and Russell said.[42]

In addition to the hardships of the trail and the fear of violence from soldiers or white settlers, "there must have been a lot of internal strife and a lot of probably, disagreement within," said Shavano's grandson Francis McKinley. Shavano "was doing what he had been directed to do by the Federal Government. He was told to move his people to this reservation. He was strong willed and very authoritarian. He wanted the people to do what he said. Because that was the only security that they had. If they violated that then they were gone, dispersed."[43]

While the Uncompahgres were being marched from Colorado to their new reservation in Utah, things were not going as smoothly as officials had hoped up north on the White River. On September 18, Colonel L. C. Hunt

sent a letter to his superiors from the army's camp there saying there had
been reports of White River Utes who had earlier moved to Utah now
returning to Colorado. "This was confirmed by the arrival at the trader's
store of two small parties led by 'Waste' [possibly Washington, who was
sometimes called "Wass"] and 'Jack' [Nicaagat] separately," Colonel Hunt
wrote. "Jack, when questioned was noncommittal about how many were
expected to return to the White River. It's impossible to prevent."[44]

One reason for their return may have been tension with the Uintah
Utes, who had lived on the reservation in northeastern Utah since Abraham Lincoln had been president, and were suddenly being asked to make
room for more than 500 White River Utes. Worse, the White River Utes
were to receive more money, as a result of the 1880 agreement, than the
Uintah Utes received in annual payments from the government. The White
River Utes made fun of their Uintah cousins for farming and trying to survive on their own, said Uintah agent J. J. Critchlow. They suggested that the
Uintah Utes go to war against the white people, as the White River Utes
had, in order to get more in government assistance.[45]

The situation on the White River was made more worrisome a few
days after Colonel Hunt wrote his letter, when it was reported that two settlers had been killed by Utes about 40 miles downstream from the site of
the White River Agency. The two settlers, named Malloney and Lee, had
reportedly been there since 1880, before the reservation had been legally
opened, and there was concern that the Indians were retaliating for their
illegal intrusion. But, as with much of the violence for which the Utes had
been blamed, this turned out not to be the Utes' fault. On October 13, 1881,
a letter from General Pope to the adjutant general of the army in Chicago
explained that a Lieutenant Porter had investigated the incident. He determined "that Malloney was killed not by Indians on White River—but most
probably by his partner, Lee, who has fled the country."[46]

By November 12, tension on the White River appeared to be dimin-
ishing. A military officer there "had council with White River Utes led by
Colorow and Jack [Nicaagat] and they agreed to return to Uintah in 20
days—after their annual hunt," said a letter sent from the army camp on
the White River. The officer who met with the Ute leaders was confident
they would fulfill their promise because "they are peaceably disposed."[47]

But Nicaagat would never make the Uintah Reservation his permanent
home. In a few months he and Colorow would be the subject of nervous
missives sent out by Indian agents, and they would be sought by military
authorities across much of the West.

THE FINAL TRAIL
FOR NICAAGAT AND JOSEPHINE

JOSEPHINE MEEKER RETURNED TO THE SUPPOSED SAFETY OF WHITE CIVI-lization after her release from captivity with the Utes, only to face new dangers less than a month later. It was her celebrity status that nearly led to her demise. She was in great demand on the lecture circuit, and in mid-November 1879, she was scheduled to speak in Leadville, high in the mountains some 200 miles southwest of her home in Greeley, in the heart of Colorado's mining country. Because the stagecoach in which she was to travel was too crowded, she was forced to wait another day—fortunately for her. A snowstorm struck the mountains, and "the stage in which she was to have gone overturned, with fatal results to one of the passengers, and serious injuries to the others."[1]

Josie, however, refused to be deterred. Her speech was rescheduled from Friday to Saturday night, and she made the stage trip safely the fol-lowing day. Despite the continuing storm, she was greeted by a large crowd. "Notwithstanding that she was greatly fatigued by the long ride and exposure to the storm on the range, her lecture was a complete success, and the applause was frequent and prolonged. At the close, Miss Meeker was requested to give a ladies matinee the next Monday afternoon, and also to repeat it in the evening; to these requests she acceded."[2]

For a time in late 1879, Josie Meeker was the nineteenth-century equivalent of a modern-day superstar. Newspapers that had covered the events at the White River sought her out not only for her account of her captivity with the Utes, but for her opinion on how best to deal with the political issue—the Indian question.

Her book, *The Ute Massacre! Brave Miss Meeker's Captivity! Her Own Account of It*, was rapidly written with the aid of her brother Ralph and hastily published by a Philadelphia company. It gave people across the nation a firsthand account of her captivity and that of her fellow hostages, and a mostly accurate story of the people and events that played parts leading up to it.

Josie took to the lecture circuit and quickly eclipsed the popularity of her sister Rozene, who also was giving lectures about the privations and suffering that her family had endured as victims of the Utes. It probably didn't help the growing rift between the sisters that audiences seemed more eager to hear Josie's exciting but more nuanced story of her time with the Utes than Rozene's shrill tale of Ute treachery and government incompetence, and her repeated calls for killing as many Utes as possible.[3] For instance, a few days before her trip to Leadville, Josie spoke to "a crowded and enthusiastic house" in Greeley, the *Greeley Tribune* reported. "The attendance was so large that the room was filled before half-past seven o'clock, and many ladies were obliged to remain standing during the entire evening.... Her effort was so successful that a 'special' was telegraphed to the Denver papers about it, and Miss Josephine has received an offer of $200 a week to travel and speak, with all her expenses paid."[4] When Rozene Meeker spoke in the same lecture hall a few days later, the Greeley newspaper carried a lengthy story about her remarks, but said nothing about the size of her audience or the reception she received.[5]

Not long afterward, Rozene spoke in Boulder and offered "a clear and concise statement of the Indian question," according to the *Boulder Courier*. Only sixty or so people turned out for her speech, but the *Courier* said there were several reasons for that: the price for a ticket was too high, there were other activities taking place the same evening, and, most importantly, "It was the wrong lady, Miss Josephine being the one our people most desired to see."[6] When Josie appeared in Boulder a week later, the same newspaper offered a glowing account of her presentation to "a large audience." "Her lecture was a decided success, and we sincerely hope that she may find a warm reception wherever she may go."[7]

By early January 1880, Josie had departed Colorado for Washington, D.C., to take a job with the Department of the Interior that Ralph Meeker had helped arrange for her. Despite all the commotion in the nation's capital that winter and spring, Josephine still garnered her share of publicity. When she testified before the House committee investigating the Ute uprising, and when she met with the Utes who had traveled to Washington, she attracted news coverage in Colorado—some of it not very flattering.[8]

Stardom is fleeting, though, and by mid-1880 Josie Meeker was no longer a popular subject for news stories. She worked quietly at her job in Washington, taught Sunday school at a church for African Americans, and teamed with her brother to try to get money from the government for her family. She also spearheaded another effort to provoke government action to get her father's remains moved from the White River, where he had been temporarily buried in October 1879, to the family plot in Greeley. That was accomplished, due largely to her letter-writing campaign, in September 1880. That month Josie and Ralph made the trip to Colorado for their father's reburial and funeral, which was attended by residents of the community that Nathan Meeker had founded a decade earlier.[9]

With that accomplished, Josie achieved something like normalcy in her life. She returned to work in Washington, D.C., and continued teaching at the Lincoln Mission Sunday School.[10] She occasionally took trips to the country to relax, but rejected Ralph's invitation to visit him in New York.[11] She wrote long, somewhat melancholy letters to her younger sister, Mary, still in Greeley.[12] And she seems to have acquired at least one secret, romantic admirer. A letter sent to her in Greeley on February 13, 1882, and forwarded to Washington, D.C., addressed her as "True Love," and said "My true heart is all thine own!"[13]

Nicaagat's life, meanwhile, was anything but normal, even compared to the lives of other Ute leaders who had made the trek to Utah at the army's insistence. Authorities in late 1881 may have been convinced he was "peaceably disposed" and was ready to move to the Uintah Reservation without problem (see chapter 21), but a few months later there was an entirely different official view.

In a letter dated February 17, 1882, Secretary of Interior Samuel J. Kirkwood informed Secretary of War Robert Lincoln that problems were
developing among "certain Utes belonging to the bands of Jack [Nicaagat]
and Colorow." Kirkwood said he had received information that the two
leaders and their followers might be anywhere from Texas to Fort Sill (in
Indian Territory, in what is now Oklahoma). According to information
that Uncompahgre Ute agent W. H. Berry had received, the pair were
going to join the Comanches in that area to start trouble. Kirkwood asked
Lincoln to instruct anyone who encountered Nicaagat, Colorow, "Unca"
Sam, "and any Utes with them" to arrest them on the spot.[14]

J. J. Critchlow, the agent at the Uintah Reservation where the absent
White River Utes were supposed to be residing, said he had no definitive
information about the movements of either Nicaagat or Colorow. But, he
said, they had refused to come into the reservation headquarters for the
distribution of annuity payments, and the last time they were seen they
were "reportedly drunk and defiant."[15]

They may have been defiant, but it is almost certain that Colorow,
Nicaagat, and their supporters did not go to Texas or the Indian Territory
in Oklahoma. Nicaagat, at least, went to Wyoming, to the Wind River
Reservation, home of the Shoshones. The Utes and Shoshones had long
been friendly and shared similar languages, and there are indications that
Nicaagat's wife was a Shoshone.[16]

By mid-March 1882, the army knew Nicaagat was on the Shoshone
reservation and was wondering what to do about him. "Jack [Nicaagat],
chief of the White River Utes…is among the Shoshones near Fort
Washaki on the Wind River Reservation," General Phil Sheridan said in a
March 18 telegram to the adjutant general of the army. "He was ordered
arrested if found in Indian Territory [Oklahoma]. Shall I arrest him for
being where he is? There are three other Utes with him."[17]

Later accounts would claim that Nicaagat was wanted for stealing
horses or other crimes,[18] but there is no evidence in the official record that
this was the case. He was to be arrested simply because he was not where
authorities with the army and Department of Indian Affairs wanted him
to be. On March 31, Secretary of Interior Kirkwood sent another letter to
Secretary of War Lincoln, this time officially requesting the arrest of "Jack
[Nicaagat], Colorow, Unca Sam," and other Utes who might be found at
Fort Washakie.[19]

Before that arrest could occur, however, Colorow made his way back to Utah. In late April 1882, he met with W. H. Berry, agent for the Uncompahgres on their new reservation south of the Uintah Reservation. Colorow promised to bring his band there, Berry said in an April 26 letter to the commander of the army's new Fort Thornburgh, just outside the Uncompahgres' Utah reservation.[20]

If Nicaagat had considered returning to the Utah reservation, he waited too long. On April 29, a small detachment of soldiers from Fort Washakie approached a house where he was reportedly staying on the Shoshone reservation. (Here's more evidence of Nicaagat's English skills: When the soldiers called for Captain Jack, "Jack replied in very good English, 'What do you want?'" according to the report of Lieutenant George Morgan.)[21]

Nicaagat chose not to surrender peacefully. General Sheridan described the resulting confrontation in a May 1, 1882, telegram to General R. C. Drum in Washington, D.C.: "Captain Jack of the White River Utes, so notorious in the Thornburgh massacre, was arrested at the Shoshone Agency April 29. Shortly after his arrest he made his escape to a neighboring teepee, where he obtained a carbine and ammunition and instantly killed Sgt. Richard Casey. A mountain howitzer was then procured and fired into the teepee, killing Captain Jack."[22]

That was the unfortunate end for the man who had tried so hard to convince authorities that Nathan Meeker was the cause of problems at the White River Indian Agency, who had attempted to negotiate with Major Thomas T. Thornburgh to prevent violence at Milk Creek, and who had been determined by the White River Ute Commission not to have committed any crime in the battle with Thornburgh. This was the Ute leader who had worked with Charles Adams and others to try to arrange the surrender of the Utes accused of killing Meeker and his employees, and who had traveled repeatedly to Washington, Denver, and other centers of white civilization to prevent violence.

Nicaagat was blown to bits by the small cannon aimed specifically at him—an ignominious end for someone who deserves to be among the pantheon of American Indian leaders, a courageous and independent man who had tried hard to work with whites and to accept their word, but a man who, in the end, decided he would live—and die—where he chose, not where the whites told him he must.

Nicaagat's demise was fodder for only small news stories in national and Colorado newspapers, with much of the focus on whether his death would cause other Utes to again go to war against the whites.[23] Josie Meeker surely must have heard of the killing of the man who had been both her antagonist and friend, but if she mentioned it to anyone, her comments don't appear to have survived.

For eight months following Nicaagat's death, Josie apparently continued working at her job in Washington, D.C. However, the same month that Nicaagat died, Secretary of Interior Samuel Kirkwood resigned and was replaced by none other than Colorado's own Senator Henry Teller.[24] By then Josie was disenchanted with her life in the city, missing the Rocky Mountains and her sister Mary. "I would a good deal rather stay out here in the country," she told Mary in a letter she wrote while vacationing outside of Washington in July of 1881. "I wish I could spend my vacatin [sic] with you this year, then we could lie on the bed and talk about things, couldn't we, would my little birdie like that? I am sure that I should."[25]

At the end of 1882, Josie's health suddenly deteriorated. She contracted pneumonia and struggled for more than a week to recuperate. She appeared to be doing so but then suffered a relapse. She died on December 30, 1882, at the age of twenty-six.[26] The newspapers, especially those in Colorado, paid far more attention to her death than they did to Nicaagat's. "The remains of Miss Josephine Meeker, who died at Washington, D.C. last Saturday of pneumonia arrived in Greeley Thursday. She held a position in Secretary Teller's office," wrote the *Gunnison Daily Review* on January 6, 1883.[27]

Her hometown newspaper, the *Greeley Tribune*, carried a notice of Josie's death on December 30. It published an obituary on January 3, 1883, and a news story on the funeral held in Greeley, followed by a January 17 tribute to the young woman written by the Lincoln Mission School in Washington, D.C., where she had taught for three years.[28] One former student, Albert J. Bailess of Washington, D.C., sent a letter to her a day too late—December 31, 1882—saying he was very sorry to hear that she was sick.[29]

The January 10 edition of the *Greeley Tribune* that reported on her funeral also told how Josie had become sick on December 21, when the weather had turned bad in Washington, and that she had wanted to return to Colorado. "Her ambition was to get money enough to buy a farm in Colorado, live on it, and invest her earnings in Colorado," reported the newspaper once run by her father. "The wicked and false statements in some of the newspapers that she suffered from poverty in Washington are simply malicious and slanderous. Miss Meeker received a pension of $500 a year and a salary of $18 a week."[30]

Pneumonia contracted in a cold and rainy Washington winter was the immediate cause listed in newspaper reports of Josie's death. But, at that time, pneumonia was frequently listed as the cause of death for any number of ailments. Josie's mother, Arvilla Meeker, suggested another, underlying cause of her daughter's demise. In a letter she wrote in 1903 to the author of a book about the founding of Greeley, Arvilla, then eighty-eight, noted that Josie had shared "all our trials" on the hostage trail "with such courage." But, she added, Josie "died in her earliest youth from the suffering that proved too heavy for her to bear."[31]

A Washington publication carried a far more scandalous suggestion for the cause of her death—an unnamed sexually transmitted disease—tied to her time as a hostage. The *National Republican* story was reprinted in the *Rocky Mountain Daily News* on January 7, 1883. "The whole story of what was done then never has been and never can be told," the article said. "It comes back now, brought up by this last result of it, with a pity and terror in it none the less vivid by reason of the time that has intervened."

The daughter of Nathan Meeker, who had accompanied him to the White River Indian Agency, "was carried off by the Indians, and for weeks, that must have been ages of despair, she was kept a captive among them, subject to treatment brutal beyond all thought, much less all naming," the article continued. "When at last she got away her health, which never had been sound, was hopelessly broken and burdened with infections from which there could be no escape short of the grave." Lest there were any doubt about the nature of her affliction, the article noted that "rich and comfortable ladies" of Washington, who at first befriended the young woman, "dropped her as soon as they learned the nature of the troubles she had known among her captors."[32] However, since the article referred to Josie as "Anna Meeker," and got several critical facts about her life and circumstances wrong, it's difficult to put too much store in this account.[33]

Little wonder that both the *Greeley Tribune* and the *Denver Tribune* condemned this story circulating in other newspapers. "The people of Greeley are justly indignant over the slanderous article published by a Washington paper about the late Josephine Meeker," the *Denver Tribune* wrote.

Several Colorado papers reproduced the article and failed to deny its import when its falsity was made known. The poor girl suffered beyond description while a prisoner among the White River Utes, and the sensational attempt to cast a stain upon her name and a reproach upon her character by reason of that misfortune is considered by her friends as among the most heartless and ghoulish deeds of the century.[34]

Such sensationalism was a shabby way to treat the memory of a young woman who had suffered the loss of her father at the White River, had been personally victimized by the events there, and had worked to protect her mother and the other hostages during their nearly three weeks of captivity. Despite all that had happened to her, however, she never displayed the bitter hatred toward the Utes that her sister and many others in Colorado did. And she never abandoned her determination to live as an independent career woman. Even so, Josie Meeker—like Nicaagat—was dead barely three years after the tragic events of September 29, 1879, in which they were both so deeply involved.

EPILOGUE

Even before Josephine Meeker and Nicaagat died in 1882, the appetite of whites in Colorado for vengeance toward the Utes involved in the killings at the White River Indian Agency in 1879 seems to have evaporated. Seeing the Utes removed from Colorado had become far more critical than individual justice.

Among its other responsibilities, the five-member White River Ute Commission, appointed by Secretary of Interior Carl Schurz in 1880, had been assigned to find and apprehend the nine remaining Utes accused of killing Nathan Meeker and his employees. (Three were in federal prison by February 1880.) But the commission apparently paid only cursory attention to that part of its duties. In its final report, issued in January 1881, the commission explained that there was little point in looking for the accused, based on what Nicaagat told them. Commission member A. B. Meacham said he spoke with Nicaagat during the summer of 1880 and learned that of the nine accused Utes still at large, "some were dead. Some had fled to Sitting Bull [with the Sioux in the Dakotas]. All had severed their connections with the tribe."[1]

That wasn't strictly true, however. One of the nine—Canalla, also known as Johnson 2—seems to have been hiding in plain sight. He signed the agreement in July 1880 in which the Utes ceded most of their land in Colorado to the U.S. government. Obtaining Ute signatures on that document was the Ute Commission's primary responsibility.[2] But shortly after signing the agreement, Canalla disappeared. There are few mentions of him again in the books or official records. Canalla's descendants believe he may have been killed by other Utes, perhaps at Ouray's direction. (Ouray died in August 1880.) Other Utes may have held Canalla responsible for bringing army troops to the White River in 1879, and all of the subsequent troubles that had befallen them, because he had shoved Nathan Meeker in early September 1879.[3]

Canalla's wife, She-towitch, survived the events of 1879–81. Known to the whites as "Susan," she lived a long life on the new reservation in Utah. According to her family, she lived to be more than a hundred.[4]

The son of Canalla and She-towitch, Tim Johnson, also lived well into the twentieth century, dying in 1935 at the age of seventy-six.[5] Along with his father, Tim Johnson was among the dozen Utes accused of the killings at the White River Agency. Unlike his father and most of the others accused, however, he was actually imprisoned for his part in the crime. Tim Johnson surrendered to Nicaagat in February 1880 and traveled to Washington, D.C., with Nicaagat, Charles Adams, and Otto Mears that same month. He was initially incarcerated at Fort Monroe, Virginia, along with Thomas, another Ute accused in the killings.[6] He may have been transferred to Fort Leavenworth some time later. In any event, he was released and returned to his family on the Uintah Reservation approximately two years after his imprisonment.[7]

What happened to Thomas, the Ute imprisoned with Tim Johnson, is unclear, but the fate of a third accused Ute is known, that of Quinkent (Douglas), the aging leader of one contingent of the White River Utes—and the man who had kept Arvilla Meeker with him during most of her time on the hostage trail. In February 1880 he also accompanied Nicaagat, Charles Adams, and Otto Mears on their trip back to Washington, D.C., but he only made it as far as Fort Leavenworth, where Adams decided to have him incarcerated. He escaped from prison a few weeks later but was recaptured in a matter of hours.[8]

By late 1880, Quinkent was a figure of pity. The Ute Commission concluded he wasn't guilty of any of the crimes for which he was accused and urged his speedy release from prison. That appeal may have brought a response. He was released from prison in early 1881 and returned to Colorado under strict secrecy because government officials feared there might be an attempt to kill him.[9]

But life on the new reservation in Utah was not the freedom the old Ute leader desired. He became morose, according to some reports, and drank heavily. In August 1884, when a group of Utes returned to the White River to race horses and trade with the white settlers who now inhabited the area, Quinkent became convinced that one white man had stolen money from him. He made plans to kill the offender, but as he waited to ambush him, a young Ute who'd had his own run-ins with Quinkent shot and killed the aging Ute leader instead. His body was hidden in a remote canyon.[10]

Colorow, the leader with Nicaagat in the battle with Thornburgh's troops at Milk Creek, did return to the Utah reservation, as he promised, in 1882. But like other Utes, he grew restless there. Several years later he was back in Colorado, and a confrontation between his band of Utes and some whites in the new town of Meeker over gambling debts and allegations of stolen horses erupted in gunfire when a sheriff and posse showed up. The brief conflict that followed became known as Colorow's War.

"September, 1884, a band of White River Utes, led by Colorow, caused trouble while on a hunt in the lower Snake River country," wrote one man who was in the region at the time. "A number of settlers undertook to drive them out. One Indian was killed during the fracas. The Utes fled toward their reservation. Soldiers from Fort Duchesne were called to gather in scattered hunting bands....Colorow died of old age in 1908." His descendants are unsure where he is buried.[11]

Pahsone, Josie Meeker's captor and would-be husband, seems to have disappeared after the women were released from captivity. He was among the accused Utes who never surrendered and were never captured. His name does not appear on any of the lists of those who signed the 1880 agreement with the federal government. He may have fled to another area, to the Shoshones in Wyoming, or to other friendly American Indian tribes. Or, as Canalla's family believes, Pahsone may have faced the wrath of other Utes who held him partially responsible for the events that transpired after the killings at the White River Agency.

Arvilla Meeker, already considered old and somewhat infirm when the White River killings and kidnappings occurred, proved more resilient than her daughter. She wrote letters to her remaining children on her eighty-second birthday in 1897, and to an author in 1903. She died in 1905 in White Plains, New York, where she had gone to live with her son, Ralph.[12]

Ralph Meeker was married but had no children. He died in 1921 in Greeley after visiting the town of Meeker and the White River area where his father had once been the Indian agent. His sister Rozene Meeker died in Greeley in 1935.[13]

Flora Ellen Price, whose real name was Sophronia, also lived a long life, dying in Tulare, California, in 1927. After she and the other captives were released, she returned to Greeley, but soon thereafter moved to Kittitas County, Washington. She eventually married a man named Weaver and, later still, John Henry Ramm. Between 1900 and 1910 she moved to California.[14]

Price's two young children who accompanied her on the hostage trail also survived the ordeal and lived into adulthood. May, whose full name was Florence May Price, was married several times, including to Henry Reed. She lived mostly in Washington and California.[15]

As for John Price, Flora Ellen's son, little is known. "I don't think he ever married," said Thomas Reed, Flora Ellen's great-grandson. "He stayed in Washington. We never heard much about him."[16] A family photograph taken in 1919 in California shows Sophronia (Flora Ellen) and her husband, John Henry Ramm, surrounded by various children and grandchildren, including Florence May Reed and her husband, Henry, as well as a daughter of Flora Ellen through her marriage to a man named Weaver. Johnny Price is not pictured or mentioned.[17]

Charles Adams—the man who arranged the release of the hostages and played a critical part in the two investigations into the White River events of 1879—came to his own unexpected end a few years later. Although he was given a State Department appointment to Bolivia in reward for his service in the White River events, Adams was back in Denver in 1895. He was one of at least twenty people killed when a steam boiler exploded at a hotel in the city.[18]

Frederick Pitkin served as governor of Colorado until 1883, a term marked by the Ute uprising, a violent miners' strike in Leadville, and a war between competing railroads. When a vacancy occurred in the U.S. Senate, Pitkin ran for the seat but lost by two votes. He moved to Pueblo and opened a law practice, but died there on December 18, 1886, at the age of forty-nine. He had long suffered from chronic illness, believed to be tuberculosis, which had forced him to visit sanatoriums in Europe before he moved to Colorado in 1872, where his health had temporarily improved.[19]

Following his service as secretary of the Interior Department, Henry Teller was re-elected in 1885 to the U.S. Senate, where he would continue to serve until 1909. He switched parties, however, becoming a Democrat in 1903. He sponsored legislation that created the Teller Indian School in Grand Junction, Colorado, which was later turned over to the state and became a home for the mentally disabled, now known as the Grand Junction Regional Center. He died in Denver on February 23, 1914, at the age of eighty-four.[20]

That briefly explains what happened to some of the people most deeply involved in the events related in this book. But it is in no way the end of the story.

Loya Arrum, a descendant of Colorow, gave an impassioned speech about the Utes and their relationship with whites during a gathering in Meeker, Colorado, in July 2007. It was a meeting laying the groundwork for the first Smoking River Pow Wow and the official visit of many White River Utes to the area where their ancestors had once lived—where the events of 1879 had led to their eventual removal. At the meeting Arrum noted how the Utes are often viewed in the twenty-first century. "Too many whites think of the Utes in the past tense," she told the crowd of mostly Caucasian Colorado residents that morning. "They think when we left Colorado we disappeared forever and that's not true. We're very much alive today."

She was right. It is easy to lapse into a mental picture of the Utes of 130 years ago, but they remain a vibrant people, dealing with the events of modern-day life. Much has happened to them since they were forced from Colorado in 1881. There have been more confrontations with whites, such as the events called Colorow's War. There have been new government demands, such as the update of the Allotment Act in 1906 that allowed still more white incursions onto what had been dedicated as Ute lands. And there was Teddy Roosevelt's creation of the Ashley National Forest, which took nearly half of the Ute reservation in Utah away from them.

In 1906, more than 380 Utes decided they'd had enough of Utah and began a trek to South Dakota, where they hoped to live with the Sioux Indians. They stayed there for two years, until most of them agreed to return to Utah and were carted back in government wagons.[21] In September and October 2008, representatives of both the Sioux and Ute tribes commemorated the centennial of those events with ceremonies in South Dakota and Utah.

There have been other legal and political battles through the many years since 1881, including recent legal efforts to assert some of the Utes' rights—including hunting rights in the Colorado mountains—that were granted to them under the Brunot Agreement of 1874. Even so, Utes have served this country and their own people. They have joined the armed services of the United States and served honorably and heroically in World War II, Vietnam, Iraq, and other foreign conflicts. Many Utes left their reservations to obtain college educations or career experience and became successful in various endeavors. Many then returned to help their people.

The landscape over which the events in this book took place has also changed dramatically. The white settlers who moved in immediately as the Utes were being forced out turned the area from the Uncompahgre Valley to the White River into a highly productive agricultural region. But more whites continued coming, first to visit the spectacular mountains, then to live and create new businesses or search for new jobs. And the mountains contained natural resources—coal, uranium, natural gas, and oil shale—that brought still more people and changed the landscape further.

As this book was being written, most of the area traversed by the hostage trail was in the midst of a major natural gas boom. New roads, gas wells, pipelines, and other facilities were being built in the very locations that Nicaagat, Josie Meeker, Colorow, and Quinkent may once have ridden. Organizations including the U.S. Bureau of Land Management, the Colorado Historical Society, and the Dominquez Archaeological Research Group joined forces to conduct the Colorado Wickiup Project, looking for evidence of old Native American sites—primarily Ute—in the region where new gas wells were going up daily. Gas wells are also going up on parts of the Ute reservation in Utah, as well as the Southern Ute and Ute Mountain Ute reservations in southwestern Colorado. That energy development is helping to fund important tribal activities.

New efforts have been undertaken by the Rio Blanco County Historical Society in Meeker to improve a monument overlooking the site of the Milk Creek battle, and to give more recognition to the Utes who participated in that battle, as well as the U.S. soldiers. The Smoking River Pow Wow—put together jointly by the U.S. Forest Service, the Rio Blanco Historical Society, and the Ute tribe—not only welcomed Utes back to the White River area around Meeker, but to nearby Forest Service locations such as the Flat Tops Wilderness Area, once an important portion of the Utes' mountain home.

This book recounts events that occurred during an important period in Ute history. But the Ute story didn't begin there, and it most certainly does not end there. The Utes live on, proud of their ancestry and history, and important players in the modern West as well.

INTRODUCTION TO THE APPENDICES

WHILE RESEARCHING THIS PROJECT, I DISCOVERED A CONSIDERABLE amount of information related to the events recounted in this book, but not critical to the primary story. I have included much of that material in the following appendices.

For example, it is interesting that members of the Church of Jesus Christ of Latter-day Saints—the Mormons—were suspected of fomenting the conflict at the White River, but there is no evidence that occurred. Consequently, it was a side issue, and is listed in the appendix to chapter 9.

Information on how many people fought at Milk Creek and what happened to the Utes' horses following their forced removal to Utah is more germane to the primary story. I have included those accounts in appendices simply to provide more detail about them without disrupting the main narrative.

I hope the information in these appendices will add to readers' knowledge of what occurred in northwestern Colorado in 1879 and shortly thereafter.

Appendix I

HOW MANY FOUGHT AT MILK CREEK?
SUPPLEMENT TO CHAPTER 2

How MANY U.S. ARMY TROOPS AND UTE WARRIORS ENGAGED IN THE battle at Milk Creek, beginning on September 29, 1879? There is considerable dispute about those numbers.

Wyoming state archaeologist and history professor Mark E. Miller has thoroughly researched the army records and published the most complete report available from the army's side of the battle. In his book, *Hollow Victory,* he notes that estimates of Major Thomas T. Thornburgh's troop strength when he left Fort Steele ran from as low as 150 to more than 200. Based on examinations of the troop rosters from the three cavalry companies and one infantry company that made up Thornburgh's White River Expedition, Miller concluded that there were at least 180 officers and enlisted men, as Captain J. Scott Payne reported at the conclusion of the battle, and perhaps as many as 200. However, Miller notes that the infantry company, consisting of thirty men, was left at Fortification Creek, about 30 miles to the north, and did not participate in the Milk Creek fight. That left 150 to 170 troops in the actual battle.[1]

Determining how many Utes were involved is substantially more difficult because the estimates vary wildly. Depending on the source, the soldiers may have been outnumbered more than two to one, or there were three times as many army troops as there were Indians.

Captain Payne, who assumed command of Thornburgh's forces after the major was killed, estimated that there were 300 to 400 Ute warriors in the battle. Lieutenant Samuel Cherry, who was in the advance guard of Thornburgh's troops and was in the middle of the first burst of gunfire, made the same estimate based on the number of Indians he said he saw lying behind trees on the ridges in front of him.[2]

General William T. Sherman, the commanding general of the army in 1879, said in his annual report, which was included in the secretary of war's report to Congress for 1879: "On the 29th of September, Major Thornburgh's command was attacked by about 300 well-armed warriors."[3]

Alarmist newspaper reports of the time put the number considerably higher—as many as 500 Ute warriors—and predicted additional warriors would join the fight from other Ute bands, as well as from the Shoshone, Arapaho, and other tribes.[4]

Others estimated the number of Utes in the battle much lower. For instance, Joe Brady, who was sent by Ouray with a message telling the White River Utes to stop fighting, thought there might have been 150 Utes around the main encampment at Milk Creek. But it was difficult to know for sure, he said, because so many Indians were coming and going.[5]

Josephine Meeker, in her testimony before Congress in early 1880, believed there were 150 to 175 Ute warriors fighting that day, with 200 as the highest possible number, based on her knowledge of the total number of White River Utes prior to the fight—about 800, including men, women, and children.[6]

Miller, citing census figures for the Indians, concludes, "There were not as many White River Ute warriors as there were troopers."[7]

Lieutenant Colonel E. V. Sumner, a member of Colonel Merritt's relief forces, who arrived on October 5 to end the siege of Thornburgh's troops, listed Thornburgh's command at Milk Creek at about 170 men and said the number of Indians opposing them was "not half that number."[8]

Charles Adams reduced that estimate even further in his testimony before Congress. "I found that only about 60 or 70 had been engaged in the fight with the soldiers," he said, basing his information on conversations he had with several Ute chiefs whom he knew and trusted.[9]

And Nicaagat cut that number still further. When asked by a member of Congress: "How many of your people were in the fight?" he replied, "About fifty."[10]

So, somewhere between 50 and 500 Utes participated in the battle at Milk Creek. Given the statements of people such as Josephine Meeker, who knew how many Utes were part of the White River band, and Charles Adams, who had also lived among them and knew their leaders, it seems likely that the number of Utes involved in the fight was on the low side of that vast range, 150 or fewer.

Appendix II

FASTER HORSES
Supplement to Chapter 6

The rapid rides made by Joe Rankin and the Uncompahgre Ute Yanco following the outbreak of hostilities at Milk Creek were unquestionably exceptional. But they were not the most famous rides of that era in the Rocky Mountain region.

Wyoming history lists several rides that surpassed Rankin's and Yanco's in distance covered. The most celebrated ride to bring news of an Indian battle occurred in December 1866, after what became known as the Fetterman massacre in north-central Wyoming. Captain William J. Fetterman and 79 cavalry troopers went to the aid of a wood-cutting detail outside of Fort Phil Kearny, near present-day Sheridan, Wyoming, on December 21, 1866. Ignoring specific orders not to pursue the retreating Sioux, Fetterman and his soldiers galloped after the Indians and into a trap in which they were cut off from the fort and surrounded by an estimated 2,000 warriors. All of the soldiers were killed.

A civilian at the fort, John "Portugese" Phillips, volunteered to ride to the telegraph office at Horseshoe Station on the North Platte, 190 miles away, in subzero weather. He carried Colonel Henry B. Carrington's dispatches regarding the massacre. He was accompanied by several different riders on various portions of the ride. Along the way he received an additional dispatch that required him to continue on to Fort Laramie. He arrived there—a distance of 236 miles—late on Christmas night, December 25. Much of his ride took place during a heavy snowstorm.[1]

But for flat-out speed over rugged terrain in difficult conditions, William Cody—"Buffalo Bill"—has the Wyoming record. He is credited with a ride in 1861 that beat the distances ridden by Rankin and Phillips significantly. Cody was a sixteen-year-old employee of the Pony Express, the company that took high-cost mail from Saint Joseph, Missouri, to Sacramento, California, using a series of small, light riders who changed swift horses frequently. Cody's normal route was long enough, 78 miles across south-central Wyoming, from Red Buttes to Three Crossings. It included a difficult crossing of the North Platte River and some of the most barren land in North America. But when he arrived at Three Crossings one day in June 1861, he learned that the rider who was supposed to take the next leg of the route had been killed the day before. So Cody had to continue that rider's leg—another 85 miles. When he arrived at that station, he learned there was no one to take the mail back in the other direction. So he turned around and retraced his entire ride. All together, Cody is credited with riding 322 miles in 21 hours and 40 minutes, using 21 different horses. Other riders for the Pony Express are said to have ridden farther at one stretch without stopping, but none is listed as having matched Cody's speedy pace.[2]

Young Bill Cody averaged just under 15 miles per hour for the duration of that great ride, but an Englishman earlier in the nineteenth century surpassed that speed rate considerably, albeit under much more controlled circumstances.

In 1831 George "Squire" Osbaldeston undertook a historic ride at Newmarket to settle a wager. A forty-four-year-old steeplechase champion and experienced fox hunter, Osbaldeston said he could ride 200 miles in 10 hours or less. Others disputed his claim, bets were made, and the race was on. Beginning at 7 a.m., on a 4 mile circular course, with grooms bringing out fresh, saddled horses after each round of the course, Osbaldeston rode at a steady gallop. He completed the 200 miles in 8 hours and 42 minutes, a rate of 23 miles per hour. If one subtracts the time Osbaldeston took for brief breaks and one quick meal, and one fall from a horse unsettled by the excitement, he actually covered the 200 miles in 7 hours and 19 minutes, for a rate of slightly better than 27 miles per hour.[3]

Few long rides, of course, occur under such controlled conditions and with so many horses available to a rider. Perhaps a more telling comparison of the rides undertaken by Joe Rankin and Yanco can be made with modern endurance riding. These competitors use only one horse for rides over a specific distance, usually 50 or 100 miles. The horses are superbly trained and health-checked by veterinarians before the start of the race. The winner of the 2009 American Endurance Riding Conference national championship completed 100 miles in 9 hours, 58 minutes, for a rate of just over 10 miles per hour.[4]

Appendix III

MORMONS ON THEIR MINDS
Supplement to Chapter 9

When Uintah Indian agent John Critchlow sent two white men in the company of several Utes to Colorado in response to Josephine Meeker's request for assistance, it sparked considerable suspicion among Colorado officials. The Uintah Agency was, after all, in Utah. And Utah, as everyone knew, was the headquarters of the Church of Jesus Christ of Latter-day Saints—the Mormons.

The United States had reached peace with Utah and the leader of the Mormon Church, Brigham Young, more than twenty years earlier. Young had died in 1877. Even so, many people in Colorado and around the West believed that the Mormons were intent on establishing hegemony of the Mountain West and would encourage Indian wars if it would help keep the non-Mormon whites out of lands in and around Utah.

Charles Adams, who arranged the release of the five white hostages following their twenty-three days of captivity, told of encountering S. B. Dillman and D. B. McLane—the men dispatched by Critchlow to try to secure the hostages' release —at the main Ute camp on the Grand (Colorado) River, at the mouth of Roan Creek, a few days after Adams met the hostages.

"When I arrived there I found two white men who told me that they were employees of the Uinta [sic] Agency, and that they had been sent there by the agent in Utah to try to get these women released," Adams reported to the House Committee on Indian Affairs. "One of them could speak Ute, and their whole actions in camp made me think that they were not what they pretended to be, and I have since learned that they were Mormons who came there to influence the Indians."[1]

That sparked interest among the committee members, who asked if the men indeed proved to be Mormons, and, if so, why they had been sent there. Adams responded that he didn't know for sure the two men were Mormons, but he said Chief Ouray later told him they were, and that they had been sent "for the purpose of keeping the Indians in hostility to the government."[2]

However, McLane, in a letter he wrote to Arvilla Meeker in January of 1880—from Wyoming, not Utah—strived to make it clear that he and his partner were not Mormons. But he did not dispute that members of the Mormon Church were trying to incite the Indians. In fact, he encouraged that notion, explaining that he understood the Ute language, but the Indians didn't know that, so he was privy to some of their conversations without them realizing it. He said he learned that the Mormons were encouraging the Utes in their fight against the other whites, and that the Utes were prepared to kill McLane and his partner if they turned out not to be Mormons.[3] McLane also talked of an unnamed "mormon Captain, who told the Indians to fight the 'mericans that god had toald [sic] him to tell the Indians to get all other tribes to join and the mormons would assist them."[4]

Although no more solid evidence than this was presented, the idea that Mormons were behind the battle was reported as fact in some contemporary newspaper articles.[5] It was even stated, again without supporting evidence, that Quinkent (Douglas) had participated in the infamous Mountain Meadows massacre on September 11, 1857, when non-Mormon immigrants in a wagon train near Cedar City, Utah, were ambushed and killed by men dressed as Indians.[6] It was later proved that the attackers were Mormons, not Indians.

In fact, the Mormons had a troubled relationship with the American Indians they encountered in Utah. Although they had sought to bring

Utes into the church, there were also battles between the Utes and Mormon settlers off and on for decades prior to the 1879 events at White River.

Furthermore, Nicaagat had a long-standing animosity toward the Mormons as a result of the time he spent with a Mormon family in his youth. It is unlikely he would have been eager to join forces with church members against the U.S. Army, whose soldiers he called his brothers and with whom he believed he had a friendly relationship until the battle started at Milk Creek.[7]

Despite the fears expressed by Adams and others, there is nothing to substantiate claims that the Mormon Church was involved in the White River Ute uprising. Ouray mentioned nothing about the Mormons in his testimony before Congress in 1880. And Governor Frederick Pitkin, who was not above spreading rumors backed by little evidence when it came to the Utes, told Congress, "I don't believe the Mormons had anything to do with it at all."[8]

Appendix IV

ONE FAMILY'S HISTORY
SUPPLEMENT TO CHAPTER 10

FOR MORE THAN A CENTURY, THE DESCENDANTS OF SHE-TOWITCH AND Canalla kept their family stories—their oral history—to themselves. "From the time of the massacre in Meeker into the 1960s, our people were afraid that families in Meeker were going to come over here [to the Uintah Reservation in Utah] and kill our family" because of the part that their ancestors had played in the events at the White River Agency in 1879, said Jonas Grant Sr. "Our family lived in fear. That's why we were told not to repeat these stories to anyone."

Still, the stories were passed down within the family, and many came directly to Jonas from his great-grandmother, Clara (Congove) Johnson Wopsock, who died in 1965. She was believed to have lived at least 120 years.

"My great-grandmother told me a lot," Jonas recalled. "My mother said I was always my great-grandmother's favorite great-grandson, so she told me the stories."

Others contributed as well. Wilson Johnson, Jonas's great-uncle, and Jonas's stepfather, Robert (Bobby) Lee Cuch, also provided information about the family's history.

Beginning about 2003, Jonas's great-uncle requested that he begin writing down the family's stories and letting others know of the family's lineage. Jonas did the latter so well that in 2005 the Southern Utes, on whose reservation Chief Ouray is buried, officially recognized Jonas Grant's family and the wider Johnson clan as direct descendants of Ouray's family through Ouray's full sister She-towitch. This is the story of the Johnson clan.

The father of She-towitch and Ouray was Guero, who was Tabeguache Ute—a band that would later become known as the Uncompahgres, with Ouray as their leader. The mother of She-towitch and Ouray, whose name is lost to time, was half Jicarilla Apache and half Tabeguache Ute.

She-towitch's husband was sometimes known as Half-breed Johnson Number Two, because he was also half Jicarilla Apache and half Ute, Jonas recounted. "His nu-yna [Ute name] was Con-nev, although he was also called Canalla. He was born around the mountains of Dulce, New Mexico, in the early 1800s."

Canalla's father was Canavish—known in the Johnson family as Johnson Number One. He was a Uintah Ute who later moved to the White River and brought with him a young runaway from the Mormons in Salt Lake City whose name was Nicaagat.

Canalla grew up in New Mexico and became friends with another young Ute who also had Apache blood—Ouray. And despite his residence far to the north, Canavish kept in contact with the Utes in New Mexico and kept tabs on his progeny. According to the family history, he reached an agreement with Guero, father of Ouray and She-towitch, that She-towitch should marry Canalla. They did, after She-towitch's capture and escape from the Arapahos. And they soon moved north to join Canalla's family on the White River.

The couple had five children. The oldest son, Augustine Vigil Johnson, eventually became a chief of the Jicarilla Apaches. A second son, Tatiz Johnson, was killed on September 29, 1879. Some published accounts say he died during the shootings at the White River Agency. Family history says he was killed in the battle with Major Thornburgh's troops at Milk Creek.

She-towitch and Canalla also had two daughters, Looking Glass and Minna Johnson. And they had a third son, Tim Johnson—Jonas Grant's great-grandfather—who was a teenager at the time of the Milk Creek battle. Decades later, Tim Johnson would become a leader of the White River Utes, then living in Utah, and would help lead several hundred Utes on an odyssey to join the Sioux in South Dakota.

Tim Johnson married two sisters at separate times. The first was Pearl Thompson, whose Ute name was Pamik-ka Kochamanasken, with whom he had a son and a daughter. He later married Pearl's sister Clara Thompson, who would eventually relate the family history to her great-grandson Jonas Grant. Tim and Clara Johnson had three children, sons Myton and Wilson and a daughter, Lula. Myton was Jonas Grant's grandfather. Wilson is the great-uncle who also told Jonas of his family's history.

Jonas Grant's father, Floyd Grant—a decorated veteran of the Philippines campaign during World War II—died at the age of thirty-two, when Jonas was a young boy. Jonas was raised by his mother, Emma Lou Johnson, and his stepfather, Bobby Cuch.

While his maternal ancestry links back to Ouray and Guero, Jonas Grant's lineage on his father's side is equally intriguing. It can be traced back to Eau-su-kur-pen, a chief of the Uintah Utes when they lived in the Salt Lake Valley, before the arrival of whites. According to family history, Eau-su-kur-pen, who became known to the whites as "Jirop," actually welcomed Brigham Young's retinue to the Salt Lake Valley. He invited the Mormons to stay "half a moon," or two weeks, while Brigham Young recovered from an illness. They stayed a good deal longer than that.

Eau-su-kur-pen and other Utes eventually retreated to the Uintah Valley and surrounding mountains under an agreement with the Mormons. His granddaughter, Evangeline Jirop, was Floyd Grant's mother and Jonas Grant's grandmother.

Meanwhile, another Grant ancestor had his own run-in with the Mormons. He became an important spiritual leader—or medicine man—after a near-death encounter during a battle with the Latter-day Saints at Spanish Fork, Utah. "He was shot in the forehead and our people thought he was dead," Jonas said. "When our people went back to gather the dead, they found him alive. The medicine man told him he was blessed, and his name was changed from whatever he was using to Bullethead."

He was Jonas Grant's great-great-grandfather, and his son was known as Grant Bullethead. But the surname and the first name were switched by some unknown official within the Bureau of Indian Affairs, and on the official records he became Bullethead Grant. Even more confounding, a separate line of Bullethead's descendants managed to keep the Bullethead last name until late in the twentieth century.

Bullethead Grant's son was Ulysses Simpson Grant, Jonas's grandfather. Each of the male descendants of Bullethead became spiritual leaders in their own right.

Then there is Nicaagat, whose strange story places him on both sides of Jonas Grant's family history.

The man who would eventually be one of the leaders in the fight at Milk Creek did indeed spend much of his youth with a Mormon family in Salt Lake City, according to stories repeated to Jonas Grant. But when he ran away, he ran first to the Uintah Ute clan headed by Eau-su-kur-pen, who adopted the young man as a nephew. After a time, Nicaagat decided to move on to the White River. And he went in the company of Canavish—Johnson Number One. There he became a member of the White River band, married and had children, served as an army scout, and became a tribal leader.

But his life before he arrived in Utah is even more intriguing. To begin with, the Grant family history relates, he was a half brother to Ouray and She-towitch. Guero was also his father. He and another half brother, Quenche, were from the same mother.

Several books tell of Ouray's brother Quenche. One reports that in 1851 Guero "decided to return to his own people with his three sons and two daughters." Ouray and Quenche are named in this account, but not the third son.[1]

How the young Nicaagat ended up with the Mormons in Utah is more perplexing. As noted in chapter 5, one source says that he was taken captive by the notorious Walkara, a Ute chief in Utah, and sold to the Mormons. But the Grant family history says he was actually a half brother to Walkara, perhaps through adoption by the famous chief, who was about thirty years older than Nicaagat. The Grant family history relates that the two ended up in northern California during the early stages of the Modoc war in the 1850s and were nearly killed. But they were rescued by Mormons who returned them to Utah. Interestingly, one of the leaders of the Modocs would later become known as "Captain Jack Kientopoos," while Nicaagat would be known as "Captain Jack" in Colorado.

Appendix V

POWELL SPEAKS OUT
SUPPLEMENT TO CHAPTER 13

EVEN AFTER TWO MONTHS OF ALMOST DAILY DOSES OF UTE NEWS, THE editors of the *Chicago Tribune* must have believed their readers needed proof that the Indians of the West were incorrigible and impossible to turn into civilized human beings—at least as they defined "civilized." So they turned to an expert.

On Christmas Day, 1879, the newspaper published a lengthy article titled "The Core of the Indian Question," featuring detailed comments from John Wesley Powell. Powell, the one-armed Civil War veteran, was already a national celebrity. In 1875 he had published his book *The Exploration of the Colorado River and Its Canyons* to great national acclaim. It recounted his nearly miraculous descent down the Green and Colorado rivers, through all of their canyons, including the Grand Canyon. He and his small group of fellow adventurers were the first people to make the entire trip—in wooden boats, no less.

He also had ties to Illinois. He had taught at several colleges in that state and had obtained funding for his expedition through them and the Illinois Natural History Society.

In 1878, Powell published an even more important, though decidedly less exciting, volume: *Report on the Lands of the Arid Region of the United States.* And by that time he was busy working for the Public Lands Commission under the auspices of the U.S. Geologic Survey in Washington, D.C.[1]

In the first book, especially, Powell gave accounts of the American Indian tribes that he had encountered—their cultures, dress, manners, and means of survival. Powell was familiar with Utes in general, and because he had spent the winter of 1868–69 in what would thereafter be called Powell Park—the location to which Nathan Meeker would move the White River Agency a decade later—he was particularly well acquainted with the White River Utes. That's why the *Chicago Tribune* sought him out for comment on the Indians in 1879.

"The history of all the Indian tribes with whom this country at different stages of its development has come in contact is practically the same," the *Tribune* quoted Powell as saying.

> They have all rebelled at the point where they have been asked to put off the habits and customs of savage life and adopt those of civilization. It is not a question of peace or war policy; it is not a question of lenient or harsh treatment; it is not a question dependent upon dishonest traders, bad whiskey, poor rations, shoddy clothes and Springfield rifles, but a question growing out of the demand made upon these people to change at once from all that makes them savage nomads to a condition of peaceful husbandry.... Any attempt whatever, whether it be by fair or foul means, to change Indians into Caucasians will be a flat failure.[2]

The anonymous *Tribune* writer then added his own opinion: "One of the phases of civilization which the Indian has most bitterly opposed and to which he has never yet yielded is the agricultural. For two centuries he has steadily refused to break the ground with a plow and cultivate it, or allow the whites to cultivate an acre of his reservation, and from this relentless determination has sprung nearly all our Indian troubles."[3]

It was nonsense, of course, ignoring not only the troubles caused by the whites' repeated incursions onto Indian lands, but the fact that more than two centuries earlier, American Indians had educated European settlers in the art of cultivating maize, tobacco, and other native plants. The argument also ignored the considerable agricultural enterprises of Indians at that time on reservations from Oklahoma to Arizona, Lake Superior to the Pacific Ocean. Furthermore, if the quote attributed to John Wesley Powell was accurate, it contradicted his own words from just a few years earlier.

In his first book, *The Exploration of the Colorado River and Its Canyons,* Powell described his visit to small Ute farms in northeastern Utah when he and two members of his party left the Green River and hiked to the Uintah Reservation to replenish their supplies. "Quite a number of Indians have each a patch of ground of two or three acres, on which they are raising wheat, potatoes, turnips, pumpkins, melons, and other vegetables," Powell wrote, noting that irrigation was necessary to grow crops in the dry climate. "Most of the crops are looking well, and it is rather surprising with what pride they show us that they are able to cultivate crops like white men."[4] Not exactly the intractable nomads he described to the *Tribune.*

Elsewhere in the same book, Powell offered accounts of other Indian tribes he encountered farther downstream and their considerable agricultural efforts. But that sort of evidence didn't fit well with the point the *Tribune* writer sought to make. "It is not so much a question of whether the Utes [in Colorado] must go to Uintah that must be solved," he wrote. "That is clear, and there should not be a moment's hesitation about removing them. The real problem is to set all the Indians to work and treat them as white citizens, or else remove them to underground reservations."[5]

Appendix VI

THE FINAL SKIRMISH
SUPPLEMENT TO CHAPTER 16

THE OCTOBER 22 SKIRMISH DESCRIBED TO CHARLES ADAMS BY UTE Indians as they rode from the Grand (Colorado) River toward the White River camp of Colonel Wesley Merritt was recounted in considerably different terms by military authorities.

General William T. Sherman listed the date of the skirmish as taking place two days earlier when he reported the incident to the secretary of war. On October 20, Merritt sent out two companies of cavalry to scout near the summit between the White and Grand rivers, Sherman said. "Lieutenant Weir, of the Ordnance, a fine young officer, asked and obtained leave to accompany Lieutenant Hall. When about twenty miles out, Lieutenant Weir and William Humme, chief of scouts, rode to one side to hunt deer [and] encountered a picket party of Indians. Shots were exchanged, and both Lieutenant Weir and Humme were killed. Their bodies were afterward recovered." Sherman also noted that the Indians insisted that they fired on the two men only after shots were fired at them, killing two of their men.[1]

Sherman at least acknowledged the Utes' side of the story. Merritt was adamant that the Utes had ambushed his unsuspecting troops. "After proceeding about twenty miles, Hall's party was fired into by Indians and taken at a disadvantage," Merritt said in a telegram to General George Crook. Humme and Weir went off deer hunting, and gunshots were heard in their direction, Merritt said. The shots were determined to be coming from the Utes' attack on the two men, he added.[2]

After reporting that he had sent out a detachment to search for Weir and Humme, Merritt expressed hope that they were alive. "The party which attacked Hall was not a large one. From all the circumstances connected with the attack of Lieut. Weir, it is believed he is safe, but has lost his horses. I hope for the best."

But it was not to be. In the same telegram, immediately after expressing his hope, Merritt wrote: "Later: The worst fears are realized. Lieut. Weir's body has been found. He was shot through the head and killed instantly! A noble, Christian gentleman and soldier has thus been made a victim to these fiends in human shape."[3]

Another account was written a dozen years later by Lieutenant Colonel E. V. Sumner, who accompanied Merritt to the White River. He was in the detachment sent to recover Lieutenant Weir's body. It was Sumner who encountered Charles Adams and his Ute entourage.

Sumner said Hall and his party were surrounded, but hunkered down in a dry streambed, "kept the Indians off until after dark," and then made it back to Merritt's camp, without Humme and Weir.[4] The battalion of the Fifth Cavalry, including Sumner, "was turned out at once, and, as it was 10 p.m., we had an all-night march ahead of us."

"Just at dawn we reached the place where Weir had left Hall, and we took his trail and followed it up until we found his dead body lying cold and stiff on the mountain side," Sumner recounted. "His face still bore the familiar and kindly expression we knew so well. An overcoat was wrapped around the body, and it was then strapped on a cavalry horse. We returned to camp as sad a funeral procession as one could well imagine."[5]

General Sherman is the only one to record that the bodies of both Lieutenant Weir and the scout Humme were recovered. Sumner mentions only that of Weir, and Merritt said it was not even clear what had happened to Humme. "It is thought Humme has escaped and he is being looked for now. Lieutenant Weir's body is being brought in and will be sent north at once."[6]

In 1993, a body was discovered near the top of Rio Blanco Hill—not far from where we believe this skirmish took place. Could it have been Humme's? Through telephone conversations with former Rio Blanco County Sheriff Ron Hilkey and assistant Colorado state archaeologist Kevin Black—both of whom examined the partially exposed skeletal remains before they were reburied in place with the aid of Utes—it appears the body was probably Ute. Black said the condition of the teeth, facial characteristics, and the type of burial definitely pointed to American Indian, possibly Ute. He said the death could have occurred any time from the mid-1700s to the late 1800s. There were remnants of an old saddle and brass buttons with the army's distinctive "U.S." imprinted on them. It is known that several of the Utes involved at the battle at Milk Creek took uniforms from fallen soldiers. Could these remains have been one of them—perhaps one of the two Utes reported killed in that final skirmish on October 22, 1879?[7]

Appendix VII

COLOROW
SUPPLEMENT TO CHAPTER 18

COLOROW, THE BEAR-SIZED UTE WHO JOINED NICAAGAT AS A LEADER IN the battle at Milk Creek, was well known by whites in Colorado long before 1879. But few of the white men's stories about him were flattering.

"He was aggressive, quarrelsome, and it would seem that his courage was well-tempered by caution," wrote one northwestern Colorado resident.[1] "Colorow was an enigma and a headache to the whites," he added. "At times his counsel and actions were of great value. But usually he made no pretense of liking the white race or of being happy under their rule."[2]

One of Colorow's descendants agreed he was no fan of the intruders moving into Ute territory. "He was a warrior, and he didn't like white people," said Loya Arrum, a great-great-granddaughter of Colorow. One family story tells of Colorow and several of his followers traveling to Hot Sulphur Springs—once considered part of Ute territory, but by the early 1870s controlled by white settlers. "They were 'harvesting horses'"—freeing horses from the burden of white ownership, Arrum explained. The white settlers objected and took to Colorow's trail.

"They were in hot pursuit through the canyons in that country, but they couldn't find him," Arrum said. Colorow drove the horses into a cave he knew, and remained hidden until the pursuers gave up. He simply vanished, in the eyes of the whites.[3]

Despite Colorow's dislike of white interlopers, he was not eager for war with them. Like Nicaagat, he met with Major Thomas T. Thornburgh before the battle at Milk Creek and urged him not to bring all of his troops onto the reservation. Months later, when an official inquest into the White River events began, Colorow was one of the few Utes to cooperate.[4]

There are differing accounts of Colorow's origins. One story says he was born a Comanche.[5] Another claims he was a Shoshone.[6]

There were also different versions of his name. One contemporary account referred to him as a chief "Colorado, pronounced and generally spelled Colorow."[7] But it appears that several Utes went by that name. In 1880, when the agreement ceding much of the Ute land in Colorado to the U.S. government was completed, three different Utes signed with some version of the name "Colorow" or "Colorado."[8]

It's clear, however, that when most people at the time talked of Colorow, they were referring to one man—and a very large man at that. He was "a huge fellow (nearly 300 pounds)," said one account.[9] And it was said that "Ranching housewives came to feel slighted if the huge-stomached Colorow didn't bluster into their kitchens occasionally with three or four squaws demanding biscuits, sugar lumps and bean soup."[10] Even during the battle at Milk Creek, food was on his mind. "Colorow would only say that he was hungry....Sitting here all this time and keeping the soldiers in that hole had only kept him from getting enough food to fill his belly."[11]

Arrum believes some of the stories of his eating and begging were exaggerated to discredit him. "He was aggressive because he didn't like the whites taking the Utes' land. He was very verbal about that. Some people didn't like that," she said. "They said he was always coming around wanting food. But I don't think that was an everyday thing. I think people used words like that because they were angry with him, or scared of him."[12]

By 1879, Colorow was about fifty years old, according to Charles Adams. He had once been a leader with a considerable following. But his standing suffered greatly when he confronted territorial governor Edward McCook at his office in Denver in the early 1870s and demanded goods for his band camped near the city. McCook took Colorow's pistol away from him, threw him down the stairs, and berated him in front of his own followers.[13]

But Colorow regained considerable respect among his fellow Utes during the battle at Milk Creek. "Colorow, the great clown of the Nupartka [the White River Utes], had proved himself one of the greatest warriors of the People. He was admired by all, yet when a man was with him, he still found it impossible not to think first of his great jokes and his talk that was big like his belly....Now the great clown had really become the great warrior."[14]

Colorow remained a respected leader, warrior, and storyteller until his death, the date of which is uncertain.

Appendix VIII

WHAT HAPPENED TO THE UTES' HORSES?
Supplement to Chapter 21

When the Uncompahgre and White River Utes were forced to Utah, they still owned many horses. But their descendants' stories and other evidence show that a large portion of those horses did not make it to Utah. One indication is that both Ute and army observers reported that many of the Utes made the journey on foot. But estimating how many horses were lost is difficult. So is determining what happened to them.

Annual reports of the secretary of Interior from that period contain census data for each American Indian tribe, including the number of people, livestock, and more. For the Utes and other tribes that moved frequently, getting an accurate count of horses must have been difficult, but these are the best numbers available.

In 1878, shortly after Nathan Meeker arrived at the White River Indian Agency, he estimated that the 890 Utes of the White River owned 3,000 horses. The Uintah Utes of northeastern Utah had a herd of 876 horses that same year. And the Uncompahgres on the Los Pinos Reservation were reported to have 5,500 horses.[1]

By 1881, as the army was preparing to move Utes from Colorado to Utah, the numbers listed were even greater: 6,100 horses for the Uncompahgres and 1,550 for the Uintahs. There was no White River Indian Agency in 1881, and no report on White River horse herds.[2]

By 1882, after the Uncompahgre and White River bands had been moved onto reservations in Utah, the numbers were quite different. The White River and Uintah Utes were forced to share the existing Uintah Reservation, and in 1882 their combined herd was 3,000 horses. The Uncompahgres, who were settled on their own Utah site, called the Ouray Reservation, were reported to have 4,000 horses.[3]

So the Uncompahgres lost between 1,500 and 2,100 horses when they moved from Colorado. For the Uintah and White River Utes, between 900 or 1,500 horses disappeared. What happened to them? "We believe the army killed many of them," said Jonas Grant Sr., a direct descendant of Canalla and She-towitch.[4]

There is certainly precedent for such action. The army had been known to destroy the horses of other American Indian tribes. In fact, Colonel Ranald Mackenzie, who oversaw the removal of Uncompahgre Utes from Colorado in 1881, had done exactly that a few years earlier. "In 1874, the regiment under Mackenzie defeated the main body of the Comanches on the Staked Plains [of west Texas], capturing nearly 2,000 horses," wrote James Parker, an officer who served with him. "Knowing from previous experience the impossibility of protecting this vast herd from a stampede by Indians, who would thus regain their hostile influence, he was compelled to order the herd destroyed."[5]

But if Mackenzie or anyone else ordered the destruction of many of the Ute horses, there is nothing in the official report of the secretary of war for 1881, or in correspondence between military officials (available through the National Archives) that indicates such action was taken.

Historians and archeologists with federal public lands agencies in Colorado I have contacted said they know of no site that would indicate a mass slaughter of horses. But they also note that in the vast territory of northwestern Colorado, hiding such a site would not be difficult, especially if the carcasses had been burned.

Killing the horses is not the only possible explanation of what happened to them. Sidney Jocknick, who was in the Uncompahgre Valley when the army was preparing to remove the Utes from that territory, said one of the reasons that the Utes pleaded for more time was to round up their livestock. When Colonel Mackenzie refused them the additional time, it is likely they had to abandon large numbers of horses.[6]

What became of them?

For one thing, even in the twenty-first century there are wild horse herds in Colorado—one in northwestern Colorado, one north and east of Grand Junction, and one southwest of the Uncompahgre Valley near the Utah border. All are believed to have originally been made up of Indian ponies, although they interbred with domestic ranch horses over many decades.

Also, as is clear from Jocknick, Parker, and others who were present at the time the Utes were removed from Colorado, white settlers moved in as rapidly as the Utes moved out. It is likely many of the abandoned Ute ponies became part of the ranch stock of new white settlers. In fact, white settlers were attempting to grab the Utes' horses even before the Indians left Colorado, according to Los Pinos Indian agent William H. Berry. "Last April, some unknown parties, supposed to have been passing through the reservation, stole and drove off twenty-three head of Indian horses and ponies, which so seemed to excite and create among them a feeling of hatred and revenge that was at the time difficult to overcome; yet from prompt action taken at the time, and success in recovering all of the horses and ponies, good feeling was restored."[7]

One thing is definite: in addition to being forced from their mountain homes in 1881, the Utes also lost many of their beloved horses.

NOTES

CHAPTER 1

1. *White River Ute Commission Investigation,* p. 46.
2. Events that would have contributed to the Utes' fear of white soldiers included the Sand Creek Massacre on Colorado's eastern plains in 1864 and the destruction of several Sioux and Cheyenne villages during the campaign of 1876–77.
3. Mark E. Miller, *Hollow Victory* (University Press of Colorado, 1997), Appendix B, p. 178; *Testimony in Relation to the Ute Indian Outbreak,* p. 202 (hereafter referred to as *Testimony*).
4. *Testimony,* pp. 194–196.
5. Ibid., p. 84.
6. Ibid.
7. Ibid., pp. 63, 171.
8. Ibid., p. 104.
9. Ibid., p. 90.
10. M. Wilson Rankin, *Reminiscences of Frontier Days* (Yellow Cat Publishing, Moab, Utah, 2000), p. 203.
11. Robert Emmitt, *The Last War Trail* (University Press of Colorado, Boulder, 2000), pp. 13–19; *Testimony,* pp. 72–73.
12. Fred H. Werner, *Meeker: The Story of the Meeker Massacre and Thornburgh Battle, September 29, 1879* (Western Publications, Greeley, Colo., 1985), p. 12; *Testimony,* p. 75.
13. Thomas F. Dawson and F. J. V. Skiff, *The Ute War: A History of the White River Massacre and the Privations and Hardships of the Captive White Women among the Hostiles on Grand River* (Tribune Publishing House, Denver, 1879), p. 101.

14. Marshall Sprague, *Massacre: The Tragedy at White River* (Ballantine Books, New York, 1972), p. 116.

15. Josephine Meeker, *The Ute Massacre! Brave Miss Meeker's Captivity! Her Own Account of It* (Old Franklin Publishing House, Philadelphia, Penn., 1879), p. 17 (hereafter referred to as *Brave Miss Meeker*).

16. Nicaagat made no mention of this meeting with Josephine in his official testimony, although he did report arriving at the camp where the hostages were held six days after the Milk Creek battle began.

CHAPTER 2

1. Peter Decker, *The Utes Must Go!* (Fulcrum Publishing, Golden, Colo., 2004), chap. 3; *Testimony*, pp. 1–15.

2. Sprague, *Massacre*, p. 6

3. Decker, *The Utes Must Go!* chap. 3.

4. Ibid.

5. Sprague, *Massacre*, p. 29.

6. Decker, *The Utes Must Go!* chap. 3.

7. Ibid.

8. Sprague, *Massacre*, chap. 5.

9. Ibid.

10. Ibid., chap. 6.

11. *Testimony*, pp. 94–126.

12. Ibid., pp. 100–101.

13. Emmitt, *The Last War Trail*, p. 91; Miller, *Hollow Victory*, p. 8.

14. *Testimony*, p. 96.

15. Ibid., pp. 72–76.

16. *White River Ute Commission*, pp. 7–9; *Testimony*, pp. 199–200.

17. *Testimony*, pp. 77, 107–108, 199.

18. Miller, *Hollow Victory*, p. 13.

19. Ibid., pp. 7–9.

20. Ibid., pp. 11–12.

21. Ibid., p. 24.

22. *Testimony*, pp. 194–195.

23. Decker, *The Utes Must Go!* pp. 30–32.

24. Emmitt, *The Last War Trail*, p. 197; John Gregory Bourke, *On the Border with Crook* (Rio Grande Press, Glorieta, N.Mex., 1969), p. 349.

25. *Testimony*, p. 199.

26. Ibid., p. 196.

27. Miller, *Hollow Victory*, pp. 33–51.

28. *Testimony*, p. 14; Emmitt, *The Last War Trail*, pp. 197–199.

29. *Testimony*, p. 196.

30. Miller, *Hollow Victory*, p. 61; *Testimony*, p. 65.

31. *Testimony,* pp. 65–66; Meeker, *Brave Miss Meeker,* p. 14.
32. Ute historian Clifford Duncan and Jonas Grant Sr., conversation with author, Milk Creek battle site, July 2007.
33. Miller, *Hollow Victory,* pp. 62–66; *Testimony,* p. 66.
34. *Testimony,* pp. 195–197.
35. *White River Ute Commission,* p. 35.
36. Meeker, *Brave Miss Meeker,* p. 6.
37. Ibid., pp. 7–8.
38. Ibid., p. 8; Sprague, *Massacre,* p. 177.
39. Meeker, *Brave Miss Meeker,* p. 24.
40. Ibid., pp. 24, 35.

CHAPTER 3

1. James F. Brooks, *Captives and Cousins: Slavery, Kinship and Community in the Southwest Borderlands* (University of North Carolina Press, Chapel Hill, 2002), pp. 19–26.
2. Ibid., chap. 1.
3. Ibid., chap. 4.
4. Ibid., pp. 133–135.
5. Ibid., pp. 143–148.
6. Meeker, *Brave Miss Meeker,* p. 19.
7. Cynthia Becker and David Smith, *Chipeta, Queen of the Utes* (Western Reflections Publishing, Montrose, Colo., 2003), pp. 11–12.
8. Ibid., pp. 31–32, 69–73.
9. Ibid., pp. 24–30.
10. Sprague, *Massacre,* pp. 119–120.
11. Emmitt, *The Last War Trail,* p. 39.
12. Ibid.
13. Ibid.
14. Emmitt, *The Last War Trail,* p. 39.
15. Bourke. *On the Border with Crook,* p. 349.
16. "This Day in History," May 19 (category, Old West). http://www.history.com.

CHAPTER 4

1. *Testimony,* p. 82.
2. Joe Sullivan, conversation with author, September 2005.
3. The moon was full on September 30, 1879. "Phases of the Moon chart." *U.S. Naval Observatory.* www.usno.navy.mil/USNO/astronimcal-applications/data-services/rs-one-day-us.
4. *White River Ute Commission,* p. 46.

5. Rankin, *Reminiscences*, p. 222. Rankin said the camp "was known as the squaw camp" in his original manuscript (p. 67), but that reference is omitted from the abridged version by Yellow Cat Publishing.

6. Meeker, *Brave Miss Meeker*, p. 35.

7. Ibid., p. 24.

8. Ibid., pp. 24–27.

9. Ibid., p. 24.

10. *Testimony*, p. 83.

11. Meeker, *Brave Miss Meeker*, p. 35.

12. *Testimony*, p. 87.

13. Ibid., pp. 179–180.

14. *White River Ute Commission*, p. 17.

15. Meeker, *Brave Miss Meeker*, p. 27.

16. Meeker, *Brave Miss Meeker*, pp. 10, 16.

17. Meeker, *Brave Miss Meeker*, p. 35.

18. Ibid., p. 36.

19. Ibid., p. 27.

20. *Testimony*, p. 83.

21. Rankin, *Reminiscences*, p. 238.

22. *Testimony*, pp. 83–84.

23. *White River Ute Commission*, p. 33.

24. Meeker, *Brave Miss Meeker*, p. 14.

25. Ibid., p. 37.

26. Rankin, *Reminiscences*, p. 244

27. Meeker, *Brave Miss Meeker*, p. 13.

CHAPTER 5

1. Val FitzPatrick, *Red Twilight, the Last Free-Roaming Days of the Ute Indians* (Yellow Cat Publishing, Moab, Utah, 2000), pp. 95–96.

2. Dawson and Skiff, *The Ute War*, pp. 15–17.

3. Val McClellan, *This Is Our Land*, vol. 2 (Western Publishers, Jamestown, Ohio, 1979), p. 737.

4. News article, *Chicago Tribune*, March 20, 1880.

5. Emmitt, *The Last War Trail*, p. 15.

6. *Testimony*, pp. 182, 191, 194.

7. Ibid., p. 198.

8. Rankin, *Reminiscences*, p. 215.

9. Decker, *The Utes Must Go!* p. 101.

10. Sprague, *Massacre*, p. 104.

11. Charles Wilkinson, *Fire on the Plateau: Conflict and Endurance in the American Southwest* (Island Press/Shearwater Books, Washington, D.C., and Covelo,

Calif., 1999), p. 132; James Goss, Texas Tech University historian, interview with the author, May 2006.

12. Rankin, *Reminiscences,* p. 200.
13. FitzPatrick, *Red Twilight,* p. 19.
14. Ibid.
15. Rankin, *Reminiscences,* p. 200.
16. Emmitt, *The Last War Trail,* p. 39.
17. Sprague, *Massacre,* p. 104.
18. Jonas Grant Sr., conversation with author, July 2007.
19. Jay C. Burrup, archivist, LDS Church History Library and Archives, e-mail communication with the author, May 2006.
20. Emmitt, *The Last War Trail,* pp. 39, 40.
21. Bourke, *On the Border with Crook,* p. 349.
22. Emmitt, *The Last War Trail,* p. 40.
23. Dawson and Skiff, *The Ute War,* pp. 171–172.
24. News article, *Chicago Tribune,* October 16, 1879.
25. Ibid.
26. News article, *Chicago Tribune,* January 1, 1880.
27. Dawson and Skiff, *The Ute War,* p. 172.
28. Sprague, *Massacre,* p. 71.
29. Ibid., p. 73.
30. Rankin, *Reminiscences,* pp. 199–200.
31. Bourke, *On the Border with Crook,* p. 350.
32. Ibid.
33. For example, Josie (in *Brave Miss Meeker)* mentions a number of Utes who were drunk after the battle at Milk Creek and the killings at the White River Agency, but no such mention is made of Nicaagat.
34. Bourke, *On the Border with Crook,* p. 350.
35. Ibid.
36. Rankin, *Reminiscences,* p. 203.
37. *Testimony,* p. 194.
38. Wilkinson, *Fire on the Plateau,* p. 134.
39. *Testimony,* p. 75.
40. Ibid., p. 162.
41. Dawson and Skiff, *The Ute War,* p. 172.

CHAPTER 6

1. Miller, *Hollow Victory,* pp. 89–90.
2. E. V. Sumner, "Besieged by the Utes," *Century Illustrated Monthly Magazine* (New York) (May 1891 to October 1891).
3. *White River Ute Commission,* p. 35.
4. *Hayden Survey of Colorado,* 1874–76, maps (published 1877), Denver Public Library.

5.   *White River Ute Commission*, p. 28.
6.   Ibid., pp. 28–29.
7.   Ibid., pp. 28–34; Dawson and Skiff, *The Ute War*, p. 78.
8.   *White River Ute Commission*, pp. 28–29.
9.   Miller, *Hollow Victory*, p. 89.
10. Ibid., pp. 89–92.
11. Dawson and Skiff, *The Ute War*, p. 47.
12. Miller, *Hollow Victory*, p. 96.
13. Ibid., p. 97.
14. Ibid., pp. 97–99.
15. Dawson and Skiff, *The Ute War*, p. 36.
16. Miller, *Hollow Victory*, p. 100.
17. Dawson and Skiff, *The Ute War*, pp. 39–40.
18. Miller, *Hollow Victory*, p. 127.
19. Ibid., pp. 128–130.
20. Ibid., pp. 126–131.
21. Ibid., pp. 125–126.
22. Ibid., pp. 135–136.
23. *White River Ute Commission*, p. 29.
24. Ibid., p. 30.
25. Ibid.
26. Ibid.
27. Ibid., pp. 30–31.
28. Ibid., p. 31.
29. Ibid., p. 49.
30. Ibid., p. 33.
31. Meeker, *Brave Miss Meeker*, p. 13.
32. *White River Ute Commission*, p. 31.
33. Miller, *Hollow Victory*, p. 143; Dawson and Skiff, *The Ute War*, pp. 50–57.

CHAPTER 7

1.   Virginia McConnell Simmons, *The Ute Indians of Utah, Colorado and New Mexico* (University Press of Colorado, Boulder, 2000), p. 140.
2.   Emmitt, *The Last War Trail*, p. 32.
3.   Samantha Tisdel, *San Juan Silver Stage Online*, vol. 10 (2005), www.silverstage.net/history.htm.
4.   D. B. Huntington, *Vocabulary of the Utah and Shoshoni*, 3rd edition, revised and enlarged. Printed at the *Salt Lake Herald* office, Salt Lake City, 1872; Jim Jefferson, telephone conversation with the author, November 2006.
5.   Frank Gilbert Roe, *The Indian and the Horse* (University of Oklahoma Press, Norman, 1955), p. 79.
6.   Simmons. *The Ute Indians*, p. 29.
7.   Sprague, *Massacre*, p. 48.

8. Roe, *The Indian and the Horse*, p. 30.

9. Ibid., p. 159.

10. Jan Pettit, *Utes, the Mountain People* (Johnson Printing Co., Boulder, Colo., 2005), p. 18.

11. Simmons, *The Ute Indians*, p. 30.

12. Pettit, *Utes, the Mountain People*, p. 42.

13. Ibid., p. 23.

14. Jim Jefferson, phone conversation with the author, September 2006; Sidney Jocknick, *Early Days on the Western Slope of Colorado* (Western Reflections Publishing Co., Montrose, Colo., 2004), p. 24.

15. Brooks, *Captives and Cousins*, pp. 157–159.

16. Roe, *The Indian and the Horse*, p. 242.

17. James Jefferson, Robert W. Delaney, and Gregory C. Thompson, *The Southern Utes: A Tribal History* (published by the Southern Ute Tribe, printed by the University of Utah Printing Service, Salt Lake City, 1972), p. 61.

18. Fred Conetah, *A History of the Northern Ute People*, edited by Kathryn L. MacKay and Floyd A. O'Neil (published by the Uintah-Ouray Ute Tribe, printed by the University of Utah Printing Service, Salt Lake City, 1982), pp. 81–82.

19. Becker and Smith, *Chipeta, Queen of the Utes*, p. 36.

20. Simmons, *The Ute Indians*, p. 175.

21. *Testimony*, p. 197.

22. Dawson and Skiff, *The Ute War*, p. 141.

23. Jefferson, *The Southern Utes*, p. 67.

24. Emmitt, *The Last War Trail*, pp. 123–125, 143–145.

25. Ibid.

26. Decker, *The Utes Must Go!* p. 106.

27. FitzPatrick, *Red Twilight*, p. 52.

Chapter 8

1. Meeker, *Brave Miss Meeker*, p. 14.

2. Ibid.

3. Ibid., p. 39.

4. Sprague, *Massacre*, p. 267.

5. *Hayden Survey of Colorado*.

6. "Phases of the Sun and Moon," U.S. Naval Observatory, www.usno.navy.mil/USNO/astronomical-applications/data-services/rs-one-day-us.

7. Meeker, *Brave Miss Meeker*, pp. 28–29.

8. Rankin, *Reminiscences*, p. 244.

9. *Testimony*, p. 6; Adams referred to Roan Creek as "the Roon River"; Meeker, *Brave Miss Meeker*, p. 14.

10. Bob Elderkin, interview with author, September 2007; author visit to Parachute Creek, September 2009.

11. *Testimony*, p. 88.
12. Ibid.; Meeker, *Brave Miss Meeker*, p. 17.

CHAPTER 9

1. News article, *Greeley Tribune*, August 4, 1875.
2. Carol Rein Shwayder, *Nathan Cook Meeker, Founder of Greeley, Colorado, a Chronology of his Life and Times, 1817–1879* (Unicorn Ventures, Greeley, Colo., 1996).
3. Peggy Ford, archivist, City of Greeley Museums, interview with author, January 16, 2006.
4. N. C. Meeker, letter to Josephine Meeker, May 13, 1878, City of Greeley Museums.
5. Shwayder, *Nathan Cook Meeker*.
6. Isabella Bird, *A Lady's Life in the Rocky Mountains* (University of Oklahoma Press, Norman, 1965), p. 95.
7. Josephine Meeker, letter to Mary Meeker, July 17, 1881, City of Greeley Museums.
8. Sprague, *Massacre*, pp. 234–235.
9. Ibid., p. 18.
10. Ibid., pp. 6–8, 21.
11. Josephine Meeker, letter to Ralph Meeker, August 11, 1878, City of Greeley Museums.
12. Emmitt, *The Last War Trail*, p. 58.
13. Ibid.
14. Werner, *Meeker: The Story of the Meeker Massacre*, p. 12.
15. Sprague, *Massacre*, p. 116.
16. Ibid.
17. Peggy Ford, phone interview with author, January 16, 2006; Sprague, *Massacre*, p. 116.
18. Dawson and Skiff, *The Ute War*, p. 101.
19. Emmitt, *The Last War Trail*, p. 66.
20. Ibid. Emmitt says the Ute word for "sister" is "Pa-veet'z." Ute elder Clifford Duncan, who read parts of this manuscript, corrected it to the word I used here.
21. Meeker, *Brave Miss Meeker*, p. 39.
22. Ibid., p. 17.
23. Ibid.
24. Ibid., p. 10.
25. Ibid.
26. Dawson and Skiff, *The Ute War*, p. 125.
27. Ibid.
28. J. J. Critchlow, letter to Mary Meeker, October 16, 1879, City of Greeley Museums.

29. D. B. McLane, letter to Arvilla Meeker, January 12, 1880, City of Greeley Museums.
30. Dawson and Skiff, *The Ute War*, p. 145. The dress that Josie made along the hostage trail is on display at the City of Greeley Museums.
31. Ibid., p. 146.
32. Ibid.

Chapter 10

1. Josie may have been exaggerating for the benefit of her readers. Utes had occasionally killed captives, but I found no record in many accounts of Ute fighting and hostage taking that suggests they burned prisoners at the stake.
2. Meeker, *Brave Miss Meeker*, p. 13.
3. Ibid., p. 30.
4. Mrs. Charles Adams, Meeker Massacre Scrapbook, p. 7. Archived at the Colorado Springs Pioneers Museum.
5. *Testimony*, pp. 1–16.
6. Becker and Smith, *Chipeta, Queen of the Utes*, pp. 11–12, 18.
7. Ibid., p. 11.
8. Ibid., pp. 23–24.
9. Ibid.
10. Ibid., pp. 29–30.
11. Ibid., p. 30.
12. Ibid.
13. Dawson and Skiff, *The Ute War*, pp. 144–145.
14. Jonas Grant Sr., interview with author, September 2006.
15. Ibid.
16. Meeker, *Brave Miss Meeker*, p. 40.
17. Ibid., p. 30.
18. Rankin, *Reminiscences*, p. 238; *Shawsheen*, document at City of Greeley Museums.
19. Simmons, *The Ute Indians*, p. 187.
20. Shirley Johnston, "Queen Chipeta," *Journal of the Western Slope*, vol. 11, no. 1 (Winter 1996), p. 8.
21. Becker and Smith, *Chipeta, Queen of the Utes*, p. 29.
22. News article, *Chicago Tribune*, October 29, 1879.

Chapter 11

1. Dawson and Skiff, *The Ute War*, p. 151.
2. *Testimony*, p. 45.
3. *White River Ute Commission*, p. 67.

4. *Testimony*, p. 162.
5. Ibid., p. 183.
6. Ibid., p. 103.
7. *White River Ute Commission*, pp. 72–73.
8. *Testimony*, pp. 158, 171, 183.
9. *White River Ute Commission*, pp. 66–75.
10. Ibid., p. 67.
11. *Testimony*, p. 171.
12. *White River Ute Commission*, p. 67.
13. Simmons, *The Ute Indians*, pp. 112–114.
14. News article, *Greeley Tribune*, December 11, 1878.
15. Accounts written at the time listed her only as "Jane," but her full name, according to descendants, was Jane Redjacket.
16. Sprague, *Massacre*, p. 120.
17. Ibid., pp. 120–121.
18. Ibid., pp. 121–122.
19. *Testimony*, p. 74.
20. Ibid., p. 76.
21. *White River Ute Commission*, p. 70.
22. Ibid., p. 66.
23. Sprague, *Massacre*, p. 136.
24. Ibid.
25. *White River Ute Commission*, p. 69.
26. Ibid., pp. 69–70.
27. Ibid., p. 70.
28. Ibid.
29. Ibid.
30. Ibid., p. 67.
31. Ibid., p. 68.
32. Ibid., pp. 68–69.
33. Ibid., p. 46.
34. Ibid.
35. *Testimony*, p. 84.
36. Ibid., p. 85.
37. Ibid., p. 173.
38. Ibid., p. 107.
39. Ibid., p. 139.
40. Ibid., p. 107.
41. *White River Ute Commission*, p. 67.
42. Ibid., p. 72.

CHAPTER 12

1.   *Hayden Survey of Colorado.*
2.   Meeker, *Brave Miss Meeker,* p. 39.
3.   Ibid., pp. 14, 39.
4.   Ibid., p. 14.
5.   Ibid., pp. 14–17.
6.   Dawson and Skiff, *The Ute War,* p. 125.
7.   Ibid., p. 145.
8.   Meeker, *Brave Miss Meeker,* p. 17.
9.   Ibid.
10. Ibid., p. 39.
11. Ibid., pp. 17, 39.
12. Rankin, *Reminiscences,* p. 245. Adams didn't receive his formal orders to attempt to rescue the hostages until October 14, but discussions for him to undertake such a mission began at least a week earlier. Rankin says the telegram ordering Merritt to halt was sent to Rawlins on October 9.
13. Ibid.
14. Ibid., pp. 245–246.
15. Meeker, *Brave Miss Meeker,* p. 17.
16. "Phases of the Sun and Moon." *U.S. Naval Observatory.* www.usno.navy.mil/USNO/astronomical-applications/data-services/rs-one-day-us.
17. Meeker, *Brave Miss Meeker,* p. 17.
18. Ibid., p. 18.
19. Rankin, *Reminiscences,* p. 244; *Testimony,* p. 6.
20. James Parker, *The Old Army: Memories, 1872–1918* (Stackpole Books, Mechanicsburg, Penn., 2003), p. 421.
21. Meeker, *Brave Miss Meeker,* p. 18.
22. Ibid., p. 39.
23. Ibid., p. 29.
24. Ibid., p. 18; *Testimony,* p. 198.
25. *White River Ute Commission,* p. 50; Meeker, *Brave Miss Meeker,* p. 18.
26. Meeker, *Brave Miss Meeker,* p. 18.

CHAPTER 13

1.   Article from unidentified newspaper included in Meeker Massacre Scrapbook; letters in "The People's Voice," *Chicago Tribune,* October 17, 1879; sermon of Rev. Mr. Harsha, at Chicago Presbyterian Church, *Chicago Tribune,* October 20, 1879.
2.   News stories, editorials, and letters, *Chicago Tribune,* September 1879 through April 1880.

3. *Chicago Tribune*, October 2, 1879.
4. News stories, *Chicago Tribune*, October 1879.
5. "Horace Greeley, Ideas and Movements, 1811–1872," www.us-history.com; Decker, *The Utes Must Go!* p. 167.
6. See, for instance, the October 11, 1879, editorial supportive of Commissioner of Indian Affairs E. A. Hayt's policies, and the November 28 editorial critical of Interior Secretary Carl Schurz's policies, even though the policies were the same.
7. Decker, *The Utes Must Go!* pp. 146–147.
8. Ibid., p. 150.
9. News article, *Chicago Tribune*, October 24, 1879.
10. *Testimony*, p. 113.
11. Decker, *The Utes Must Go!* p. 150; *White River Ute Commission*, p. 66.
12. *Testimony*, p. 1.
13. Miller, *Hollow Victory*, pp. 149, 172.
14. *White River Ute Commission*, p. 25.
15. Dawson and Skiff, *The Ute War*, p. 56.
16. Decker, *The Utes Must Go!* p. 144; McClellan, *This Is Our Land*, p. 369.
17. Decker, *The Utes Must Go!* pp. 145–153.
18. Rio Blanco Historical Society Museum. Several buildings still stand and are part of the museum.
19. Rankin, *Reminiscences*, p. 245.
20. Ibid.

CHAPTER 14

1. Meeker, *Brave Miss Meeker*, p. 39.
2. Ibid., p. 18; *White River Ute Commission*, p. 45.
3. Meeker, *Brave Miss Meeker*, p. 18.
4. *Testimony*, pp. 2, 6.
5. Meeker, *Brave Miss Meeker*, p. 18.
6. George D. Sherman, *The Solid Muldoon* (Ouray, Colo.), November 7, 1879.
7. *Testimony*, p. 6.
8. Sprague, *Massacre*, p. 267.
9. *Testimony*, p. 88. There is a discrepancy here with Josie's other story that the rescue site was not on Plateau Creek, but another small stream 12 or 15 miles away from Plateau Creek. Adams and others make it clear it was at this second location—a camp on Mesa Creek—that the hostages were found and released.
10. *White River Ute Commission*, p. 45.
11. *Hayden Survey of Colorado*; Sprague, *Massacre*, p. 267.

CHAPTER 15

1. Sprague, *Massacre,* p. 239.
2. Ibid.
3. News article, *Chicago Tribune,* January 7, 1880.
4. News article, *Greeley Tribune,* January 7, 1880.
5. *Report of the Ute Commission,* p. 7.
6. *Testimony,* p. 48; also, Jonas Grant Sr., conversation with the author, July 2008.
7. *Testimony,* p. 3.
8. Ibid.
9. Ibid.
10. Ibid., p. 2.
11. Ibid., p. 8.
12. Ibid.
13. *White River Ute Commission,* pp. 17–18. Presumably Flora Ellen was referring to Canalla, who was in charge of her during most of her captivity. But there is some indication that she was referring to Canavish, Canalla's father. Adams asked her, "Johnson. You mean the old man himself?" and she replied, "Yes sir, the old man himself."
14. Jonas Grant Sr., conversation with the author, July 2008. Flora Ellen Price's great-grandson, Thomas Henry Reed, said he believes the rapes did occur. Phone conversation with the author, January 2008.
15. *White River Ute Commission,* p. 26.
16. Ibid., pp. 43–44.
17. Ibid., p. 44.
18. Ibid.
19. Ibid., p. 43.
20. Ibid., p. 17.
21. Ibid., p. 43.
22. Meeker, *Brave Miss Meeker,* p. 11.
23. News article, *Greeley Tribune,* June 26, 1878.
24. Meeker, *Brave Miss Meeker,* p. 9.
25. Ibid., p. 17.
26. Ibid., p. 19.
27. Dawson and Skiff, *The Ute War,* p. 101.
28. *White River Ute Commission,* p. 44.
29. Ibid., p. 75.
30. Ibid., p. 76.
31. Ibid.
32. Ralph Meeker, letter to the *Denver Tribune,* January 19, 1880, reprinted in the *Chicago Tribune,* January 28, 1880.
33. Ibid.

34. Josephine Meeker, letter to Ralph Meeker, January 30, 1880. Colorado Historical Society, Denver.
35. Ralph Meeker, letter to the *Denver Tribune,* January 19, 1880, reprinted in the *Chicago Tribune,* January 28, 1880.
36. Sprague, *Massacre,* pp. 234–238.
37. Josephine Meeker, letter to Ralph Meeker, January 30, 1880, Colorado Historical Society, Denver.
38. Josephine Meeker, letter to Ralph Meeker, February 22, 1880, Colorado Historical Society, Denver.
39. *Testimony,* p. 9.
40. Ibid., p. 48.
41. Arvilla D. Meeker, letter to her children, March 5, 1897, City of Greeley Museums.
42. *Report of the Ute Commission,* p. 7.
43. Ibid., p. 42.
44. News article, *Greeley Tribune,* December 31, 1879.
45. Ralph Meeker, letter to Arvilla Meeker, January 5, 1880, Colorado Historical Society, Denver.
46. Charles Adams, letter to Arvilla Meeker, December 31, 1879, City of Greeley Museums.
47. News article, *Chicago Tribune,* January 11, 1880; *White River Ute Commission,* pp. 64, 76.
48. Decker, *The Utes Must Go!* p. 156.
49. Sprague, *Massacre,* pp. 235, 241.
50. *Colorado Miner* (Georgetown), January 17, 1880.
51. Ibid., January 24, 1880.

Chapter 16

1. *Testimony,* p. 1.
2. Ibid., p. 109.
3. Ibid., pp. 1–2.
4. Ibid.; news article, *Chicago Tribune,* October 14, 1879.
5. "Denver and Rio Grande Railroad, Scenic Line of the World," http//:ghostdepot.com.
6. *Testimony,* p. 3.
7. Sprague, *Massacre,* pp. 79–80.
8. Ibid., pp. 80–89.
9. Ibid., p. 187.
10. George D. Sherman, *The Solid Muldoon* (Ouray, Colo.), November 7, 1879.
11. Ibid.; Sprague, *Massacre,* p. 198; Meeker, *Brave Miss Meeker,* p. 20.
12. Sherman, *The Solid Muldoon* (Ouray, Colo.), November 7, 1879.

13. Ibid.
14. See appendix VI.
15. Sprague, *Massacre*, p. 199.
16. Sherman, *The Solid Muldoon* (Ouray, Colo.), November 7, 1879.
17. Ibid.
18. Meeker, *Brave Miss Meeker,* p. 19.
19. *Testimony,* p. 2.
20. Ibid.
21. Ibid.
22. Ibid., pp. 2–3.
23. Ibid., p. 3.
24. Ibid., p. 4.
25. Ibid., p. 4.
26. Ibid.
27. Ibid., p. 5.
28. Ibid.
29. Ibid., pp. 5–6.
30. Ibid.
31. Ibid.
32. Meeker, *Brave Miss Meeker,* p. 20.
33. Ibid., pp. 43–44.
34. Ibid., p. 20.

Chapter 17

1. Editorial, *Chicago Tribune,* November 4, 1879.
2. Ibid.
3. Ibid.
4. Swisshelm, letter, *Chicago Tribune,* December 15, 1879.
5. Ibid.
6. From Arthur J. Larsen's introduction to Jane Grey Swisshelm, *Crusader and Feminist: Letters of Jane Grey Swisshelm, 1858–1865* (Minnesota Historical Society, Saint Paul, 1934).
7. Swisshelm letter, *Chicago Tribune,* October 4, 1879.
8. Ibid.
9. Editorial, *Chicago Tribune,* November 28, 1879.
10. Swisshelm letter, *Chicago Tribune,* November 7, 1879.
11. Swisshelm letter, *Chicago Tribune,* December 15, 1879.
12. Editorial, *Colorado Sun,* January 10, 1880.
13. *Petition on behalf of Susan* (SEN 46A–H10), Record Group 46, Records of the U.S. Senate.

14. Staff members with the National Archives in Washington, D.C., who tracked down a copy of the petition at my request, were unable to find any evidence that Congress ever took action on it. E-mail exchange, November 2006, between the author and William H. Davis, Archival Programs Branch, Center for Legislative Archives, National Archives and Records Administration.
15. Simmons, *The Ute Indians*, p. 187.
16. Jonas Grant Sr., conversation with the author, March 22, 2008; Becker and Smith, *Chipeta, Queen of the Utes*, p. 237.
17. Swisshelm letter, *Chicago Tribune*, December 29, 1879.

Chapter 18

1. News article, *Chicago Tribune*, December 9, 1879, quoting from a special report to the *Denver Tribune* dated December 6.
2. Ibid. There is no mention of this incident in transcripts of the White River Ute Commission investigation, but other newspapers mentioned it; *Greeley Tribune*, December 10, 1879.
3. *White River Ute Commission.*
4. For instance, the *Greeley Tribune* referred to it as "The Ute Peace Commission" in a news article on November 19, 1879.
5. *Testimony*, p. 8.
6. *White River Ute Commission*, p. 2.
7. Ibid., pp. 27, 78.
8. Ibid., p. 2; *Greeley Tribune*, November 19, 1879.
9. *White River Ute Commission*, p. 2.
10. Ibid., various pages.
11. Ibid., pp. 3–6.
12. Ibid., pp. 11–12.
13. Ibid., pp. 12, 76.
14. Ibid., p. 64. Several sources report that the White River Ute listed in the transcripts as "Colorado" was actually Colorow. See Emmitt, *The Last War Trail*, p. 266.
15. *White River Ute Commission*, pp. 62–65.
16. Ibid., pp. 66–74.
17. Ibid., pp. 74–75.
18. Ibid., p. 75.
19. Ibid., pp. 75–76.
20. News articles, *Chicago Tribune*, December 23, 1879, and January 7, 1880.
21. *White River Ute Commission*, p. 80.
22. Ibid., p. 81.
23. Ibid., p. 76. What happened to Johnny is a mystery. There is no record that he was taken east to Fort Leavenworth with Quinkent and Tim Johnson early in 1880.

24. *White River Ute Commission,* p. 78.
25. Ibid., p. 80.
26. Ibid., p. 81. Exclamation point after Ouray's statement is in original.
27. The official transcripts simply say, at various times, that documents were translated for Ouray. For example, on November 17, 1879, a dispatch from the secretary of Interior was read into the record and translated for him; *White River Ute Commission,* p. 20. The *Greeley Tribune,* on November 19, 1879, described the process as items being translated for Ouray into Spanish, who then translated them into Ute for the other Indians present. The process worked the opposite way when a Ute was speaking.
28. *White River Ute Commission,* p. 82.
29. Ibid., p. 83.
30. Ibid., pp. 83–84.
31. Editorial, *Greeley Tribune,* December 31, 1879.

CHAPTER 19

1. News article, *Chicago Tribune,* January 11, 1880; Sprague, *Massacre,* p. 240.
2. News article, *Chicago Tribune,* January 11, 1880.
3. Ibid.
4. Ibid.
5. Ibid.
6. Ibid.
7. Sprague, *Massacre,* p. 240.
8. Josephine Meeker, letter to Ralph Meeker, January 11, 1880. Colorado Historical Society, Denver.
9. News article, *Colorado Miner,* January 17, 1880.
10. *Testimony,* pp. 1–61. Fisk's dispute with Hayt was outlined in several *Chicago Tribune* articles in early 1880. For instance, January 10: "Fisk preparing a variety of charges against Commissioner Hayt."
11. News article, *Chicago Tribune,* January 30, 1880.
12. Ibid.
13. Ibid., January 24, 1880.
14. Josephine Meeker, letter to Ralph Meeker, January 25, 1880, Colorado Historical Society, Denver.
15. *Testimony,* pp. 71–93.
16. News articles, *Chicago Tribune,* January 27, 1880; February 4, 1880.
17. Ibid., February 27, 1880.
18. Ibid., January 26, 1880; February 7, 1880.
19. Ibid., February 18, 1880.
20. Ibid., February 27, 1880.
21. Ibid., February 18, 1880.
22. Ibid.

23. Ibid.
24. Ibid.
25. Ibid., March 1, 1880.
26. Ibid., February 27, 1880.
27. Ibid.
28. Sprague, *Massacre*, p. 241; Jonas Grant Sr., conversation with the author, April 2008.
29. News article, *Chicago Tribune*, February 29, 1880.

CHAPTER 20

1. News article, *Chicago Tribune*, December 3, 1879.
2. Simmons, *The Ute Indians*, p. 178.
3. William Wyckoff, *Creating Colorado: The Making of the Western American Landscape, 1860–1940* (Yale University Press, 1999), p. 222.
4. Ralph K. Andrist, *The Long Death: The Last Days of the Plains Indians* (University of Oklahoma Press, Norman, 2001), p. 331.
5. *Testimony*, pp. 125–127.
6. News article, *Chicago Tribune*, December 10, 1879.
7. Ibid., December 12, 1879.
8. Ibid., January 22, 1880.
9. Ibid., January 14, 1880.
10. Ibid., January 22, 1880.
11. *Testimony*, p. 127.
12. Ibid.
13. Ibid., p. 113.
14. Ibid. Canalla (Johnson) said his brother died from wounds suffered during the fight at the White River Agency; *White River Ute Commission*, p. 8. Johnson family history says it was Canalla's son who was killed. That son would have been Ouray's nephew.
15. *Testimony*, p. 122.
16. Ibid., p. 168.
17. News article, *Chicago Tribune*, January 10, 1880.
18. Ibid.
19. Ibid.
20. Ibid., March 7, 1880.
21. Ibid.; also March 4, 1880.
22. Decker, *The Utes Must Go!* pp. 167–168.
23. News articles, *Chicago Tribune*, March 1–April 13, 1880.
24. Ibid., March 7.
25. Simmons, *The Ute Indians*, p. 191.

26. Ibid. Other accounts have slightly different details, particularly about the annuity payments. See Decker, *The Utes Must Go!* p. 163; and Conetah, *History of the Northern Ute People*, pp. 63, 115.
27. Sprague, *Massacre*, p. 245.
28. Conetah, *History of the Northern Ute People*, pp. 63–64.
29. Ibid., p. 64.
30. *Report of the Ute Commission*, p. 41.
31. Conetah, *History of the Northern Ute People*, p. 64.
32. Simmons, *The Ute Indians*, pp. 192–193.

CHAPTER 21

1. Jonas Grant Sr., conversations with the author, September 2008. Grant said that for most of his life he was cautioned by elders in his family not to discuss what happened on that trip, but in later years his great-uncle Wilson Johnson encouraged him to tell what really occurred. Other modern-day Utes said their parents and grandparents rarely talked of the events of 1879 and the subsequent move in 1881, and frequently discouraged their children from talking about it because they still feared repercussions from the whites.
2. See appendix VIII.
3. *Report of the Secretary of Interior*, 1881, p. 79.
4. *Report of the Secretary of Interior*, 1878, p. 778; 1882, pp. 400–403.
5. *Testimony*, p. 90.
6. *Report of the Secretary of Interior*, 1878, p. 778.
7. *Report of the Secretary of Interior*, 1882, pp. 400–403.
8. *Report of the Secretary of Interior*, 1878, pp. 778, 790; 1882, pp. 390, 402.
9. Loya Arrum, phone conversation with author, August 6, 2008; Parker, *The Old Army*, p. 53.
10. Francis McKinley, interviewed by Leslie Kelen, August 11, 1988, *University of Utah's Oral History Project*, p. 8.
11. Marietta Reed, interviewed by Norma Denver, January 3, 1969, *Doris Duke American History Project*, pp. 1–2.
12. Sprague, *Massacre*, p. 245.
13. Parker, *The Old Army*, p. 126.
14. McKinley, *University of Utah's Oral History Project*, p. 6.
15. Parker, *The Old Army*, p. 130.
16. Ibid.
17. *Report of the Secretary of Interior*, 1881, p. 384.
18. News article, *Daily Sentinel* (Grand Junction, Colo.), August 11, 2008.
19. Jocknick, *Early Days on the Western Slope*, p. 219.
20. *Report of the Secretary of Interior*, 1881, p. 385.
21. Ibid.

22. Ibid., p. 386.

23. Jocknick, *Early Days on the Western Slope*, p. 220.

24. Ibid., p. 221.

25. Arvis Gilson, letter to Colonel Ranald Mackenzie, June 21, 1881, National Archives, Lakewood, Colo.

26. Arvis Gilson, letter to Colonel Ranald Mackenzie, July 25, 1881, National Archives, Lakewood, Colo.

27. Jocknick, *Early Days on the Western Slope*, pp. 221–222.

28. Parker, *The Old Army*, pp. 51–52.

29. Colonel Ranald Mackenzie, telegram to army headquarters for the region of the Missouri, August 12, 1881; Secretary of Interior Samuel Kirkwood, letter to Secretary of War Robert Lincoln, August 20, 1881; Secretary of Interior Samuel Kirkwood, letter to Ute Commission member Thomas McMorris, August 24, 1881. All at National Archives, Lakewood, Colo.

30. Colonel A. B. Meacham, letter to Assistant Secretary of Interior A. Dill, June 18, 1881, National Archives, Lakewood, Colo.

31. Author unknown, White River military headquarters, letter to General John Pope, June 23, 1881, National Archives, Lakewood, Colo.

32. Major Orlando H. Moore, letter to U.S. Army, Department of the Missouri Headquarters, Fort Leavenworth, Kan., National Archives, Lakewood, Colo.

33. Secretary of Interior Samuel Kirkwood, letter to Secretary of War Robert Lincoln, August 20, 1881, National Archives, Lakewood, Colo.

34. Colonel Ranald Mackenzie, telegram to U.S. Army Headquarters, Washington, D.C., August 28, 1881, National Archives, Lakewood, Colo.

35. Jocknick, *Early Days on the Western Slope*, pp. 224–225.

36. Parker, *The Old Army*, pp. 52–53.

37. *Report of the Secretary of War*, 1881, p. 116.

38. Parker, *The Old Army*, pp. 53, 135.

39. Jocknick, *Early Days on the Western Slope*, p. 226.

40. General George Crook, telegram to U.S. Army, Department of the Missouri Headquarters, Fort Leavenworth, Kan., October 3, 1881, National Archives, Lakewood, Colo.

41. *Report of the Secretary of War*, 1881, p. 116.

42. *Report of the Secretary of Interior*, 1881, p. 385.

43. Francis McKinley, *University of Utah's Oral History Project*, pp. 5–7.

44. Colonel L. C. Hunt, letter to U.S. Army, Department of the Missouri Headquarters, Fort Leavenworth, Kan., September 18, 1881, National Archives, Lakewood, Colo.

45. *Report of the Secretary of Interior*, 1881, p. 215.

46. General John Pope, letter to Adjutant General of the Army, Chicago, October 13, 1881, National Archives, Lakewood, Colo.

47. Anonymous, White River military headquarters, letter to military authorities, November 12, 1881, National Archives, Lakewood, Colo.

CHAPTER 22

1.　News article, *Greeley Tribune,* November 19, 1879.
2.　Ibid.
3.　Ibid.
4.　Ibid., November 12, 1879.
5.　Ibid., November 19, 1879.
6.　News article, *Boulder Courier,* November 21, 1879.
7.　Ibid., November 28, 1879.
8.　See chapter 15.
9.　U.S. Army Headquarters, Military Division of the Missouri, Chicago, letter to Miss Josephine Meeker, September 11, 1880, Greeley City Museums; news article, *Colorado Sun,* September 18, 1880.
10.　Albert J. Bailess, letter to Josephine Meeker, December 31, 1882, Colorado Historical Society, Denver.
11.　Josephine Meeker, letter to Mary Meeker, July 17, 1881, City of Greeley Museums.
12.　Ibid.
13.　Anonymous letter to Josephine Meeker, February 13, 1882, Colorado Historical Society, Denver.
14.　Secretary of Interior Samuel Kirkwood, letter to Secretary of War Robert Lincoln, February 17, 1882, National Archives, Lakewood, Colo.
15.　J. J. Critchlow, letter to Department of Interior, January 30, 1882, National Archives, Lakewood, Colo.
16.　Jonas Grant Sr., telephone conversation with author, August 8, 2008.
17.　General Phillip Sheridan, telegram to Adjutant General of the Army, March 18, 1882, National Archives, Lakewood, Colo.
18.　McClellan, *This is Our Land,* p. 737.
19.　Secretary of Interior Samuel Kirkwood, letter to Secretary of War Robert Lincoln, March 31, 1882, National Archives, Lakewood, Colo.
20.　W. H. Berry, letter to Army Commander at Fort Thornburgh, Utah, April 26, 1882, National Archives, Lakewood, Colo.
21.　Lieutenant George Morgan, report on death of Nicaagat, May 1882, National Archives, Lakewood, Colo.
22.　General Sheridan, telegram to General R. C. Drum, Washington, D.C., May 1, 1882, National Archives, Lakewood, Colo.
23.　News article, *Chicago Tribune,* May 2, 1882.
24.　"Henry M. Teller (1882–1885): Secretary of the Interior," *American President, an Online Reference Source,* Miller Center of Public Affairs, University of Virginia, http://www.millercenter.org/academic/americanpresident.
25.　Josephine Meeker, letter to Mary Meeker, July 17, 1881, City of Greeley Museums.

26. News article, *Greeley Tribune*, December 31, 1882.

27. News article, *Gunnison Daily Review*, January 6, 1883.

28. News articles, *Greeley Tribune*, December 30, 1882; January 3, 1883; January 10, 1883; and January 17, 1883.

29. Albert J. Bailess, letter to Josephine Meeker, December 31, 1882, Colorado Historical Society, Denver.

30. News article, *Greeley Tribune*, January 10, 1883.

31. Arvilla Meeker, letter to Sarah E. Howard, April 25, 1903, City of Greeley Museums.

32. News article, *Rocky Mountain Daily News,* January 7, 1883.

33. Ibid. For instance, the article claims Josie's health was poor prior to joining her mother and father at the White River Agency, when she was actually a robust young woman. It said she worked hard at a tent and awning manufacturer for very little money immediately prior to going to the White River, when family letters show she was attending business school in Denver. It also said the young woman witnessed her father's death, which was clearly not true, based on Josie's own accounts.

34. News article, *Greeley Tribune*, January 24, 1883.

Epilogue

1. *Report of the Ute Commission*, p. 7.

2. Ibid., p. 42.

3. Jonas Grant Sr., phone conversation with author, September 21, 2008.

4. Ibid.

5. Ibid.

6. News article, *Chicago Tribune,* February 27, 1880.

7. Jonas Grant Sr., phone conversation with author, September 21, 2008.

8. News articles, *Chicago Tribune,* February 27, 1880; March 5, 1880.

9. Sprague, *Massacre*, p. 255.

10. Rankin, *Reminiscences,* pp. 269–270.

11. Ibid., pp. 268–269. Simmons says Colorow's War occurred in 1887, and he died in 1888 (*The Ute Indians*, pp. 205–206).

12. Sprague, *Massacre*, p. 251.

13. Ibid.

14. *Descendants of Thomas Price,* a Price family genealogy.

15. Thomas Reed, phone interview with author, January 27, 2008.

16. Ibid.

17. Photo provided to City of Greeley Museums by Thomas Reed, 2003.

18. Sprague, *Massacre*, p. 254.

19. Governor Pitkin Collection, Colorado State Archives, http://www.colorado.gov/dpa/doit/archives/govs/pitkin.html.

20. "Teller, Henry Moore, (1830–1914)," *Biographical Directory of the United States Congress;* http://www.bioguide.congress.gov/biosearch/biosearch.asp; Donald A. MacKendrick, "Cesspools, Alkali and White Lily Soap: The Grand Junction Indian School, 1886–1911," *Journal of the Western Slope,* vol. 8, no. 3 (Summer 1993).
21. Floyd A. O'Neil, "An Anguished Odyssey: The Flight of the Utes, 1906–1908," *Utah Historical Quarterly,* vol. 36, no. 4 (Fall 1968). Reprinted for the Western History Center, University of Utah, 2008.

Appendix I

1. Miller, *Hollow Victory*, pp. 24–25.
2. *Testimony*, pp. 65, 174.
3. *Report of the Secretary of War*, 1879, p. 10.
4. News article, *Chicago Tribune*, October 12, 1879.
5. *White River Ute Commission*, p. 32.
6. *Testimony*, p. 90.
7. Miller, *Hollow Victory*, p. 147.
8. Sumner, "Besieged by the Utes," p. 838.
9. *Testimony*, p. 7.
10. Ibid., p. 192.

Appendix II

1. John D. McDermott, "The Famous Ride of John 'Portugese' Phillips," www.philkearny.vcn.com/phillips.htm.
2. Wyoming historical marker, Split Rock Monument, on State Highway 287 near Muddy Gap; also Margot Lawrence, *Flyers and Stayers: The Book of the World's Greatest Rides* (George G. Harrap & Co. Ltd., London, 1980), pp. 232–233.
3. Lawrence, *Flyers and Stayers*, pp. 221–225.
4. "2009 Results," American Endurance Riding Conference website, www.aerc.org.

Appendix III

1. *Testimony*, pp. 6–7.
2. Ibid., p. 7.
3. D. B. McLane, letter to Arvilla Meeker, January 12, 1880, City of Greeley Museums.
4. Ibid.
5. News article, *Chicago Tribune*, December 27, 1879.

6.   Dawson and Skiff, *The Ute War*, p. 171.
7.   Emmitt, *The Last War Trail*, pp. 39–40.
8.   *Testimony*, p. 132.

Appendix IV

1.   Becker and Smith, *Chipeta, Queen of the Utes*, pp. 11–18. Jonas Grant has acted as an adviser to me, sharing information about the Johnson family and the Utes in general, and correcting errors I have made. He and his wife, Joy, who is half Uncompahgre Ute and half Navajo, live in Fort Duchesne, Utah.

Appendix V

1.   Wallace Stegner, *Beyond the Hundredth Meridian: John Wesley Powell and the Second Opening of the West* (Penguin Books, New York, 1992), p. 245.
2.   News article, *Chicago Tribune*, December 25, 1879.
3.   Ibid.
4.   John Wesley Powell, *The Exploration of the Colorado River and Its Canyons* (Penguin Books, New York, 2003), p. 184.
5.   News article, *Chicago Tribune*, December 25, 1879.

Appendix VI

1.   *Report of the Secretary of War*, 1879, p. 12.
2.   Colonel Wesley Merritt, telegram to General George Crook, [October] 22, 1879 (date shown is "22nd"). Records Group 75, National Archives, Lakewood, Colo.
3.   Ibid.
4.   Sumner, "Besieged by the Utes," pp. 846–847.
5.   Ibid.
6.   Colonel Wesley Merritt, telegram to General George Crook, [October] 22, 1879.
7.   Ron Hilkey, phone conversation with author, March 2008; Kevin D. Black, e-mail communication with author, June 2008; *Southwestern Lore, Journal of Colorado Archaeology*, vol. 63, no. 3 (Fall 1997), pp. 13–14.

Appendix VII

1.   FitzPatrick, *Red Twilight*, p. 30.
2.   Ibid., p. 96.
3.   Loya Arrum, conversation with author, October 4, 2008.

4. *White River Ute Commission*, pp. 61–65.
5. FitzPatrick, *Red Twilight*, p. 96.
6. Simmons, *The Ute Indians*, p. 63.
7. Dawson and Skiff, *The Ute War*, p. 174.
8. *Report of the Ute Commission*, pp. 42–49.
9. FitzPatrick, *Red Twilight*, p. 97.
10. Sprague, *Massacre*, p. 94.
11. Emmitt, *The Last War Trail*, p. 214.
12. Loya Arrum, phone interview, August 6, 2008.
13. Dawson and Skiff, *The Ute War*, pp. 175–176.
14. Emmitt, *The Last War Trail*, p. 223.

Appendix VIII

1. *Report of the Secretary of Interior*, 1878, pp. 795, 805.
2. *Report of the Secretary of Interior*, 1881, pp. 351, 363.
3. *Report of the Secretary of Interior*, 1882, pp. 422, 423.
4. Jonas Grant Sr., interview with author, September 2007.
5. Parker, *The Old Army*, p. 44.
6. Jocknick, *Early Days on the Western Slope*, p. 222.
7. *Report of the Secretary of Interior*, 1881, p. 78.

BIBLIOGRAPHY

Primary Sources
Official Documents

Annual Report of the Secretary of Interior for the Year ended June 30, 1878. Vol. I.
    Government Printing Office, 1878. Copy on file at the Denver Public Library.
Annual Report of the Secretary of Interior for the Year ended June 30, 1879. Vol. I.
    Government Printing Office, 1879. Copy on file at the Denver Public Library.
*Annual Report of the Secretary of Interior on the operations of the Department for the
    year ended June 30, 1880.* Vol. I. Government Printing Office, 1880. Copy on file
    at the Denver Public Library.
*Annual Report of the Secretary of Interior, on the operations of the Department for the
    Year ended June 30, 1881.* Vol. II. Government Printing Office, 1881. Copy on file
    at the Denver Public Library.
*Annual Report of the Secretary of Interior on the operations of the Department for the
    year ended June 30, 1882.* Vol. II. Government Printing Office, 1882. Copy on
    file at the Denver Public Library.
Hayden Survey of Colorado, 1874–1876. Maps. Published 1877. Originals in the
    Western History Collection at the Denver Public Library.
"Petition on behalf of Susan" (SEN 46A-H10). Record Group 46, Records of
    the U.S. Senate, Committee on Indian Affairs, Petitions and Memorials,
    Various Subjects. Copy sent to author from the National Archives and
    Records Administration, 700 Pennsylvania Avenue, NW, Washington, D.C.,
    November 16, 2006.
Report of the Secretary of War for the year ended June 30, 1879. Vol. I. Government
    Printing Office, 1879. Copy on file at the Denver Public Library.

Report of the Secretary of War for the year ended June 30, 1881. Vol. I. Government Printing Office, 1881. Copy on file at the Denver Public Library.

Report of the Ute Commission. January 20, 1881. Included in Letter from the Secretary of Interior to Congress, February 2, 1881. 46th Congress, 3rd Session, Senate Ex. Doc. No. 31. Copy on file at the Denver Public Library.

Testimony in Relation to the Ute Indian Outbreak Taken before the Committee on Indian Affairs of the House of Representatives. 46th Congress, 2nd Session, House of Representatives, Misc. Doc. No. 38. Government Printing Office, 1880. From microfilm available at the Mesa State College Library, Western Americana Series, Yale University, 1975. F591, W48, Reel No. 558, Item 5698.

White River Ute Commission Investigation, Letter from the Secretary of the Interior, Transmitting Copy of evidence taken before White River Ute Commission, May 14, 1880—Referred to the Committee on Indian Affairs. 46th Congress, 2nd Session, House of Representatives, Ex. Doc. No. 83. Government Printing Office, 1880. From microfilm available at the Mesa State College Library, Western Americana Series, Yale University, 1975. F591, W48, Reel No. 575, Item No. 5916.

Letters and Other Communications

Meeker, Josephine; Meeker, Arvilla; Meeker, Nathan; others. Letters. 1878 to 1906. Meeker Collection, City of Greeley Museums.

Meeker, Josephine; Meeker, Ralph. Meeker Family Collection, Colorado Historical Society, Manuscript Collection 426, Carton No. 4, File Folders 158–162.

Merritt, Colonel Wesley. Telegram to General George Crook, dated only "22nd." National Archives files, Lakewood, Colo., Records Group 75, M 666, File 3319, Roll 514, 4278 AGO, 1879.

U.S. Department of Interior and U.S. War Department. Miscellaneous letters. National Archives, Lakewood, Colo., M. 666, File 4278-AGO 1870, Rolls 513–517.

HISTORICAL BOOKS AND ARTICLES

Bird, Isabella. *A Lady's Life in the Rocky Mountains.* University of Oklahoma Press, 1965. Originally published by John Murray of London and G. P. Putnam's Sons, New York, 1879.

Bourke, John Gregory, Captain, Third Cavalry, U.S.A. *On the Border with Crook.* Rio Grande Press, Inc., Glorieta, N.Mex., 1969. Originally published by Charles Scribner's Sons, 1891.

Dawson, Thomas F., and F. J. V. Skiff. *The Ute War: A History of the White River Massacre and the Privations and Hardships of the Captive White Women among the Hostiles on Grand River.* Tribune Publishing House, Denver, 1879. From microfilm available at Mesa State College Library, Western Americana Series, Yale University, 1975. F591, W48, Reel 147, Item No. 1554.

Finerty, John. *War-Path and Bivouac, the Conquest of the Sioux.* University of Oklahoma Press, Norman, 1961. Originally published in 1890.

FitzPatrick, Val. *Red Twilight: The Last Free Roaming Days of the Utes.* Yellow Cat Publishing, Moab, Utah, 2000.

Huntington, D. B., Indian interpreter. *Vocabulary of the Utah and Shoshoni.* 3rd edition, revised and enlarged. Printed at the Salt Lake Herald Office, Salt Lake City, Utah, 1872. From microfilm available at Mesa State College Library, Western Americana Series, Yale University, 1975. F591, W48, Reel 277, Item No. 2730.

Jocknick, Sidney. *Early Days on the Western Slope of Colorado.* Western Reflections Publishing Co., Montrose, Colo., 2004. Originally published by the author in 1913.

Meeker, Josephine. *The Ute Massacre! Brave Miss Meeker's Captivity! Her Own Account of It, Also, the Narratives of Her Mother and Mrs. Price.* The Old Franklin Publishing House, Philadelphia, 1879. From microfilm available at Mesa State College Library, Western Americana Series, Yale University, 1975. F591, W48, Reel No. 365, Item No. 3544.

Meeker Massacre Scrapbook. Clippings from various newspapers, 1879. Compiled by Mrs. Charles Adams. Archived at the Colorado Springs Pioneer Museum. Acc. No. 548, Archives Location 15 A.

Merritt, Wesley. *Memoirs of Wesley Merritt.* 1892. Copy at Denver Public Library.

Parker, James. *The Old Army: Memories, 1872–1918.* Stackpole Books, Mechanicsburg, Penn., 2003. Originally published by Dorrance & Co., Philadelphia, 1929.

Powell, John Wesley. *The Exploration of the Colorado River and Its Canyons.* Penguin Books, New York, 2003. Originally published as *Exploration of the Colorado River of the West and its Tributaries,* Government Printing Office, 1875.

Rankin, M. Wilson. *Reminiscenses of Frontier Days.* Self–published ca. 1935. From microfilm available at Mesa State College Library, Western Americana Series, Yale University, 1975. F 591, W48, Reel No. 437, Item No. 4418. Abridged version included in *Red Twilight: The Last Free Days of the Ute Indians,* by Val FitzPatrick, Yellow Cat Publishing, Moab, Utah, 2000.

Sumner, E. V., Lt. Col., Fifth Cavalry – USA. "Besieged by the Utes." *Century Illustrated Monthly Magazine,* May 1891 to October 1891. The Century Co., New York. Vol. XLII. New Series Vol. XX. Copy on file at the City of Greeley Museums.

HISTORICAL NEWSPAPERS

Boulder [Colo.] Courier. November 21, 1879. Colorado Historic Newspaper Collections. http://coloradohistoricnewspapers.org.

Chicago Tribune. September 1879 to January 1883. From microfilm supplied by the Abraham Lincoln Library, Springfield, Ill. WPA Project No. 30098, Rolls 100–103, 119. Loaned to the Mesa County Public Library for use by the author in 2007.

Colorado Miner (Georgetown). January 17 and January 24, 1880. From microfilm at the Colorado Historical Society, Stephen H. Hart Library, Denver.

Colorado Sun (Greeley). January 10, 1880. Originals on file at the City of Greeley Museums.

Greeley [Colo.] Tribune. 1875–1883. Originals on file at the City of Greeley Museums.

Gunnison [Colo.] Daily Review. January 6, 1883. From microfilm at the Colorado Historical Society, Stephen H. Hart Library, Denver.

Rocky Mountain Daily News (Denver). January 7, 1883. From microfilm at the Colorado Historical Society, Stephen H. Hart Library, Denver.

Books and Articles

Andrist, Ralph K. *The Long Death: The Last Days of the Plains Indians.* University of Oklahoma Press, Norman, 2001. Originally published by Simon & Schuster, New York, 1964.

Becker, Cynthia, and David Smith. *Chipeta, Queen of the Utes.* Western Reflections Publishing Co., Montrose, Colo., 2003.

Brooks, James F. *Captives and Cousins: Slavery, Kinship and Community in the Southwest Borderlands.* Published for the Omohundro Institute of Early American History and Culture, Williamsburg, Va., by the University of North Carolina Press, Chapel Hill and London, 2002.

Conetah, Fred. *A History of the Northern Ute People.* Edited by Kathryn L. MacKay and Floyd A. O'Neil. Published by the Uintah-Ouray Ute Tribe. Printed by the University of Utah Printing Service, Salt Lake City, 1982.

Decker, Peter. *The Utes Must Go! American Expansion and the Removal of a People.* Fulcrum Publishing Co., Golden, Colo., 2004.

Emmitt, Robert. *The Last War Trail: The Utes and the Settlement of Colorado.* University Press of Colorado, Boulder, 2000. Originally published by the University of Oklahoma Press, Norman, 1954.

Jefferson, James, Robert W. Delaney, and Gregory C. Thompson. *The Southern Utes: A Tribal History.* The Southern Ute Tribe, University of Utah Printing Service, Salt Lake City, 1972.

Johnston, Shirley. "Queen Chipeta." *Journal of the Western Slope* (Mesa State College, Grand Junction, Colo.), vol. 11, no. 1 (Winter 1996), p. 8.

Lawrence, Margot. *Flyers and Stayers: The Book of the World's Greatest Rides.* George G. Harrap & Co. Ltd., London, 1980.

MacKendrick, Donald A. "Cesspools, Alkali and White Lily Soap: The Grand Junction Indian School, 1886–1911." *Journal of the Western Slope* (Mesa State College, Grand Junction, Colo.), vol. 8, no. 3 (Summer 1993).

McClellan, Val. *This Is Our Land*. Vol. 2. Western Publishers, Jamestown, Ohio, 1979.

Miller, Mark E. *Hollow Victory: The White River Expedition of 1879 and the Battle of Milk Creek*. University Press of Colorado, Niwot, 1997.

O'Neil, Floyd A. "An Anguished Odyssey: The Flight of the Utes, 1906–1908." *Utah Historical Quarterly*, vol. 36, no. 4 (Fall 1968). Reprinted for the Western History Center, University of Utah, Salt Lake City, 2008.

Petit, Jan. *Utes, the Mountain People*. Revised edition by Johnson Printing Co., Boulder, Colo., 2005. Originally printed by Century One Press, Colorado Springs, 1982.

Roe, Frank Gilbert. *The Indian and the Horse*. University of Oklahoma Press, Norman, 1955.

Shwayder, Carol Rein. *Nathan Cook Meeker, Founder of Greeley, Colorado, a Chronology of His Life and Times, 1817–1879*. Unicorn Ventures, Greeley, Colo., 1996. Copy on file at the Greeley Public Library.

Simmons, Virginia McConnell. *The Ute Indians of Utah, Colorado and New Mexico*. University Press of Colorado, Boulder, 2000.

Sprague, Marshall. *Massacre: The Tragedy at White River*. Ballantine Books, New York, 1972. Originally published by Little, Brown and Co., Boston, Mass., 1957.

Stegner, Wallace. *Beyond the Hundredth Meridian: John Wesley Powell and the Second Opening of the West*. Penguin Books, New York, 1992. Originally published by Houghton Mifflin Company, Boston, 1954.

Swisshelm, Jane Grey. *Crusader and Feminist: Letters of Jane Grey Swisshelm, 1858–1865*. Introduction by Arthur J. Larsen. Minnesota Historical Society, Saint Paul, 1934.

Urquart, Lena M. *Colorow, the Angry Chieftain*. Golden Bell Press, Denver, 1968. Copy available at the Mesa County Public Library, Grand Junction, Colo.

Werner, Fred H. *Meeker: The Story of the Meeker Massacre and Thornburgh Battle, September 29, 1879*. Western Publications, Greeley, Colo., 1985.

Wilkinson, Charles. *Fire on the Plateau: Conflict and Endurance in the American Southwest*. Island Press/Shearwater Books, Washington, D.C., and Covelo, Calif., 1999.

"The Woodward Ranch Burial (5RB3570)." *Southwestern Lore, Journal of Colorado Archaeology*, vol. 63, no. 3 (Fall 1997). Copy provided by the Colorado Historical Society, Denver.

Wyckoff, William. *Creating Colorado: The Making of the Western American Landscape, 1860–1940*. Yale University Press, New Haven, Conn., 1999.

Other Documents and Sources

"Descendants of Thomas Price." A Price family genealogy supplied to the author by Thomas Reed of Kalispell, Mont., great-grandson of Flora Ellen Price.

Doris Duke American History Project. Western History Center, University of Utah, Salt Lake City. Transcripts from the University of Utah Libraries.

Price Family Materials, submitted by Thomas Reed to the City of Greeley Museums, October 1, 2003.

"Shawsheen." An unsourced document about She-towitch (Susan), on file at the City of Greeley Museums.

University of Utah's Oral History Project. Western History Center, University of Utah, Salt Lake City. Transcripts from the University of Utah Libraries.

INTERNET SOURCES

American Endurance Riding Conference website. "2009 Results." http://www.aerc. org.

"Denver and Rio Grande Railroad, Scenic Line of the World." http://www. GhostDepot.com.

"The Famous Ride of John 'Portugese' Phillips." Reprinted from *Portraits of Fort Phil Kearny,* http://www.philkearny.vcn.com/phillips.htm.

"First Sgt. Moses Williams." http://www.9thcavalry.com.

"Governor Frederick W. Pitkin Collection." Colorado State Archives, http://www. colorado.gov/dpa/doit/archives/govs/pitkin.html.

"Henry M. Teller (1882–1885): Secretary of the Interior." Miller Center of Public Affairs, University of Virginia. http://www.millercenter.org/academic/ americanpresident.

"Horace Greeley, Ideas and Movements, 1811–1872." http://www.u-s-history.com.

"Phases of the Sun and Moon." U.S. Naval Observatory. http;//www.usno.navy. mil/USNO/astronomical-applications/data-services/rs-one-day-us.

San Juan Silver Stage Online, vol. 10, 2005. http://www.silverstage.net/history.htm.

"Teller, Henry Moore, (1830–1914)." http://www.bioguide.congress.gov/biosearch/ biosearch.asp.

"This Day in History" (category, "Old West") http://www.history.com.

INTERVIEWS CONDUCTED BY THE AUTHOR

Loya Arrum, educator and great-great-granddaughter of Colorow, Fort Duchesne, Utah. Phone conversation, August 6, 2008; personal interview, Fort Duchesne, Utah, October 4, 2008.

Kevin D. Black, assistant Colorado state archaeologist, Denver. E-mail communication, June 2008.

Jay C. Burrup, archivist, Church of Latter-day Saints, Church History Library and Archives, Salt Lake City. E-mail communication, May 2006.

William H. Davis, Archival Programs Branch, Center for Legislative Archives, National Archives and Records Administration, Washington, D.C. E-mail communication, November 2006.

Clifford Duncan, Ute elder and historian, Roosevelt, Utah. Personal interviews in Grand Junction, Colo., March 2006; Roosevelt, Utah, September 2006; Meeker, Colo., July 2007.

Bob Elderkin, retired Bureau of Land Management official, Silt, Colo. Phone interview, September 2007.

Peggy Ford, archivist at the City of Greeley Museums. Phone interview, January 16, 2006.

James Goss, Texas Tech University historian, Lubbock. Personal interview, May 2006.

Jonas Grant Sr., descendant of Canalla and She-towitch, Fort Duchesne, Utah. Ongoing communications in person and by phone beginning in September 2006, with personal interviews conducted at his home.

Ron Hilkey, former Rio Blanco County Sheriff, Meeker, Colo. Phone interview, March 2008.

Jim Jefferson, Southern Ute historian, Ignacio, Colo. Personal interview, May 2006; phone interviews, September and November 2006.

Thomas Reed, great-grandson of Flora Ellen Price, Kalispell, Mont. Phone interview, January 27, 2008.

Joe Sullivan, rancher on whose property Section 1 of the hostage trail begins, Meeker, Colo. Personal interview and horseback ride, October 2005.

Adelbert Tavashuts, descendant of Jane Redjacket, Fort Duchesne, Utah. Personal interview, October 2008.

INDEX